Praise for *Intel Threading Building Blocks*

"The Age of Serial Computing is over. With the advent of multi-core processors, parallel-computing technology that was once relegated to universities and research labs is now emerging as mainstream. Intel Threading Building Blocks updates and greatly expands the 'work-stealing' technology pioneered by the MIT Cilk system of 15 years ago, providing a modern industrial-strength C++ library for concurrent programming.

"Not only does this book offer an excellent introduction to the library, it furnishes novices and experts alike with a clear and accessible discussion of the complexities of concurrency."

> —Charles E. Leiserson, MIT Computer Science and Artificial
> Intelligence Laboratory

"We used to say make it right, then make it fast. We can't do that anymore. TBB lets us design for correctness and speed up front for Maya. This book shows you how to extract the most benefit from using TBB in your code."

> —Martin Watt, Senior Software Engineer, Autodesk

"TBB promises to change how parallel programming is done in C++. This book will be extremely useful to any C++ programmer. With this book, James achieves two important goals:

- Presents an excellent introduction to parallel programming, illustrating the most common parallel programming patterns and the forces governing their use.
- Documents the Threading Building Blocks C++ library—a library that provides generic algorithms for these patterns.

"TBB incorporates many of the best ideas that researchers in object-oriented parallel computing developed in the last two decades."

> —Marc Snir, Head of the Computer Science Department, University of
> Illinois at Urbana-Champaign

"This book was my first introduction to Intel Threading Building Blocks. Thanks to the easy-to-follow discussion of the features implemented and the reasons behind the choices made, the book makes clear that Intel's Threading Building Blocks are an excellent synthesis of some of the best current parallel programming ideas. The judicious choice of a small but powerful set of patterns and strategies makes the system easy to learn and use. I found the numerous code segments and complete parallel applications presented in the book of great help to understand the main features of the library and illustrate the different ways it can be used in the development of efficient parallel programs."

> —David Padua, University of Illinois

"Future generations of chips will provide dozens or even hundreds of cores. Writing applications that benefit from the massive computational power offered by these chips is not going to be an easy task for mainstream programmers who are used to sequential algorithms rather than parallel ones.

"Intel's TBB is providing a big step forward into this long path, and what is better, all in the C++ framework."

> —Eduard Ayguade, Barcelona Supercomputer Center, Technical University of Catalunya

"Intel's TBB is to parallel programming what STL was to plain C++. Generic programming with STL dramatically improved C++ programming productivity. TBB offers a generic parallel programming model that hides the complexity of concurrency control. It lowers the barrier to parallel code development, enabling efficient use of 'killer' multicores."

> —Lawrence Rauchwerger, Texas A&M University, Inventor of STAPL

"For the last eighteen years the denizens of the thinly populated world of supercomputers have been looking for a way to write really pretty and practical parallel programs in C++. We knew templates and generic programming had to be part of the answer, but it took the arrival of multi-core (and soon many-core) processors to create a fundamental change in the computing landscape. Parallelism is now going to be everyday stuff.

"Every C++ programmer is going to need to think about concurrency and parallelism and Threading Building Blocks provides the right abstractions for them to do it correctly.

"This book is not just a discussion of a C++ template library. It provides a lovely and in-depth overview of much of what we have learned about parallel computing in the last 25 years. It could be a great textbook for a course on parallel programming."

> —Dennis Gannon, Science Director, Pervasive Technology Labs at Indiana University, former head of DARPA's High Performance Computing (HPC++) project, and steering committee member of the Global Grid Forum

"TBB hits the application developer's sweet spot with such advantages as uniprocessor performance, parallel scalability, C++ programming well beyond OpenMP, compatibility with OpenMP and hand threads, Intel Threading Tools support for performance and confidence, and openness to the software development community. TBB avoids several constraints surrounding the sweet spot: language extension risks, specific compiler dependences and hand-threading complexities.

"This book should make developers productive without a steep training curve, and the applications they produce should be of high quality and performance."

> —David Kuck, Intel Fellow, founder of KAI and former director of the Center for Supercomputing Research and Development

Intel Threading Building Blocks

Outfitting C++ for Multi-Core Processor Parallelism

Other resources from O'Reilly

Related titles

C++ Cookbook™

Practical C++ Programming

C++ in a Nutshell

Pthreads Programming: A POSIX Standard for Better Multiprocessing

Secure Programming Cookbook for C and C++

High Performance Linux Clusters with OSCAR, Rocks, OpenMosix, and MPI

oreilly.com

oreilly.com is more than a complete catalog of O'Reilly books. You'll also find links to news, events, articles, weblogs, sample chapters, and code examples.

oreillynet.com is the essential portal for developers interested in open and emerging technologies, including new platforms, programming languages, and operating systems.

Conferences

O'Reilly brings diverse innovators together to nurture the ideas that spark revolutionary industries. We specialize in documenting the latest tools and systems, translating the innovator's knowledge into useful skills for those in the trenches. Visit *conferences.oreilly.com* for our upcoming events.

Safari Bookshelf (*safari.oreilly.com*) is the premier online reference library for programmers and IT professionals. Conduct searches across more than 1,000 books. Subscribers can zero in on answers to time-critical questions in a matter of seconds. Read the books on your Bookshelf from cover to cover or simply flip to the page you need. Try it today for free.

Intel Threading Building Blocks

Outfitting C++ for Multi-Core
Processor Parallelism

James Reinders

O'REILLY®

Beijing · Cambridge · Farnham · Köln · Paris · Sebastopol · Taipei · Tokyo

Intel Threading Building Blocks
by James Reinders

Published by O'Reilly Media, Inc., 1005 Gravenstein Highway North, Sebastopol, CA 95472.

O'Reilly books may be purchased for educational, business, or sales promotional use. Online editions are also available for most titles (*safari.oreilly.com*). For more information, contact our corporate/institutional sales department: (800) 998-9938 or *corporate@oreilly.com*.

Editor: Andy Oram	**Indexer:** Reg Aubry
Production Editor: Sarah Schneider	**Cover Designer:** Karen Montgomery
Copyeditor: Audrey Doyle	**Interior Designer:** David Futato
Proofreader: Sarah Schneider	**Illustrator:** Jessamyn Read

Printing History:

July 2007:   First Edition.

 This book uses RepKover™, a durable and flexible lay-flat binding.

ISBN-10: 0-596-51480-8
ISBN-13: 978-0-596-51480-8
[M]

Table of Contents

Foreword

Building libraries is an important task. The activity goes back to the earliest days of computing, when Wilkes, Wheeler, and Gill introduced subroutines as instruments for packaging useful software. Sadly, this activity lost its academic glamour and is often relegated to the boiler room of programming. It is essential that we start building libraries based on rigorous scientific foundations.

Let us define a good library. It should not be intrusive. The old code should run as is without any modifications. It should not be exclusive. Other libraries should be able to coexist alongside it. It should be orthogonal. Instead of defining similar facilities in different contexts, it should factor them out into different dimensions. It should be open and not hide useful information from the client for the sake of illusory security. It should be efficient. Using the library should not penalize the application.

Concurrent programming is a very difficult task. At the same time, the evolution of hardware makes it more and more mainstream. Although there have been major advances in our theoretical understanding of concurrency, we need to have practical libraries that encapsulate this knowledge. It is great that the Intel team led by Arch Robison made a major step designing and implementing Threading Building Blocks, which could become a basis for the concurrency dimension of the C++ standard library.

I would also like to congratulate Intel management for not just sponsoring this activity, but also releasing it as open source. I hope that they will keep funding the team so that they can further extend their work.

—Alexander Stepanov
Palo Alto, California

Alexander Stepanov was the key person behind the creation of the C++ Standard Template Library (STL). While at HP, he developed it with Meng Lee and David Musser. With the encouragement and persistence of Andy Koenig and Bjarne Stroustrup, STL became a key part of the C++ standard. Alexander is presently a Principal Scientist at Adobe Systems.

Note from the Lead Developer of Intel Threading Building Blocks

Parallel computing has become personal, in both liberating and demanding ways.

I remember using an IBM 1130 mainframe in high school in the 1970s, and how frustrating it was because only one person could use the machine at a time, feeding it via a card reader. Then, in the 1980s, computers became personal, and I had all the time I wanted to run and debug sequential programs.

Parallel computing has undergone a similar shift. In the 1980s and 1990s, parallel computers were institutional. They were fascinating to program, but access was limited. I was fortunate at one point to share a 256-processor nCUBE with only a few other people. Now, with multi-core chips, every programmer can have cheap access to a parallel computer—perhaps not with 256 processors yet, but with a growing number every year.

The downside, of course, is that parallel programming is no longer optional because parallel computers have become personal for consumers, too. Now parallel programming is mandatory for performance-sensitive applications.

There is no *one true way* to do parallel programming. Many paradigms have been proposed and have been cast in the form of new languages, language extensions, and libraries. One such paradigm defines tasks that run in shared memory. This paradigm is well suited to achieving parallel speedup on multi-core chips. The key notion is to separate logical task patterns from physical threads, and to delegate task scheduling to the system.

The paradigm has been around for a long time. Intel Threading Building Blocks was written to evangelize the paradigm, and to provide it off the shelf so that programmers would not have to reinvent it (and debug and tune it!).

Threading Building Blocks is strictly a library, not a new language or language extension. Though new languages and extensions are attractive, they raise a high barrier to adoption in the near term, particularly in commercial settings, where continuity from the existing code base is paramount. (Indeed, it is so important that businesses are still selling systems that are upward-compatible with some of those mainframes from the 1970s.)

Starting in 2004, I chaired a study group inside Intel that drafted the initial Threading Building Blocks proposal. Despite an early commitment to a library-only solution, we drew much of our inspiration from new languages and extensions for parallel programming. Our goal was to borrow as many good ideas as we could put into library form. Sticking to a library was a requirement so that Threading Building Blocks could slip easily into existing C++ programming environments.

C++ makes the library approach practical because it is designed for writing libraries. Stroustrup cites a 10X reduction in line count for the Booch components written in C++ versus Ada. Perhaps C++ will be even more powerful in the future. For example, the addition of lambda functions (see Chapter 12) would simplify the mechanics of using the Threading Building Blocks parallel_for.

A library-only solution is not perfect. We had to leave out some features that really require compiler support. For example, data-parallel array operations such as Fortran 90, ZPL, and NESL were deemed impractical because they rely heavily on optimizing compilers. There have been some C++ libraries such as POOMA that do some of the optimizations via template metaprogramming, but the complexity of such libraries is high. Parallel functional programming is another powerful paradigm, but alas, it requires significant compiler support.

Several systems were particularly influential in the development of Threading Building Blocks; these (and others) are listed in the bibliography of this book.

The Chare Kernel (now Charm++) showed the advantages of breaking a program into many small tasks. In particular, distributing load is simplified. By analogy, it's a lot easier to evenly distribute many small objects among the cases instead of a few large objects.

Cilk showed the power of combining a scheduling technique called *task stealing* with recursive tasks. Recursion is often slower than iteration for serial programming, but it turns out that recursive parallelism has some big advantages over iterative parallelism with respect to load balancing and cache reuse. Cache reuse is critical because restructuring for cache sometimes improves program speed by 2X or more, possibly delivering better improvement than multithreading alone. Fortunately, the Cilk approach tends to steer programmers to solutions that both are parallel and have good cache behavior.

The C++ Standard Template Library (STL) showed how a library could be both generic *and* efficient. As we gain experience, we're learning how to be more generic. STAPL showed how to bring generic binding of algorithms to containers into the parallel world, by substituting the fundamentally sequential STL iterator with parallel recursive ranges (pRanges in STAPL). This enabled parallel algorithms to operate on parallel containers and opened up the ability to apply parallel recursive ranges to multidimensional spaces (e.g., blocked_range2d), and even reuse (some would say abuse) them to write a parallel quicksort.

If you are accustomed to heavyweight threads, lightweight tasks require a new mindset. For example, heavyweight threads tend to drive designs toward relatively few threads because they are costly. Furthermore, they tend to introduce a lot of explicit synchronization, such as locks. Lightweight tasks drive designs that use many tiny tasks with implicit synchronization. Each task combines some work and a little bit of synchronization. An extreme case is the Threading Building Blocks empty_task class, which does nothing *except* synchronization. For instance, it is used by parallel_for to synchronize completion without using any (explicit) locking. The synchronization is implied by the task pattern. Locks are still sometimes necessary, but I encourage you to exploit implicit task synchronization instead where possible.

Performance matters. By definition, parallel programming for speedup is wasted effort if the sequential equivalent outruns it. Merely decomposing a problem into a zillion parallel race-free tasks is typically *not* enough to achieve speedup because each of those zillion tasks needs space. Threading Building Blocks is intended to guide programmers toward patterns that are space-efficient.

I'll close with my favorite principle for parallel programming: KISS (Keep It Simple, Stupid). Writing parallel programs can be as complicated as you want it to be. However, the successful parallel programs that I've seen stick with simple patterns. Threading Building Blocks provides a good foundation layer for these patterns.

—Arch D. Robison
Champaign, Illinois

Arch D. Robison is currently the lead developer of Intel Threading Building Blocks. Previously, Arch worked at Shell on massively parallel codes for seismic imaging, and then was the lead developer for KAI C++, a portable, cross-platform, high-performance, C++ compiler. He received his Ph.D. from the University of Illinois.

Preface

Multi-core processors have made parallel programming a topic of interest for every programmer. Computer systems without multiple processor cores have become relatively rare. This book is about a solution for C++ programmers that does not ask you to abandon C++ or require the direct use of raw, native threads.

This book introduces Intel Threading Building Blocks. Threading Building Blocks is a C++ template library for parallelism that extends C++ by abstracting away thread management and allowing straightforward parallel programming. To use the library, you specify tasks, not threads, and let the library map tasks onto threads in an efficient manner. This has many advantages in a world where you need your application to survive as more processor cores become available.

Threading Building Blocks will enable you to specify parallelism far more conveniently than using raw threads, while improving performance, portability, and scalability.

 You can download a copy of Intel Threading Building Blocks from *http://www.threadingbuildingblocks.org* or *http://www.intel.com/software/ products*.

Assumptions This Book Makes

You do not need to have any experience with parallel programming or multi-core processors to use this book. Whether you have a great deal of experience with parallel programming, or none at all, this book will be useful. No prior understanding of threading is required.

Prior knowledge of C++ templates and template libraries such as the Standard Template Library (STL), or knowledge of generic programming, will allow some concepts in the book to come more easily. Learning this template library, even if it is your first template library, should be no more difficult a place to start than any other.

If you want to gain more background on the concepts of generic programming, or the standard template library for C++, there are many fine books to read. Doing so is not necessary before reading this book, but this book will make no attempt to cover those topics.

This book is intended to be approachable for a C programmer or a C++ programmer without experience with templates, but it will require some patience as occasional references to STL and templates will require some study. The examples throughout the book, and particularly those in Chapter 11, are clear enough to follow, even if you do not understand all the constructs perfectly.

Contents of This Book

Chapter 1, *Why Threading Building Blocks?*, introduces the motivation for Intel Threading Building Blocks and gives you a high-level feel for how this solution is superior to other options for C++ programmers.

Chapter 2, *Thinking Parallel*, is a brief introduction to parallelism. Understanding how to "Think in Parallel" is fundamental to being able to write a good parallel program. This is the one place in the book where terms such as *scalability* are defined and the motivation for focusing on it is provided.

The rest of the book deals with using Threading Building Blocks.

Chapter 3, *Basic Algorithms*, covers the basic algorithmic capabilities. This is the key chapter to learning Threading Building Blocks. Here you will come to understand the concepts of recursion, task stealing, and algorithm patterns that are uniquely combined in Intel Threading Building Blocks. This will make the capabilities of Threading Building Blocks available to you.

Chapter 4, *Advanced Algorithms*, covers more advanced algorithmic capabilities.

Chapter 5, *Containers*, covers the data structure capabilities: the containers.

Chapter 6, *Scalable Memory Allocation*, covers the scalable memory allocator. Making sure your memory allocation is handled by a *scalable* memory allocator is very important.

Chapter 7, *Mutual Exclusion*, discusses mutual exclusion, both by locks and by atomic operations.

Chapter 8, *Timing*, discusses timing using a global timestamp capability built into Threading Building Blocks.

Chapter 9, *Task Scheduler*, discusses the core of the Threading Building Blocks runtime: the task scheduler.

Chapter 10, *Keys to Success*, pulls everything together to offer key tips to success, including the five steps to making the best use of Threading Building Blocks. The chapter also covers debugging, thread safety, mixing with other threading models, and general performance considerations.

Chapter 11, *Examples*, is a rich collection of examples ranging from simple to moderately complex and from obvious uses to more esoteric uses to meet specific needs. This may be a chapter you jump to if you are eager to type in some code and take it for a "spin." This chapter expands on the short samples of code shown throughout the book to explain individual features.

Chapter 12, *History and Related Projects*, departs from the goal of teaching the use of Intel Threading Building Blocks and talks instead about its design and the influences on it. The chapter includes a recap of the research that inspired Intel Threading Building Blocks and a bibliography with many pointers to additional readings on parallel programming.

Conventions Used in This Book

The following typographical conventions are used in this book:

Italic

> Indicates new terms.

`Constant width`

> Indicates variables, functions, data types, classes, the contents of files, and the output from commands.

`Constant width bold`

> Shows commands or other text that should be typed literally by the user.

`Constant width italic`

> Indicates elements of code that you should replace with your own values.

 This icon signifies a tip, suggestion, or general note.

 This icon indicates a warning or caution.

Informal Class Declarations

As a convention in this book, class members are summarized by informal class declarations that describe the class as it seems to clients, not how it is actually implemented. For example, here is an informal declaration of class Foo:

```
class Foo {
public:
    int x( );
    int y;
    ~Foo( );
};
```

The actual implementation might look like this:

```
class FooBase {
protected:
    int x( );
};

class Foo: protected FooBase {
private:
    int internal_stuff;
public:
    using FooBase::x;
    int y;
};
```

The example shows two cases where the actual implementation departs from the informal declaration:

- Method x( ) is inherited from a protected base class.
- The destructor is an implicitly generated method.

The informal declarations are intended to show you how to use the class without the distraction of irrelevant clutter particular to the implementation.

Using Code Examples

This book is here to help you get your job done. In general, you may use the code in this book in your programs and documentation. You do not need to contact us for permission unless you're reproducing a significant portion of the code. For example, writing a program that uses several chunks of code from this book does not require permission. Selling or distributing a CD-ROM of examples from O'Reilly books does require permission. Answering a question by citing this book and quoting example code does not require permission. Incorporating a significant amount of example code from this book into your product's documentation does require permission.

We appreciate, but do not require, attribution. An attribution usually includes the title, author, publisher, and ISBN. For example: "*Intel Threading Building Blocks*, by James Reinders. Copyright 2007 James Reinders, 978-0-596-51480-8."

If you feel your use of code examples falls outside fair use or the permission given above, feel free to contact us at *permissions@oreilly.com*.

How to Contact Us

Please address comments and questions concerning this book to the publisher:

O'Reilly Media, Inc.
1005 Gravenstein Highway North
Sebastopol, CA 95472
800-998-9938 (in the United States or Canada)
707-829-0515 (international or local)
707-829-0104 (fax)

We have a web page for this book, where we list errata, examples, and any additional information. You can access this page at:

http://www.oreilly.com/catalog/9780596514808

Intel Threading Building Blocks itself is available from:

http://threadingbuildingblocks.org

and:

http://intel.com/software/products

To comment on or ask technical questions about this book, send email to:

bookquestions@oreilly.com

For more information about our books, conferences, Resource Centers, and the O'Reilly Network, see our web site at:

http://www.oreilly.com

Acknowledgments

I have the good fortune to work with a passionate and driven team at Intel. The Intel Software Development Products team is very dedicated to helping software developers get the most out of parallelism, and none more so than the Threading Building Blocks team.

Arch Robison was the principle architect and lead developer of Intel Threading Building Blocks. Arch has been more than gracious in talking with me about Threading Building Blocks, answering my questions, and providing me with the reference and tutorial material that forms the basis of specifications and many explanations in this book. Arch was the most prolific reviewer of the book in terms of helping keep things accurate.

Dave Poulsen is the project manager for a number of products, including Intel Threading Building Blocks, who does his best to protect his team from random interruptions. He has been most gracious at allowing my interruptions to be productive through his kind but direct style of feedback.

Victoria Gromova has been the most active in helping our customers use Intel Threading Building Blocks. She has a reputation for bending the use of Threading Building Blocks to make sure our customers get what they need. She provided examples and commentary for Chapter 11 and helped with short examples elsewhere in the book. The experiences she has shared through many examples provide an important contribution to this book.

Bob Kuhn generated a couple of key examples on packet processing and domain decomposition, which you can find in Chapter 11, along with his fine explanations.

Dennis Lin took the examples explained in Chapter 11 and made them ready to download from the web site and use. He helped correct several key issues for which I am very grateful.

Tim Mattson, co-author of the book *Parallel Programming Patterns* (Addison-Wesley), gave feedback on how to connect his general work with the specifics I sought to convey in this book. He was most kind to tell me I should know better than to write another book, since he and I both know how much work it is. Another person who told me not to write the book, as a way to push me into doing it, was **Greg Stoner**. Thank you for the push and the frequent back-and-forth discussions over our shared belief in how exciting the future of processing cores everywhere is going to be.

Laura Cane was instrumental in helping to create the product Reference Guide and the Tutorial from which I drew much material for the core of this book. Laura has helped make the material quite clear and accurate.

Sanjiv Shah manages the lab, as we call it, where our Intel Threading Building Blocks, Intel Thread Profiler, Intel Thread Checker, OpenMP runtime, and Cluster OpenMP runtime are developed, readied for the marketplace, and supported. He has been a relentless champion for customers and strong engineering, as well as a friend. Sanjiv's support helped make this book possible and he offered feedback on the book as well. In a bigger sense, he made Threading Building Blocks available to us all through his championing it as a product.

Mike Davis, **Shobhan Jha**, **Robert Reed**, and **Randy Smith** have been tireless supporters of Threading Building Blocks and helped with feedback on drafts of this book.

Mike Voss and **Alexey Kukanov** contributed to the development of Threading Building Blocks and provided key feedback on the draft of this book.

John Taylor Jr. provided feedback nearly cover to cover, which helped a great deal. He provided good insights and his very fresh eyes caught issues we had overlooked a hundred times because they were too familiar to us.

Anton Malkhov, **Elena Gavrina**, **Susan Milbrandt**, and **Asia Nezhdanova** all contributed to the development of Threading Building Blocks and its project management and, therefore, this book.

Clay Breshears, **David Mackay**, **Anton Pegushin**, and **Vasanth Tovinkere** work tirelessly to train and help customers. They shared experiences, examples, and feedback. Their experience with Threading Building Blocks feeds back to the product and to our ability to explain it better.

I also want to thank the OSCON team at O'Reilly, who encouraged me to get the book pulled together sooner rather than later. In particular, **Andy Oram** provided guidance as the editor, which helped this book a great deal. And thank you to the Tools team at O'Reilly who provided such excellent tools for the book template along with accurate and useful documentation.

And I want to especially thank my wife, **Beth**, and children, **Andrew** and **Katie**, for supporting and encouraging me as I wrote this book. Beth reviewed the opening chapters with a teacher's eye. Andrew made sure the citations in Chapter 12 are both accurate and properly documented. Katie provided encouragement so that we could work on other things soon.

CHAPTER 1

Why Threading Building Blocks?

Intel Threading Building Blocks offers a rich and complete approach to expressing parallelism in a C++ program. It is a library that helps you leverage multi-core processor performance without having to be a threading expert. Threading Building Blocks is not *just* a threads-replacement library; it represents a higher-level, task-based parallelism that abstracts platform details and threading mechanisms for performance and scalability.

This chapter introduces Intel Threading Building Blocks and how it stands out relative to other options for C++ programmers. Although Threading Building Blocks relies on templates and the C++ concept of generic programming, this book does not require any prior experience with these concepts or with threading.

Chapter 2 explains the challenges of parallelism and introduces key concepts that are important for using Threading Building Blocks. Together, these first two chapters set up the foundation of knowledge needed to make the best use of Threading Building Blocks.

Download and Installation

You can download Intel Threading Building Blocks, along with instructions for installation, from *http://threadingbuildingblocks.org* or *http://intel.com/software/products/tbb*.

Threading Building Blocks was initially released in August 2006 by Intel, with prebuilt binaries for Windows, Linux, and Mac OS X. Less than a year later, Intel provided more ports and is now working with the community to provide additional ports. The information on how to install Threading Building Blocks comes with the product downloads.

Overview

Multi-core processors are becoming common, yet writing even a simple `parallel_for` loop is tedious with existing threading packages. Writing an efficient *scalable* program is much harder. Scalability embodies the concept that a program should see benefits in performance as the number of processor cores increases.

Threading Building Blocks helps you create applications that reap the benefits of new processors with more and more cores as they become available.

Threading Building Blocks is a library that supports scalable parallel programming using standard C++ code. It does not require special languages or compilers. The ability to use Threading Building Blocks on virtually any processor or any operating system with any C++ compiler makes it very appealing.

Threading Building Blocks uses templates for common parallel iteration patterns, enabling programmers to attain increased speed from multiple processor cores without having to be experts in synchronization, load balancing, and cache optimization. Programs using Threading Building Blocks will run on systems with a single processor core, as well as on systems with multiple processor cores. Threading Building Blocks promotes scalable data parallel programming. Additionally, it fully supports nested parallelism, so you can build larger parallel components from smaller parallel components easily. To use the library, you specify tasks, not threads, and let the library map tasks onto threads in an efficient manner. The result is that Threading Building Blocks enables you to specify parallelism far more conveniently, and with better results, than using raw threads.

Benefits

As mentioned, the goal of a programmer in a modern computing environment is scalability: to take advantage of both cores on a dual-core processor, all four cores on a quad-core processor, and so on. Threading Building Blocks makes writing scalable applications much easier than it is with traditional threading packages.

There are a variety of approaches to parallel programming, ranging from the use of platform-dependent threading primitives to exotic new languages. The advantage of Threading Building Blocks is that it works at a higher level than raw threads, yet does not require exotic languages or compilers. You can use it with any compiler supporting ISO C++. This library differs from typical threading packages in these ways:

Threading Building Blocks enables you to specify tasks *instead of threads*
> Most threading packages require you to create, join, and manage threads. Programming directly in terms of threads can be tedious and can lead to inefficient programs because threads are low-level, heavy constructs that are close to the hardware. Direct programming with threads forces you to do the work to efficiently map logical tasks onto threads. In contrast, the Threading Building

Blocks runtime library automatically schedules tasks onto threads in a way that makes efficient use of processor resources. The runtime is very effective at load-balancing the many tasks you will be specifying.

By avoiding programming in a raw native thread model, you can expect better portability, easier programming, more understandable source code, and better performance and scalability in general.

Indeed, the alternative of using raw threads directly would amount to programming in the *assembly language of parallel programming*. It may give you maximum flexibility, but with many costs.

Threading Building Blocks targets threading for performance

Most general-purpose threading packages support many different kinds of threading, such as threading for asynchronous events in graphical user interfaces. As a result, general-purpose packages tend to be low-level tools that provide a foundation, not a solution. Instead, Threading Building Blocks focuses on the particular goal of parallelizing computationally intensive work, delivering higher-level, simpler solutions.

Threading Building Blocks is compatible *with other threading packages*

Threading Building Blocks can coexist seamlessly with other threading packages. This is very important because it does not force you to pick among Threading Building Blocks, OpenMP, or raw threads for your entire program. You are free to add Threading Building Blocks to programs that have threading in them already. You can also add an OpenMP directive, for instance, somewhere else in your program that uses Threading Building Blocks. For a particular part of your program, you will use one method, but in a large program, it is reasonable to anticipate the convenience of mixing various techniques. It is fortunate that Threading Building Blocks supports this.

Using or creating libraries is a key reason for this flexibility, particularly because libraries are often supplied by others. For instance, Intel's Math Kernel Library (MKL) and Integrated Performance Primitives (IPP) library are implemented internally using OpenMP. You can freely link a program using Threading Building Blocks with the Intel MKL or Intel IPP library.

Threading Building Blocks emphasizes scalable, data-parallel programming

Breaking a program into separate functional blocks and assigning a separate thread to each block is a solution that usually does not scale well because, typically, the number of functional blocks is fixed. In contrast, Threading Building Blocks emphasizes *data-parallel* programming, enabling multiple threads to work most efficiently together. Data-parallel programming scales well to larger numbers of processors by dividing a data set into smaller pieces. With data-parallel programming, program performance increases (scales) as you add processors. Threading Building Blocks also avoids classic bottlenecks, such as a global task queue that each processor must wait for and lock in order to get a new task.

Threading Building Blocks relies on generic programming

Traditional libraries specify interfaces in terms of specific types or base classes. Instead, Threading Building Blocks uses generic programming, which is defined in Chapter 12. The essence of generic programming is to write the best possible algorithms with the fewest constraints. The C++ Standard Template Library (STL) is a good example of generic programming in which the interfaces are specified by *requirements* on types. For example, C++ STL has a template function that sorts a sequence abstractly, defined in terms of iterators on the sequence.

Generic programming enables Threading Building Blocks to be flexible yet efficient. The generic interfaces enable you to customize components to your specific needs.

Comparison with Raw Threads and MPI

Programming using a raw thread interface, such as POSIX threads (pthreads) or Windows threads, has been an option that many programmers of shared memory parallelism have used. There are wrappers that increase portability, such as Boost Threads, which are a very portable raw threads interface. Supercomputer users, with their thousands of processors, do not generally have the luxury of shared memory, so they use message passing, most often through the popular Message Passing Interface (MPI) standard.

Raw threads and MPI expose the control of parallelism at its lowest level. They represent the *assembly languages of parallelism*. As such, they offer maximum flexibility, but at a high cost in terms of programmer effort, debugging time, and maintenance costs.

In order to program parallel machines, such as multi-core processors, we need the ability to express our parallelism without having to manage every detail. Issues such as optimal management of a thread pool, and proper distribution of tasks with load balancing and cache affinity in mind, should not be the focus of a programmer when working on expressing the parallelism in a program.

When using raw threads, programmers find basic coordination and data sharing to be difficult and tedious to write correctly and efficiently. Code often becomes very dependent on the particular threading facilities of an operating system. Raw thread-level programming is too low-level to be intuitive, and it seldom results in code designed for scalable performance. Nested parallelism expressed with raw threads creates a lot of complexities, which I will not go into here, other than to say that these complexities are handled for you with Threading Building Blocks.

Another advantage of tasks versus logical threads is that tasks are much lighter weight. On Linux systems, starting and terminating a task is about 18 times faster than starting and terminating a thread. On Windows systems, the ratio is more than 100-fold.

With threads and with MPI, you wind up mapping tasks onto processor cores explicitly. Using Threading Building Blocks to express parallelism with tasks allows developers to express more concurrency and finer-grained concurrency than would be possible with threads, leading to increased scalability.

Comparison with OpenMP

Along with Intel Threading Building Blocks, another promising abstraction for C++ programmers is OpenMP. The most successful parallel extension to date, OpenMP is a language extension consisting of pragmas, routines, and environment variables for Fortran and C programs. OpenMP helps users express a parallel program and helps the compiler generate a program reflecting the programmer's wishes. These directives are important advances that address the limitations of the Fortran and C languages, which generally prevent a compiler from automatically detecting parallelism in code.

The OpenMP standard was first released in 1997. By 2006, virtually all compilers had some level of support for OpenMP. The maturity of implementations varies, but they are widespread enough to be viewed as a natural companion of Fortran and C languages, and they can be counted upon when programming on any platform.

When considering it for C programs, OpenMP has been referred to as "excellent for Fortran-style code written in C." That is not an unreasonable description of OpenMP since it focuses on loop structures and C code. OpenMP offers nothing specific for C++. The loop structures are the same loop nests that were developed for vector supercomputers—an earlier generation of parallel processors that performed tremendous amounts of computational work in very tight nests of loops and were programmed largely in Fortran. Transforming those loop nests into parallel code could be very rewarding in terms of results.

A proposal for the 3.0 version of OpenMP includes tasking, which will liberate OpenMP from being solely focused on long, regular loop structures by adding support for irregular constructs such as while loops and recursive structures. Intel implemented tasking in its compilers in 2004 based on a proposal implemented by KAI in 1999 and published as "Flexible Control Structures in OpenMP" in 2000. Until these tasking extensions take root and are widely adopted, OpenMP remains reminiscent of Fortran programming with minimal support for C++.

OpenMP has the programmer choose among three scheduling approaches (static, guided, and dynamic) for scheduling loop iterations. Threading Building Blocks does not require the programmer to worry about scheduling policies. Threading Building Blocks does away with this in favor of a single, automatic, divide-and-conquer approach to scheduling. Implemented with *work stealing* (a technique for moving tasks from loaded processors to idle ones), it compares favorably to dynamic or guided scheduling, but without the problems of a centralized dealer. Static scheduling is sometimes faster on systems undisturbed by other processes or concurrent sibling code. However, divide-and-conquer comes close enough and fits well with nested parallelism.

The generic programming embraced by Threading Building Blocks means that parallelism structures are not limited to built-in types. OpenMP allows reductions on only built-in types, whereas the Threading Building Blocks `parallel_reduce` works on any type.

Looking to address weaknesses in OpenMP, Threading Building Blocks is designed for C++, and thus to provide the simplest possible solutions for the types of programs written in C++. Hence, Threading Building Blocks is not limited to statically scoped loop nests. Far from it: Threading Building Blocks implements a subtle but critical recursive model of task-based parallelism and generic algorithms.

Recursive Splitting, Task Stealing, and Algorithms

A number of concepts are fundamental to making the parallelism model of Threading Building Blocks intuitive. Most fundamental is the reliance on breaking problems up recursively as required to get to the right level of parallel tasks. It turns out that this works much better than the more obvious static division of work. It also fits perfectly with the use of task stealing instead of a global task queue. This is a critical design decision that avoids using a global resource as important as a task queue, which would limit scalability.

As you wrestle with which algorithm structure to apply for your parallelism (for loop, `while` loop, pipeline, divide and conquer, etc.), you will find that you want to combine them. If you realize that a combination such as a `parallel_for` loop controlling a *parallel set of pipelines* is what you want to program, you will find that easy to implement. Not only that, the fundamental design choice of recursion and task stealing makes this work yield efficient scalable applications.

 It is a pleasant surprise to new users to discover how acceptable it is to code parallelism, even inside a routine that is used concurrently itself. Because Threading Building Blocks was designed to encourage this type of nesting, it makes parallelism easy to use. In other systems, this would be the start of a headache.

With an understanding of why Threading Building Blocks matters, we are ready for the next chapter, which lays out what we need to do in general to formulate a parallel solution to a problem.

Thinking Parallel

This chapter is about how to "Think Parallel." It is a brief introduction to the mental discipline that helps you make a program parallelizable in a safe and scalable manner. Even though Intel Threading Building Blocks does much of the work that traditional APIs require the programmer to do, this kind of thinking is a fundamental requirement to writing a good parallel program.

This is the place in the book that defines terms such as *scalability* and provides the motivation for focusing on these concepts. The topics covered in this chapter are decomposition, scaling, threads, correctness, abstraction, and patterns.

If you don't already approach every computer problem with parallelism in your thoughts, this chapter should be the start of a new way of thinking. If you are already deeply into parallel programming, this chapter can still show how Threading Building Blocks deals with the concepts.

How should we think about parallel programming? This is now a common question because, after decades in a world where most computers had only one central processing unit (CPU), we are now in a world where only "old" computers have one CPU. Multi-core processors are now the norm. Parallel computers are the norm. Therefore, every software developer needs to Think Parallel.

Today, when developers take on a programming job, they generally think about the best approach before programming. We already think about selecting the best algorithm, implementation language, and so on. Now, we need to think about the inherent parallelism in the job first. This will, in turn, drive algorithm and implementation choices. Trying to consider the parallelism after everything else is not Thinking Parallel, and will not work out well.

Elements of Thinking Parallel

Threading Building Blocks was designed to make expressing parallelism much easier by abstracting away details and providing strong support for the best ways to program for parallelism. Here is a quick overview of how Threading Building Blocks addresses the topics we will define and review in this chapter:

Decomposition
> Learning to decompose your problem into concurrent tasks (tasks that can run at the same time).

Scaling
> Expressing a problem so that there are enough concurrent tasks to keep all the processor cores busy while minimizing the overhead of managing the parallel program.

Threads
> A guide to the technology underlying the concurrency in programs—and how they are abstracted by Threading Building Blocks so that you can just focus on your tasks.

Correctness
> How the implicit synchronization inherent in Threading Building Blocks helps minimize the use of *locks*. If you still must use locks, there are special features for using the Intel Thread Checker to find *deadlocks* and *race conditions*, which result from errors involving locks.

Abstraction and patterns
> How to choose and utilize algorithms, from Chapters 3 and 4.

Caches
> A key consideration in improving performance. The Threading Build Blocks task scheduler is already tuned for caches.

Intuition
> Thinking in terms of tasks that can run at the same time (concurrent tasks), data decomposed to minimize conflicts among tasks, and recursion.

In everyday life, we find ourselves thinking about parallelism. Here are a few examples:

Long lines
> When you have to wait in a long line, you have undoubtedly wished there were multiple shorter (faster) lines, or multiple people at the front of the line helping serve customers more quickly. Grocery store checkout lines, lines to get train tickets, lines to buy coffee, and lines to buy books in a bookstore are examples.

Lots of repetitive work

When you have a big task to do, which many people could help with at the same time, you have undoubtedly wished for more people to help you. Moving all your possessions from an old dwelling to a new one, stuffing letters in envelopes for a mass mailing, and installing the same software on each new computer in your lab are examples.

The point here is simple: parallelism is not unknown to us. In fact, it is quite natural to think about opportunities to divide work and do it in parallel. It just might seem unusual for the moment to program that way. Once you dig in and start using parallelism, you will Think Parallel. You will think first about the parallelism in your project, and only then think about coding it.

Decomposition

When you think about your project, how do you find the parallelism?

At the highest level, parallelism exists either in the form of data on which to operate in parallel, or in the form of tasks to execute concurrently. And these forms are *not* mutually exclusive.

Data Parallelism

Data parallelism (Figure 2-1) is easy to picture. Take lots of data and apply the same transformation to each piece of the data. In Figure 2-1, each letter in the data set is capitalized and becomes the corresponding uppercase letter. This simple example shows that given a data set and an operation that can be applied element by element, we can apply the same task concurrently to each element. Programmers writing code for supercomputers love this sort of problem and consider it so easy to do in parallel that it has been called *embarrassingly parallel*. A word of advice: if you have lots of data parallelism, do not be embarrassed—take advantage of it and be very happy. Consider it *happy parallelism*.

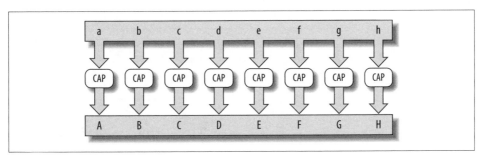

Figure 2-1. Data parallelism

Task Parallelism

Data parallelism is eventually limited by the amount of data you want to process, and your thoughts will then turn to task parallelism (Figure 2-2). Task parallelism means lots of different, independent tasks that are linked by sharing the data they consume. This, too, can be *embarrassingly parallel*. Figure 2-2 uses as examples some mathematical operations that can each be applied to the same data set to compute values that are independent. In this case, the average value, the minimum value, the binary OR function, and the geometric mean of the data set are computed.

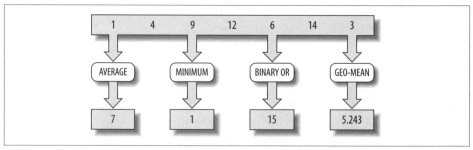

Figure 2-2. Task parallelism

Pipelining (Task and Data Parallelism Together)

Pure task parallelism is harder to find than pure data parallelism. Often, when you find task parallelism, it's a special kind referred to as *pipelining*. In this kind of algorithm, many independent tasks need to be applied to a stream of data. Each item is processed by stages as they pass through, as shown by the letter A in Figure 2-3. A stream of data can be processed more quickly if you use a pipeline because different items can pass through different stages at the same time, as shown in Figure 2-4. A pipeline can also be more sophisticated than other processes: it can reroute data or skip steps for chosen items. Automobile assembly lines are good examples of pipelines; materials flow through a pipeline and get a little work done at each step (Figure 2-4).

Figure 2-3. Pipeline

Figure 2-4. A pipeline in action with data flowing through it

Mixed Solutions

Consider the task of folding, stuffing, sealing, addressing, stamping, and mailing letters. If you assemble a group of six people for the task of stuffing many envelopes, you can arrange each person to specialize in and perform one task in a pipeline fashion (Figure 2-5). This contrasts with data parallelism, where you divide the supplies and give a batch of everything to each person (Figure 2-6). Each person then does all the steps on his collection of materials as his task.

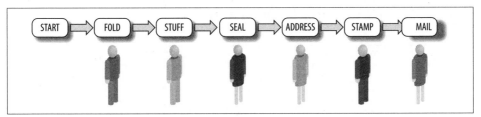

Figure 2-5. Pipelining—each person has a different job

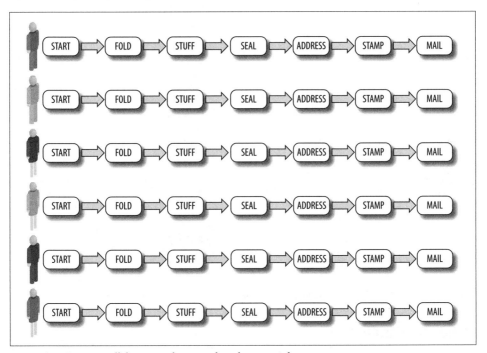

Figure 2-6. Data parallelism—each person has the same job

Figure 2-6 is clearly the right choice if every person has to work in a different location far from each other. That is called *coarse-grained* parallelism because the interactions between the tasks are infrequent (they only come together to collect envelopes, then leave and do their task, including mailing). The other choice shown in Figure 2-5 is known as *fine-grained* parallelism because of the frequent interactions (every envelope is passed along to every worker in various steps of the operation).

Neither extreme tends to fit reality, although sometimes they may be close enough to be useful. In our example, it may turn out that addressing an envelope takes enough time to keep three people busy, whereas the first two steps and the last two steps require only one person on each pair of steps to keep up. Figure 2-7 illustrates the steps with the corresponding size of the work to be done. The resulting pipeline (Figure 2-8) is really a hybrid of data and task parallelism.

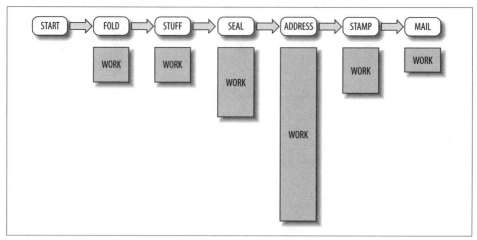

Figure 2-7. Unequal tasks are best combined or split to match people

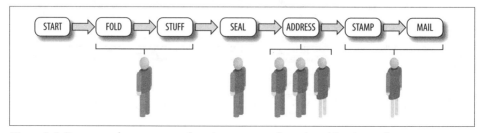

Figure 2-8. Because tasks are not equal, assign more people to the addressing task

Achieving Parallelism

Coordinating people around the job of preparing and mailing the envelopes is easily expressed by the following two conceptual steps:

1. Assign people to tasks (and feel free to move them around to balance the workload).

2. Start with one person on each of the six tasks, but be willing to split up a given task so that two or more people can work on it together.

The six tasks are folding, stuffing, sealing, addressing, stamping, and mailing. We also have six people (resources) to help with the work. That is exactly how Threading Building Blocks works best: you define tasks and data at a level you can explain and then split or combine data to match up with resources available to do the work.

The first step in writing a parallel program is to consider where the parallelism is. Many textbooks wrestle with task and data parallelism as though there were a clear choice. Threading Building Blocks allows any combination of the two that you express.

If you are lucky, your program will be cleanly data-parallel only. To simplify this work, Threading Building Blocks requires you only to specify tasks and how to split them. For a completely data-parallel task, in Threading Building Blocks you will define one task to which you give all the data. That task will then be split up automatically to use the available hardware parallelism. The implicit synchronization will often eliminate the need for using locks to achieve synchronization.

People have been exploring decomposition for decades, and some patterns have emerged. We'll cover this more later when we discuss design patterns for parallel programming.

Scaling and Speedup

The scalability of a program is a measure of how much *speedup* the program gets as you add more and more processor cores. Speedup is the ratio of the time it takes to run a program without parallelism versus the time it runs in parallel. A speedup of 2X indicates that the parallel program runs in half the time of the sequential program. An example would be a sequential program that takes 34 seconds to run on a one-processor machine and 17 seconds to run on a quad-core machine.

As a goal, we would expect that our program running on two processor cores should run faster than the program running on one processor core. Likewise, running on four processor cores should be faster than running on two cores.

We say that a program does not *scale* beyond a certain point when adding more processor cores no longer results in additional speedup. When this point is reached, it is common for performance to fall if we force additional processor cores to be used. This is because the overhead of distributing and synchronizing begins to dominate. Threading Building Blocks has some algorithm templates which use the notion of a *grain size* to help limit the splitting of data to a reasonable level to avoid this problem. Grain size will be introduced and explained in detail in Chapters 3 and 4.

As Thinking Parallel becomes intuitive, structuring problems to scale will become second nature.

How Much Parallelism Is There in an Application?

The topic of how much parallelism there is in an application has gotten considerable debate, and the answer is "it depends."

It certainly depends on the size of the problem to be solved and on the ability to find a suitable algorithm to take advantage of the parallelism. Much of this debate previously has been centered on making sure we write efficient and worthy programs for expensive and rare parallel computers. The definition of size, the efficiency required, and the expense of the computer have all changed with the emergence of multi-core processors. We need to step back and be sure we review the ground we are standing on. The world has changed.

Amdahl's Law

Gene Amdahl, renowned computer architect, made observations regarding the maximum improvement to a computer system that can be expected when only a portion of the system is improved. His observations in 1967 have come to be known as *Amdahl's Law*. It tells us that if we speed up *everything* in a program by 2X, we can expect the resulting program to run 2X faster. However, if we improve the performance of only half the program by 2X, the overall system improves only by 1.33X. Amdahl's Law is easy to visualize. Imagine a program with five equal parts that runs in 500 seconds, as shown in Figure 2-9. If we can speed up two of the parts by 2X and 4X, as shown in Figure 2-10, the 500 seconds are reduced to only 400 and 350 seconds, respectively. More and more we are seeing the limitations of the portions that are not speeding up through parallelism. No matter how many processor cores are available, the serial portions create a barrier at 300 seconds that will not be broken (see Figure 2-11).

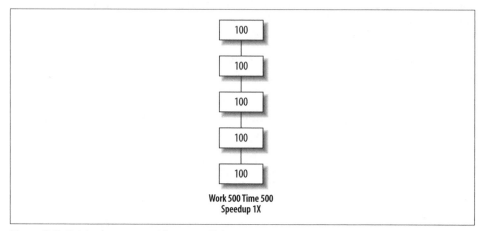

Figure 2-9. Original program without parallelism

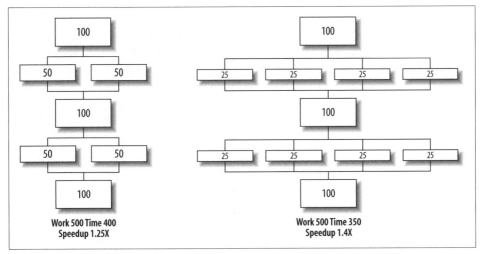

Figure 2-10. Progress on adding parallelism

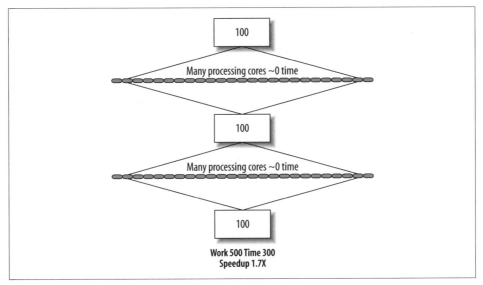

Figure 2-11. Limits according to Amdahl's Law

Parallel programmers have long used Amdahl's Law to predict the maximum speedup that can be expected using multiple processors. This interpretation ultimately tells us that a computer program will never go faster than the sum of the parts that do *not* run in parallel (the serial portions), no matter how many processors we have.

Many have used Amdahl's Law to predict doom and gloom for parallel computers, but there is another way to look at things that shows much more promise.

Gustafson's observations regarding Amdahl's Law

Amdahl's Law views programs as fixed, while we make changes to the computer. But experience seems to indicate that as computers get new capabilities, applications change to take advantage of these features. Most of today's applications would not run on computers from 10 years ago, and many would run poorly on machines that are just five years old. This observation is not limited to obvious applications such as games; it applies also to office applications, web browsers, photography software, DVD production and editing software, and Google Earth.

More than two decades after the appearance of Amdahl's Law, John Gustafson, while at Sandia National Labs, took a different approach and suggested a reevaluation of Amdahl's Law. Gustafson noted that parallelism is more useful when you observe that workloads grow as computers become more powerful and support programs that do more work rather than focusing on a fixed workload. For many problems, as the problem size grows, the work required for the parallel part of the problem grows faster than the part that cannot be parallelized (the so-called serial part). Hence, as the problem size grows, the serial fraction decreases and, according to Amdahl's Law, the scalability improves. So we can start with an application that looks like Figure 2-9, but if the problem scales with the available parallelism, we are likely to see the advancements illustrated in Figure 2-12. If the sequential parts still take the same amount of time to perform, they become less and less important as a percentage of the whole. The algorithm eventually reaches the conclusion shown in Figure 2-13. Performance grows at the same rate as the number of processors, which is called *linear* or *order of n scaling*, denoted as O(n).

Even in our example, the efficiency of the program is still greatly limited by the serial parts. The efficiency of using processors in our example is about 40 percent for large numbers of processors. On a supercomputer, this might be a terrible waste. On a system with multi-core processors, one can hope that other work is running on the computer concurrently to use the processing power our application does not use. This new world has many complexities. In any case, it is still good to minimize serial code, whether you take the "glass half empty" view and favor Amdahl's Law or you lean toward the "glass half full" view and favor Gustafson's observations.

Both Amdahl's Law and Gustafson's observations are correct. The difference lies in whether you want to make an existing program run faster with the same workload or you envision working on a larger workload. History clearly favors programs getting more complex and solving larger problems. Gustafson's observations fit the historical evidence better. Nevertheless, Amdahl's Law is still going to haunt us as we work today to make a single application work faster on the same benchmark. You have to look forward to see a brighter picture.

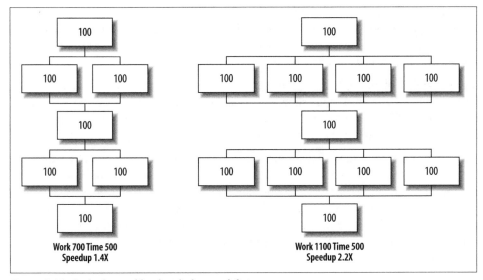

Figure 2-12. Scale the workload with the capabilities

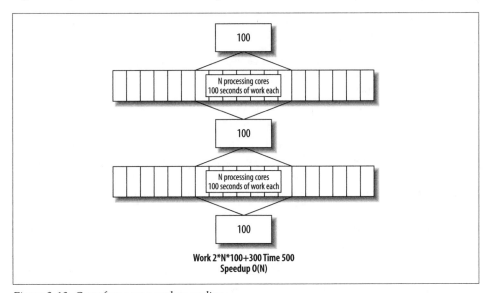

Figure 2-13. Gustafson saw a path to scaling

 The value of parallelism is easier to prove if you are looking forward than if you assume the world is not changing.

Making today's application run faster by switching to a parallel algorithm without expanding the problem is harder than making it run faster on a larger problem. The value of parallelism is easier to prove when we are not constrained to speeding up an application that already works well on today's machines.

The scalability of an application comes down to increasing the work done in parallel and minimizing the work done serially. Amdahl motivates us to reduce the serial portion, whereas Gustafson tells us to consider larger problems, where the parallel work is likely to increase relative to the serial work.

Some have defined scaling that requires the problem size to grow as *weak scaling*. It is ironic that the term *embarrassingly parallel* is commonly applied to other types of scaling. Because almost all true scaling happens only when the problem size scales with the parallelism available, we should call that just *scaling*. We can apply the term *embarrassing scaling* to scaling that occurs without growth in the size. As with *embarrassing parallelism*, if you have *embarrassing scaling*, take advantage of it and do not be embarrassed.

What did they really say?

Here is what Amdahl and Gustafson actually said in their famous papers, which have generated much dialog ever since:

> ...the effort expended on achieving high parallel processing rates is wasted unless it is accompanied by achievements in sequential processing rates of very nearly the same magnitude. —Amdahl, 1967

> ...speedup should be measured by scaling the problem to the number of processors, not by fixing the problem size. —Gustafson, 1988

Combining these ideas, you can conclude that the value of parallelism is easier to prove if you are looking forward than if you assume the world is not changing. If we double the number of cores every couple of years, we should be working to double the amount of work we want our computer to do every couple of years as well.

Serial versus parallel algorithms

One of the truths in programming is this: the best serial algorithm is seldom the best parallel algorithm, and the best parallel algorithm is seldom the best serial algorithm.

This means that trying to write a program that runs well on a system with one processor core, and also runs well on a system with a dual-core processor or quad-core processor, is harder than just writing a good serial program or a good parallel program.

Supercomputer programmers know from practice that the work required in concurrent tasks grows quickly as a function of the problem size. If the work grows faster than the sequential overhead (e.g., communication, synchronization), you can fix a program that scales poorly just by increasing the problem size. It's not uncommon at all to take a program that won't scale much beyond 100 processors and scale it nicely to 300 or more processors just by doubling the size of the problem.

To be ready for the future, write parallel programs and abandon the past. That's the simplest and best advice to offer. Writing code with one foot in the world of efficient single-threaded performance and the other foot in the world of parallelism is the hardest job of all.

What Is a Thread?

If you know what a *thread* is, skip ahead to the section "Safety in the Presence of Concurrency." It's important to be comfortable with the concept of a thread, even though the goal of Intel Threading Building Blocks is to abstract away thread management. Fundamentally, you will still be constructing a threaded program and you will need to understand the implications of this underlying implementation.

All modern operating systems are *multitasking* operating systems that typically use a *preemptive* scheduler. *Multitasking* means that more than one program can be active at a time. You may take it for granted that you can have an email program and a web browser program running at the same time. Yet, not that long ago, this was not the case.

A *preemptive* scheduler means the operating system puts a limit on how long one program can use a processor core before it is forced to let another program use it. This is how the operating system makes it appear that your email program and your web browser are running at the same time when only one processor core is actually doing the work.

Generally, each process (program) runs relatively independent of other processes. In particular, the memory where your program variables will reside is completely separate from the memory used by other processes. Your email program cannot directly assign a new value to a variable in the web browser program. If your email program can communicate with your web browser—for instance, to have it open a web page from a link you received in email—it does so with some form of communication that takes much more time than a memory access.

Breaking a problem into multiple processes and using *only* a restricted, mutually agreed-upon communication between them has a number of advantages. One of the advantages is that an error in one process will be less likely to interfere with other processes. Before multitasking operating systems, it was much more common for a single program to be able to crash the entire machine. Putting tasks into processes, and limiting interaction with other processes and the operating system, has greatly added to system stability.

Multiple processes work with coarse-grained parallelism where the tasks to be done do not require frequent *synchronization*. You can think of synchronization as the computer equivalent of people working on different parts of the same job and stopping occasionally to talk, to hand over finished work to another person, and perhaps to get work from another person. Parallel tasks need to coordinate their work as well. The more fine-grained their parallelism is, the more time is spent communicating between tasks. If parallelism is too fine, the amount of communication between tasks can become unreasonable.

Therefore, all modern operating systems support the subdivision of processes into multiple *threads* of execution. Threads run independently, like processes, and no thread knows what other threads are running or where they are in the program unless they synchronize explicitly. The key difference between threads and processes is that the threads within a process share all the data of the process. Thus, a simple memory access can accomplish the task of setting a variable in another thread.

Each thread has its own *instruction pointer* (a register pointing to the place in the program where it is running) and *stack* (a region of memory that holds subroutine return addresses and local variables for subroutines), but otherwise a thread shares its memory. Even the stack memory of each thread is accessible to the other threads, though when they are programmed properly, they don't step on each other's stacks.

Threads within a process that run independently but share memory have the obvious benefit of being able to share work quickly, because each thread has access to the same memory as the other threads in the same process. The operating system can view multiple threads as multiple processes that have essentially the same permissions to regions of memory.

Programming Threads

A process usually starts with a single thread of execution and is allowed to request that more threads be started. Threads can be used to logically break down a program into multiple tasks, such as a user interface and a main program. Threads are also useful for programming for parallelism, such as with multi-core processors.

Many questions arise once you start programming to use threads. How should you divide and assign tasks to keep each available processor core busy? Should you create a thread each time you have a new task, or should you create and manage a pool of threads? Should the number of threads depend on the number of cores? What should you do with a thread running out of tasks?

These are important questions for the implementation of multitasking, but that doesn't mean you as the application programmer should answer them. They detract from the objective of expressing the goals of your program. Likewise, assembly language programmers once had to worry about memory alignment, memory layout, stack pointers, and register assignments. Languages such as Fortran and C were created to abstract away those important details and leave them to be solved with compilers and libraries. Similarly, today we seek to abstract away thread management so that programmers can express parallelism directly.

 Threading Building Blocks takes care of all thread management so that programmers can express parallelism directly with tasks.

A key notion of Threading Building Blocks is that you should break up the program into many more tasks than there are processors. You should specify as much parallelism as practical and let Threading Building Blocks choose how much of that parallelism is actually exploited.

Safety in the Presence of Concurrency

When code is written in such a way that it cannot be run in parallel without the concurrency causing problems, it is said *not* to be *thread-safe*. Even with the abstraction that Threading Building Blocks offers, the concept of thread safety is essential. You need to understand how to build a program that is thread-safe, which essentially means that each function can be invoked by more than one thread at the same time.

Single-threaded programs contain only one flow of control, so their parts need not be reentrant or thread-safe. In multithreaded programs, the same functions and the same resources may be utilized concurrently by several flows of control. Code written for multithreaded programs must therefore be reentrant and thread-safe.

Any function that maintains a persistent state between invocations requires careful writing to ensure it is thread-safe. In general, functions should be written to have no side effects so that concurrent use is not an issue. In cases where global side effects— which might range from setting a single variable to creating or deleting a file—do need to occur, the programmer must be careful to call for *mutual exclusion*, ensuring that only one thread at a time can execute the code that has the side effect, and that other threads are excluded from that section of code.

Be sure to use thread-safe libraries. All the libraries you use should be reviewed to make sure they are thread-safe. The C++ library has some functions inherited from C that are particular problems because they hold internal state between calls, specifically `asctime`, `ctime`, `gmtime`, `localtime`, `rand`, and `strtok`. Be sure to check the documentation if you need to use these functions to see whether thread-safe versions are available. The C++ Standard Template Library (STL) container classes are in general *not* thread-safe (hence, some of the containers defined by Threading Building Blocks are not thread-safe either).

Mutual Exclusion and Locks

You need to think about whether concurrent accesses to the same resources will occur in your program. The resource with which you will most often be concerned is data held in memory, but you also need to think about files and I/O of all kinds.

The best policy is to decompose your problem in such a way that synchronization is implicit instead of explicit. You can achieve this by breaking up the tasks so that they can work independently, and the only synchronization that occurs is waiting for all the tasks to be completed at the end.

Instead of locks, which are shown in Figure 2-14, you can use a small set of operations that the system guarantees to be *atomic*. An atomic operation is equivalent to an instruction that cannot be interrupted.

When explicit synchronization and atomic operations are insufficient, locks needs to be used. Chapter 7 covers the various options for mutual exclusion.

Consider a program with two threads. We start with X = 44. Thread A executes X = X + 10. Thread B executes X = X – 12. If we add locking (Figure 2-14) so that only Thread A or Thread B can execute its statement at a time, we end up with X = 42. If both threads try to obtain a lock at the same time, one will be excluded and will have to wait before the lock is granted. Figure 2-14 shows how long Thread B might have to wait if it requested the lock at the same time as Thread A but did not get the lock because Thread A had it first.

Thread A	Thread B	Value of X
LOCK (X)	*(wait)*	44
Read X (44)	*(wait)*	44
add 10	*(wait)*	44
Write X (54)	*(wait)*	54
UNLOCK (X)	*(wait)*	54
	LOCK (X)	54
	Read X (54)	54
	subtract 12	54
	Write X (42)	42
	UNLOCK (X)	**42**

Figure 2-14. Predictable outcome due using mutual exclusion

Without the locks, a race condition exists and at least two more results are possible: X = 32 or X = 54. X = 42 can still occur as well (Figure 2-15). Three results are now possible because each statement reads X, does a computation, and writes to X. Without locking, there is no guarantee that a thread reads the value of X before or after the other thread writes a value.

Thread A	Thread B	Value of X
Read X (44)		44
add 10	Read X (44)	44
Write X (54)	subtract 12	54
	Write X (32)	32

RACE – A first, B second

Thread A	Thread B	Value of X
	Read X (44)	44
	subtract 12	44
	Write X (32)	32
Read X (32)		32
add 10		32
Write X (42)		42

DESIRED

Thread A	Thread B	Value of X
	Read X (44)	44
Read X (44)	subtract 12	44
add 10	Write X (32)	32
Write X (54)		54

RACE – B first, A second

Figure 2-15. Results of race condition (no mutual exclusion)

Correctness

The biggest challenge of learning to Think Parallel is understanding correctness as it relates to concurrency. *Concurrency* means you have multiple threads of control that are active at one time. The operating system is going to schedule those threads in a number of ways. Each time the program runs, the precise order of operations will potentially be different. Your challenge as a programmer is to make sure that every legitimate way the operations in your concurrent program can be ordered will still lead to the correct result. A high-level abstraction such as Threading Building Blocks helps a great deal, but there are a few issues you have to grapple with on your own: potential variations in results when programs compute results in parallel, and new types of programming bugs when locks are used incorrectly.

Computations done in parallel often get different results than the original sequential program. Round-off errors are the most common surprise for many programmers when a program is modified to run in parallel. You should expect numeric results to vary slightly when computations are changed to run in parallel. For example, computing (A+B+C+D) as ((A+B)+(C+D)) enables A+B and C+D to be computed in parallel, but the final sum may be slightly different from other evaluations such as (((A+B)+C)+D). Even the parallel results can differ from run to run, depending on the order of the operations.

A few types of program failures can happen only in a parallel program because they involve the coordination of tasks. These failures are known as *deadlocks* and *race conditions*. Although Threading Building Blocks simplifies programming so as to reduce the chance for such failures, they are still quite possible. Multithreaded programs can be *nondeterministic* as a result, which means the same program with the same input can follow different execution paths each time it is invoked. When this occurs, failures do not repeat consistently and debugger intrusions can easily change the failure, thereby making debugging frustrating, to say the least.

Tracking down and eliminating the source of unwanted nondeterminism is not easy. Specialized tools such as the Intel Thread Checker help, but the first step is to understand these issues and try to avoid them.

There is also another very common problem when moving from sequential code to parallel code: getting different results because of subtle changes in the order in which work is done. Some algorithms may be unstable, whereas others simply exercise the opportunity to reorder operations that are considered to have multiple correct orderings.

Here are two key errors in parallel programming:

Deadlock

Deadlock occurs when at least two tasks wait for each other and each will not resume until the other task proceeds. This happens easily when code requires the acquisition of multiple locks. If Task A needs Lock R and Lock X, it might get Lock R and then try to get Lock X. Meanwhile, if Task B needs the same two locks but grabs Lock X first, we can easily end up with Task A wanting Lock X while holding Lock R, and Task B waiting for Lock R while it holds only Lock X. The resulting impasse can be resolved only if one task releases the lock it is holding. If neither yields, deadlock occurs and the tasks are stuck forever.

Solution

Use implicit synchronization to avoid the need for locks. In general, avoid using locks, especially multiple locks at one time. Acquiring a lock and then invoking a function or subroutine that happens to use locks is often the source of multiple lock issues. Because access to shared resources must sometimes occur, the two most common solutions are to acquire locks in a certain order (always A and then B, for instance) or to release all locks whenever a lock cannot be acquired and begin again.

Race conditions

A race condition occurs when multiple tasks read from and write to the same memory without proper synchronization. The "race" may finish correctly sometimes and therefore complete without errors, and at other times it may finish incorrectly. Figure 2-15 illustrates a simple example with three different possible outcomes due to a race condition.

Race conditions are less catastrophic than deadlocks, but more pernicious because they don't necessarily produce obvious failures and yet can lead to corrupted data: an incorrect value being read or written. The result of some race conditions can be a state that is not legal because a couple of threads may each succeed in updating half their state (multiple data elements).

Solution

Manage shared data in a disciplined manner using the synchronization mechanisms described in Chapter 7 to ensure a correct program. Avoid low-level methods based on locks because it is so easy to get things wrong.

Explicit locks should be a last effort. In general, the programmer is better off using the synchronization implied by the algorithm templates and task scheduler when possible. For instance, use `parallel_reduce` instead of creating your own with shared variables. The `join` operation in `parallel_reduce` is guaranteed not to run until the subproblems it is joining are completed.

Abstraction

When writing a program, choosing an appropriate level of abstraction is important. Few programmers use assembly language anymore. Programming languages such as C and C++ have abstracted away the low-level details. Hardly anyone misses the old programming method.

Parallelism is no different. You can easily get caught up in writing code that is too low-level. Raw thread programming requires you to manage threads, which is time-consuming and error-prone.

Programming in Threading Building Blocks offers an opportunity to avoid thread management. This will result in code that is easier to create, easier to maintain, and more elegant. However, it does require thinking of algorithms in terms of what work can be divided and how data can be divided.

Patterns

Mark Twain once observed, "The past does not repeat itself, but it does rhyme." And so it is with computer programs: code may not be reused over and over without change, but patterns do emerge.

Condensing years of parallel programming experience into patterns is not an exact science. However, we can explain parallel programming approaches in more detail than just talking about task versus data decomposition.

Object-oriented programming has found value in the Gang of Four (Gamma, Helm, Johnson, and Vlissides) and their landmark work, *Design Patterns: Elements of Reusable Object-Oriented Software* (Addison Wesley). Many credit that book with bringing more order to the world of object-oriented programming. The book gathered the collective wisdom of the community and boiled it down into simple "patterns" with names, so people could talk about them.

A more recent book, *Patterns for Parallel Programming*, by Mattson et al. (Addison Wesley), has similarly collected the wisdom of the parallel programming community. Its point is that the field of parallel programming has moved from chaos to established practice. Experts use common tricks and have their own language to talk about these tricks. With these patterns in mind, programmers can quickly get up to speed in this new field, just as object-oriented programmers have done for years with the famous Gang of Four book.

Patterns for Parallel Programming is a serious and detailed look at how to approach parallelism. Tim Mattson often lectures on this topic, and he helped me summarize how the patterns relate to Threading Building Blocks. This will help connect the concepts of this book with the patterns for parallelism that his book works to describe.

Mattson et al. propose that programmers need to work through four design spaces when moving from first thoughts to a parallel program (Table 2-1 summarizes these explanations):

Finding concurrency

This step was discussed earlier in this chapter, in the section "Decomposition." Threading Building Blocks simplifies finding concurrency by encouraging you to find one or more tasks without worrying about mapping them to hardware threads. For some algorithms (e.g., parallel_for), you will supply an iterator that determines how to make a task split in half when the task is considered large enough. In turn, Threading Building Blocks will then divide large data ranges repeatedly to help spread work evenly among processor cores. Other algorithms, such as tbb::pipeline, help express the opportunity to create lots of tasks differently. The key for you is to express parallelism in a way that allows Threading Building Blocks to create many tasks.

Algorithm structures

This step embodies your high-level strategy. Figure 2-16 shows an organizational view for decompositions. In the "Decomposition" section, Figure 2-4 illustrated a Pipeline and Figure 2-2 illustrated Task Parallelism. Threading Building Blocks is a natural fit for these two patterns. Threading Building Blocks also excels at recursion because of its fundamental design around recursion, so the patterns of Divide and Conquer and Recursive Data are easily handled. The Event-Based Coordination pattern is a poor fit for parallelism because it is unstructured and unpredictable. In some cases, using the task scheduler of Threading Building Blocks directly may be an option.

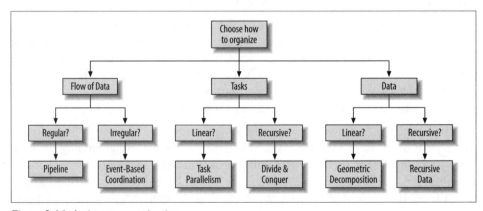

Figure 2-16. A view on organization

Supporting structures

> This step involves the details for turning our algorithm strategy into actual code. For the traditional parallel programmer, these issues are critical and have an impact that reaches across the entire parallel programming process. But Threading Building Blocks offers enough support for this design pattern that the programmer rarely has to be concerned with it.

Implementation mechanisms

> This step includes thread management and synchronization. Threading Building Blocks handles all the thread management, leaving you free to worry only about tasks at a higher level of design. The design encourages implicit synchronization so as to reduce the need for explicit locking. Chapter 7 describes the use of synchronization with Threading Building Blocks.

Table 2-1. Design spaces and Threading Building Blocks

Design space	Key	Your job or not?
Finding concurrency	Think Parallel	Your job
Algorithm structures	Algorithms from Chapters 3 and 4	You express yourself using the algorithm templates; the rest is taken care of for you
Supporting structures	Algorithms from Chapters 3 and 4	Threading Building Blocks
Implementation mechanisms	Write code to avoid the need for explicit synchronization, or use mutual exclusion from Chapter 7	Threading Building Blocks does most of the work for you

Our envelope-stuffing example from Figure 2-8 can be translated into code by addressing these four design spaces. For the *finding concurrency* design space, the concurrency is both data parallelism (the materials: envelopes, stamps, papers) and task parallelism (the jobs of folding, stuffing, etc.). For the *algorithm structures* design space, we chose a pipeline. With Threading Building Blocks, we can use tbb::pipeline. Because the synchronization is all implicit, there is no need for locks. Therefore, Threading Building Blocks handles the last two design spaces—*supporting structures* and *implementation mechanisms*—for us.

Intuition

After reading this chapter, you should be able to explain Thinking Parallel in terms of decomposition, scaling, correctness, abstraction, and patterns.

Once you understand these five concepts, and you can juggle them in your head when considering a programming task, you are Thinking Parallel. You will be developing an intuition about parallelism that will serve you well. Already, programmers seek to develop a sense of when a problem should use a parser, call on a sort algorithm, involve a database, use object-oriented programming, and so on. We look for patterns, think about decomposition, understand abstractions, and anticipate what approaches will be easier to debug. Parallelism is no different in this respect.

Developing an intuition to Think Parallel requires nothing more than understanding this chapter and trying it on a few projects. Intel Threading Building Blocks helps with each type of thinking presented in the chapter. Combined with Think Parallel intuition, Threading Building Blocks simply helps with parallel programming.

Basic Algorithms

This is *the* key chapter in learning Intel Threading Building Blocks. Here you will come to understand the recursion, task-stealing, and algorithm templates that Threading Building Blocks uniquely combines.

The most visible contribution of Threading Building Blocks is the *algorithm templates* covered in this chapter and the next chapter. This chapter introduces the simplest loop-oriented algorithms based on recursive ranges, and the next chapter expands on that with more advanced algorithm support. Future chapters offer details that round out features needed to make your use of Threading Building Blocks complete.

Threading Building Blocks offers the following types of generic parallel algorithms, which are covered in this chapter:

Loop parallelization

> `parallel_for` and `parallel_reduce`
> > Load-balanced, parallel execution of a fixed number of independent loop iterations

> `parallel_scan`
> > A template function that computes a prefix computation (also known as a scan) in parallel ($y[i] = y[i-1]$ *op* $x[i]$)

The validity of the term *Building Block* is clearer when you see how fully Threading Building Blocks supports nested parallelism to enable you to build larger parallel components from smaller parallel components. A Quicksort example shown in Chapter 11, for instance, was implemented using `parallel_for` recursively. The recursion is implicit because of Threading Building Blocks' inherent concept of *splitting*, as embodied in the parallel iterator.

> When you thoroughly understand why a recursive algorithm such as Quicksort should use the `parallel_for` template with a recursive range instead of using a recursion template, you will understand a great deal about how to apply Threading Building Blocks to your applications.

Understanding some fundamental concepts can make the parallelism model of Threading Building Blocks intuitive. Most fundamental is the reliance on breaking up problems recursively as required to get to the right level of parallel tasks. The proper degree of breakdown in a problem is embodied in a concept called *grain size*. Grain size started as a mysterious manual process, which has since been facilitated with some automation (heuristics) in the latest versions of Threading Building Blocks. This chapter offers rules of thumb, based on experience with Threading Building Blocks, for picking the best grain size.

Recursively breaking down a problem turns out to be much better than the more obvious static division of work. It also fits perfectly with the use of task stealing instead of a global task queue. Reliance on task stealing is a critical design decision that avoids implementing something as important as a task queue as a global resource that becomes a bottleneck for scalability.

Furthermore, as you wrestle to decide which algorithm template to apply to parallelism (for loop, while loop, pipeline, divide and conquer, etc.), you will find that you want to mix and nest them. More often than not, you realize that in a C++ program, a combination—such as a parallel_for loop controlling a parallel set of *pipelines*—is what you want to program. Threading Building Blocks makes such mixtures surprisingly easy to implement. Not only that, but the fundamental design choice of recursion and task stealing makes the resulting program work very well.

Initializing and Terminating the Library

Intel Threading Building Blocks components are defined in the tbb namespace. For brevity's sake, the namespace is explicit in the first mention of a component in this book, but implicit afterward.

Any thread that uses an algorithm template from the library or the task scheduler must have an initialized tbb::task_scheduler_init object. A thread may have more than one of these objects initialized at a time. The task scheduler shuts down when all task_scheduler_init objects terminate. By default, the constructor for task_scheduler_init does the initialization and the destructor does the termination. Thus, declaring a task_scheduler_init in main( ), as in Example 3-1, both starts and shuts down the scheduler.

Example 3-1. Initializing the library

```
#include "tbb/task_scheduler_init.h"
using namespace tbb;

int main( ) {
    task_scheduler_init init;
    ...
    return 0;
}
```

The using directive in the example enables you to use the library identifiers without having to write out the namespace prefix tbb before each identifier. The rest of the examples assume that such a using directive is present.

Automatic startup/shutdown was not implemented because, based on Intel's experience in implementing OpenMP, we knew that parts are too problematic on some operating systems to do it behind the scenes. In particular, always knowing when a thread shuts down can be quite problematic.

Calling the initialization more than once will not cause the program to fail, but it is a bit wasteful and can cause a flurry of extra warnings from some debugging or analysis tools, such as the Intel Thread Checker.

The section "Mixing with Other Threading Packages" in Chapter 10 explains how to construct task_scheduler_init objects if your program creates threads itself using another interface.

The constructor for task_scheduler_init takes an optional parameter that specifies the number of desired threads, including the calling thread. The optional parameter can be one of the following:

- The value task_scheduler_init::automatic, which is the default when the parameter is not specified. It exists for the sake of the method task_scheduler_init::initialize.
- The value task_scheduler_init::deferred, which defers the initialization until the task_scheduler_init::initialize(*n*) method is called. The value *n* can be any legal value for the constructor's optional parameter.
- A *positive integer* specifying the number of threads to use.

The deferred form of the task scheduler allows you to create the init object at the right scope so that the destruction will happen when that scope is exited. The actual initialization call can then occur inside a subroutine without having the destruction implicit in the return cause a problem.

The argument should be specified only when doing scaling studies during development. Omit the parameter, or use task_scheduler_init::automatic, for production code. The reason for not specifying the number of threads in production code is that in a large software project, there is no way for various components to know how many threads would be optimal for other components. Hardware threads are a shared global resource. It is best to leave the decision of how many threads to use to the task scheduler.

The parameter is ignored if another task_scheduler_init object is active. Disagreements in the number of threads are resolved in favor of the first task_scheduler_init that has not been deferred.

Design your programs to try to create many more tasks than there are threads, and let the task scheduler choose the mapping from tasks to threads.

In general, you will let the library be terminated automatically by the destructor when all `task_scheduler_init` objects terminate.

For cases where you want more control, there is a method named `task_scheduler_init::terminate` for terminating the library early, before the `task_scheduler_init` is destroyed. Example 3-2 defers the decision of the number of threads to be used by the scheduler (line 3 defers, line 5 commits), and terminates it early (line 8).

Example 3-2. Early scheduler termination

```
1  int main( int argc, char* argv[] ) {
2      int nthread = strtol(argv[0],0,0);
3      task_scheduler_init init(task_scheduler_init::deferred);
4      if( nthread>=1 )
5        init.initialize(nthread);
6      ... code that uses task scheduler only if nthread>=1 ...
7      if( nthread>=1 )
8          init.terminate( );
9      return 0;
10 }
```

In Example 3-2, you can omit the call to `terminate( )` because the destructor for `task_scheduler_init` checks whether the `task_scheduler_init` was initialized and, if so, performs the termination.

The task scheduler is somewhat expensive to start up and shut down, so it's recommended that you put the `task_scheduler_init` in your main routine or when a thread is born, and do not try to create a scheduler every time you use a parallel algorithm template.

Loop Parallelization

The simplest form of scalable parallelism is a loop of iterations that can each run simultaneously without interfering with each other. The following sections demonstrate how to parallelize such simple loops.

`parallel_for` *and* `parallel_reduce`

Load-balanced, parallel execution of a fixed number of independent loop iterations

`parallel_scan`

A template function that computes a parallel prefix (`y[i] = y[i-1] op x[i]`)

parallel_for

Suppose you want to apply a function Foo to each element of an array, and it is safe to process each element concurrently. Example 3-3 shows the sequential code to do this.

Example 3-3. Original loop code

```
void SerialApplyFoo( float a[], size_t n ) {
    for( size_t i=0; i<n; ++i )
        Foo(a[i]);
}
```

The iteration space here is of type size_t, and it goes from 0 to n-1. The template function tbb::parallel_for breaks this iteration space into chunks and runs each chunk on a separate thread.

The first step in parallelizing this loop is to convert the loop body into a form that operates on a chunk. The form is a Standard Template Library (STL)-style function object, called the *body* object, in which operator( ) processes a chunk. Example 3-4 declares the body object.

Example 3-4. A class for use by a parallel_for

```
#include "tbb/blocked_range.h"

class ApplyFoo {
    float *const my_a;
public:
    void operator()( const blocked_range<size_t>& r ) const {
        float *a = my_a;
        for( size_t i=r.begin(); i!=r.end(); ++i )
            Foo(a[i]);
    }
    ApplyFoo( float a[] ) :
        my_a(a)
    {}
};
```

Note the iteration space argument to operator( ). A blocked_range<T> is a template class provided by the library. It describes a one-dimensional iteration space over type T. Class parallel_for works with other kinds of iteration spaces, too. The library provides blocked_range2d for two-dimensional spaces. A little later in this chapter, in the section "Advanced Topic: Other Kinds of Iteration Spaces," I will explain how you can define your own spaces.

An instance of ApplyFoo needs member fields that remember all the local variables that were defined outside the original loop but were used inside it. Usually, the constructor for the body object will initialize these fields, though parallel_for does not care how the body object is created. The template function `parallel_for` requires that the body object have a copy constructor, which is invoked to create a separate copy (or copies) for each worker thread. It also invokes the destructor to destroy these copies.

In most cases, the implicitly generated copy constructor and destructor work correctly. You may need an explicit destructor if you've designed it such that the destructor must perform some action, such as freeing memory. If the copy constructor and destructor are both implicit, there will be no such side effects. But, if the destructor is explicit, most likely the copy constructor will need to be explicit as well.

Because the body object might be copied, its `operator( )` should not modify the body. Thus, in Example 3-4, the `operator( )` function should not modify data member `my_a`. It *can* modify what `my_a` points to. This distinction is emphasized by declaring `my_a` as const and what it points to as (non-const) `float`. Otherwise, the modification might or might not become visible to the thread that invoked `parallel_for`, depending upon whether `operator( )` is acting on the original or a copy. As a reminder of this nuance, `parallel_for` requires that the body object's `operator( )` be declared as const.

 Threading Building Blocks is designed to help guard against mistakes that would lead to failures: thus, `operator( )` is required to be const-qualified as a syntactic guard against trying to accumulate side effects that would be lost by the thread-private copies.

The example `operator( )` loads `my_a` into a local variable, a. Though it's not necessary, there are two reasons for doing this in the example:

Style

It makes the loop body look more like the original.

Performance

Sometimes, putting frequently accessed values into local variables helps the compiler optimize the loop better, because local variables are often easier for the compiler to track.

After you have written the loop body as a body object, invoke the template function `parallel_for`, as shown in Example 3-5.

Example 3-5. Use of parallel_for

```
#include "tbb/parallel_for.h"

void ParallelApplyFoo( float a[], size_t n ) {
    parallel_for(blocked_range<size_t>(0,n,YouPickAGrainSize), ApplyFoo(a) );
}
```

The blocked_range constructed here represents the entire iteration space from 0 to n-1, which parallel_for divides into subspaces for each processor. The general form of the constructor is:

```
blocked_range<T>(begin,end,grainsize)
```

The T specifies the value type. The arguments begin and end specify the iteration space in STL style as a half-open interval [begin,end). Half-open intervals are convenient because the empty set is easily represented by [X,X). If Y is less than X, a range [X,Y) is considered invalid and will raise an assertion if the debug macro TBB_DO_ASSERT is defined and is nonzero.

Half-Open Intervals

Intervals are specified using a square bracket [or] to indicate inclusion, or a rounded bracket (or) to indicate exclusion. An interval of [2,7] indicates the numbers 2, 3, 4, 5, 6, 7, whereas the interval (2,7) means 3, 4, 5, 6. The half-open interval [2,7) indicates 2, 3, 4, 5, 6.

Threading Building Blocks uses half-open intervals. This means that the interval [X,Y) effectively creates an iteration which will be covered by the loop for (i=X;i<Y;i++).

Example 3-6 defines a routine, ParallelAverage, using parallel_for, that sets output[i] to the average of input[i-1], input[i], and input[i+1], for $0 \leq i < n$.

Example 3-6. Parallel average

```
#include "tbb/parallel_for.h"
#include "tbb/blocked_range.h"

using namespace tbb;

struct Average {
    float* input;
    float* output;
    void operator()( const blocked_range<int>& range ) const {
        for( int i=range.begin(); i!=range.end(); ++i )
            output[i] = (input[i-1]+input[i]+input[i+1])*(1/3.0f);
    }
};

// Note: The input must be padded such that input[-1] and input[n]
// can be used to calculate the first and last output values.
void ParallelAverage( float* output, float* input, size_t n ) {
    Average avg;
    avg.input = input;
    avg.output = output;
    parallel_for( blocked_range<int>( 0, n, 1000 ), avg );
}
```

Grain size

The third argument, grainsize, specifies the number of iterations for a *reasonable size* chunk to deal out to a processor. If the iteration space has more than grainsize iterations, parallel_for splits it into separate subranges that are scheduled separately.

The grainsize amortizes parallel scheduling overhead. Having a grainsize independent of the number of processors tends to keep, in common cases, the parallel scheduling overhead in constant proportion to real work. This is because the packaging-and-handling overhead is relatively constant per grain and therefore independent of the number of processors.

The grainsize enables you to avoid excessive parallel overhead. A parallel loop construct incurs overhead cost for every subrange. If the subranges are too small, the overhead may exceed the useful work. By specifying a grain size, you can limit the overhead. The grainsize effectively sets a minimum threshold for parallelization.

Figure 3-1 illustrates the impact of overhead by showing the useful work as lettered squares surrounded by the overhead of a grain of work (the darker surrounding areas). On the left, the problem is broken into four pieces (4X), and on the right, with a finer grain size, the problem is broken into 36 pieces (36X).

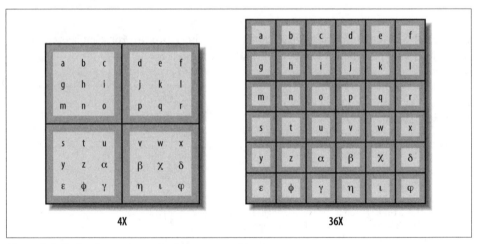

Figure 3-1. Packaging versus grain size, same workload

The total work to be done on the system is represented by the light and dark gray regions combined—the overall box. The 36X case shows how too small a grain size leads to a relatively high proportion of overhead. The 4X case shows how a large grain size reduces this proportion, at the cost of reducing potential parallelism. The overhead as a fraction of useful work depends on the grain size, not on the number of grains. Consider this relationship and not the total number of iterations or number of processors when setting a grain size.

A recommended rule of thumb is that grainsize iterations of operator( ) should take at least 10,000 to 100,000 instructions to execute, which typically means more than a few thousand mathematic calculations. When in doubt, do the following:

1. Set the grainsize parameter higher than necessary. Setting it to 10,000 is usually a good starting point.
2. Run your algorithm on one processor core.
3. Start halving the grainsize parameter and see how much the algorithm slows down as the value decreases.

A slowdown of about 5 to 10 percent when running with a single thread is a good setting for most purposes. The drawback of setting a grain size too high is that it can reduce parallelism. For example, if your grainsize value is 10,000 and the loop has 20,000 iterations, the parallel_for distributes the loop across only two processors, even if more are available. However, if you are unsure, err on the side of being a little too high instead of a little too low because too low a value hurts serial performance, which in turns hurts parallel performance if other parallelism is available higher in your program.

 Grain size is not an exact science; you do not have to set it very precisely.

To illustrate the inexact nature of setting the best value, Figure 3-2 shows a typical "bathtub curve" for execution time versus grain size, based on the floating-point a[i]=b[i]*c computation over 1 million indices. There is very little work per iteration.

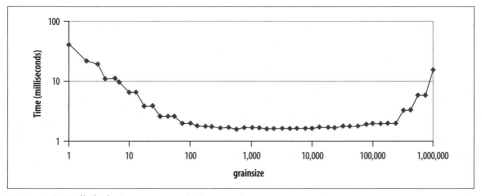

Figure 3-2. Wall clock time versus grainsize

The scale is logarithmic. The downward slope on the left side indicates that with a grain size of 1, most of the time is spent on packaging (dark gray in Figure 3-1). An increase in grain size brings a proportional decrease in parallel overhead. Then the curve flattens out because the packaging (overhead) becomes insignificant for a sufficiently large grain size. At the extreme right, the curve turns up because the chunks are so large that there are fewer chunks than available hardware threads. Notice that any grain size over the wide range of 100 to 100,000 works quite well.

 A general rule of thumb for parallelizing loop nests is to parallelize the outermost one possible. The reason is that each iteration of an outer loop is likely to provide a bigger grain of work than an iteration of an inner loop.

For a sufficiently simple function Foo, the examples might not show significant speedup when written as parallel loops. The cause could be insufficient system bandwidth between the processors and memory. In that case, you may have to rethink your algorithm to take better advantage of cache. Restructuring to better utilize the cache usually benefits the parallel program as well as the serial program.

Automatic grain size

The parallel loop templates in the original release of Threading Building Blocks required a grainsize parameter. We have been looking into ways to automatically determine the right value, but it's not easy.

Feedback from users is that they want automatic grain size determination, even if it is not always optimal, so the grainsize parameter is now optional in creating the iterator. When grainsize is not specified, a *partitioner* should be supplied to the algorithm template.

If both the partitioner and the grainsize are omitted, it's the same as specifying a grainsize of 1. If there are more than 10,000 instructions per iteration, it will work okay. With fewer than a thousand or so, there will be a serious performance hit.

A partitioner is an object that guides the chunking of a range. Currently, only auto_ partitioner makes sense without a grainsize.

The auto_partitioner provides an alternative that heuristically chooses the grain size so that you do not have to specify one. The heuristic attempts to limit overhead while still providing ample opportunities for load balancing. Guessing the grain size with the heuristic is not easy, but it does have a connection with the task scheduler that allows it to get dynamic guidance, which can make it better than a static choice of grain size.

Example 3-7 shows how to use an auto_partitioner instead of a grainsize. Notice that the grainsize parameter is omitted when constructing the blocked_range and that an auto_partitioner object is passed as a third argument to the parallel_for.

Example 3-7. Use of auto_partitioner

```
#include "tbb/parallel_for.h"

void ParallelApplyFoo( float a[], size_t n ) {
    parallel_for(blocked_range<size_t>(0,n), ApplyFoo(a),
                 auto_partitioner() );
}
```

As with most heuristics, there are situations in which auto_partitioner might not guess optimally and simple_partitioner would yield better performance. We recommend using auto_partitioner unless you have the time to experiment and tune the grain size for machines of interest.

> Support for partitioners is a new feature in Threading Building Blocks and will almost certainly have some additions in the future. You should check the documentation with the latest release to see whether there are new features.

Notes on automatic grain size

The optimal grain size depends upon implementation. This issue is not limited to parallelism. Try writing a large file using a single-character write-and-flush operation on each character. Picking appropriate chunk sizes is common in programming. Thus, automatic determination of an optimal grain size is still a research problem.

parallel_for with partitioner

parallel_for takes an optional third argument to specify a partitioner. See the earlier section "Automatic grain size" for more information.

This example shows a simple use of the partitioner concept with a parallel_for. The code shown in Example 3-8 is an extension of Example 3-6. An auto_partitioner is used to guide the splitting of the range.

Example 3-8. Parallel average with partitioner

```
#include "tbb/parallel_for.h"
#include "tbb/blocked_range.h"

using namespace tbb;

struct Average {
    float* input;
    float* output;
    void operator()( const blocked_range<int>& range ) const {
        for( int i=range.begin(); i!=range.end(); ++i )
            output[i] = (input[i-1]+input[i]+input[i+1])*(1/3.0f);
    }
};
```

Example 3-8. Parallel average with partitioner (continued)

```
// Note: The input must be padded such that input[-1] and input[n]
// can be used to calculate the first and last output values.
void ParallelAverage( float* output, float* input, size_t n ) {
    Average avg;
    avg.input = input;
    avg.output = output;
    parallel_for( blocked_range<int>( 0, n ), avg, auto_partitioner() );
```

Two important changes from Example 3-6 should be noted:

- The call to parallel_for takes a third argument, an auto_partitioner object.
- The blocked_range constructor is not provided with a grainsize parameter.

parallel_reduce

Applying a function such as sum, max, min, or logical AND across all the members of a group is called a *reduction* operation. Doing a reduction in parallel can yield a different answer from a serial reduction because of rounding. For instance, A+B+C+D+E+F may be evaluated in serial as (((((A+B)+C)+D)+E)+F), whereas the parallel version may compute ((A+B)+((C+D)+(E+F))). Ideally, the results would be the same, but if rounding can occur, the answers will differ. Traditional C++ programs perform reductions in loops, as in the summation shown in Example 3-9.

Example 3-9. Original reduction code

```
float SerialSumFoo( float a[], size_t n ) {
    float sum = 0;
    for( size_t i=0; i!=n; ++i )
        sum += Foo(a[i]);
    return sum;
}
```

If the iterations are independent, you can parallelize this loop using the template class parallel_reduce, as shown in Example 3-10.

Example 3-10. A class for use by a parallel_reduce

```
class SumFoo {
    float* my_a;
public:
    float sum;
    void operator()( const blocked_range<size_t>& r ) {
        float *a = my_a;
        for( size_t i=r.begin(); i!=r.end(); ++i )
            sum += Foo(a[i]);
    }

    SumFoo( SumFoo& x, split ) : my_a(x.my_a), sum(0) {}

    void join( const SumFoo& y ) {sum+=y.sum;}
```

Example 3-10. A class for use by a parallel_reduce (continued)

```
    SumFoo(float a[] ) :
        my_a(a), sum(0)
    {}
};
```

Threading Building Blocks defines parallel_reduce similar to parallel_for. The principle difference is that thread-private copies of the *body* must be merged at the end, and therefore the operator( ) is *not* const. Note the differences with class ApplyFoo from Example 3-4. The operator( ) is not const because it must update SumFoo::sum. Another difference is that SumFoo has a *splitting constructor* and a method named join that must be present for parallel_reduce to work.

The splitting constructor takes as arguments a reference to the original object, and has a dummy argument of type split. This dummy argument serves, simply by its presence, to distinguish the splitting constructor from a copy constructor (which would not have this argument). More information appears later in this chapter in a section titled "Advanced Topic: Other Kinds of Iteration Spaces."

The join method is invoked whenever a task finishes its work and needs to merge the result back with the main body of work. The parameter passed to the method is the result of the work, so the method will just repeat the same operation that was performed in each task on each element (in this case, a sum).

When a worker thread is available, as decided by the task scheduler, parallel_reduce hands off work to it by invoking the splitting constructor to create a subtask for the processor. When the task completes, parallel_reduce uses the join method to accumulate the result of the subtask. The diagram in Figure 3-3 shows the split-join sequence.

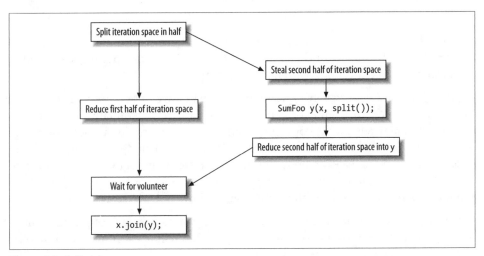

Figure 3-3. Split-join sequence

A line in Figure 3-3 indicates order in time. Notice that the splitting constructor might run concurrently while object x is being used for the first half of the reduction. Therefore, all actions of the splitting constructor that create y must be made thread-safe with respect to x. If the splitting constructor needs to increment a reference count shared with other objects, it should use an atomic increment (described in Chapter 8).

Define join to update this to represent the accumulated result for this and the right-hand side. The reduction operation should be associative, but it does not have to be commutative. For a noncommutative operation op, left.join(right) should update left to be the result of left op right.

A body is split only if the range is split, but the converse is not necessarily true. Figure 3-4 diagrams a sample execution of parallel_reduce. The root represents the original body b_0 being applied to the half-open interval [0,20). The range is recursively split at each level into two subranges. The grain size for the example is 5, which yields four leaf ranges. The slash marks (/) denote where copies (b_1 and b_2) of the body were created by the body splitting constructor. Bodies b_0 and b_1 each evaluate one leaf. Body b_2 evaluates leaf [10,15) and leaf [15,20), in that order. On the way back up the tree, parallel_reduce invokes b_0.join(b_1) and b_0.join(b_2) to merge the results of the leaves.

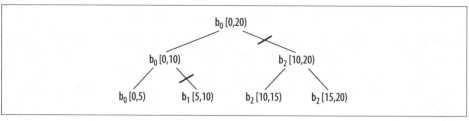

Figure 3-4. parallel_reduce over blocked_range<int>(0,20,5)

Figure 3-4 shows only one of the possible executions. Other valid executions include splitting b_2 into b_2 and b_3, or doing no splitting at all. With no splitting, b_0 evaluates each leaf in left to right order, with no calls to join.

A given body always evaluates one or more consecutive subranges in left to right order. For example, in Figure 3-4, body b_2 is guaranteed to evaluate [10,15) before [15,20). You may rely on the consecutive left to right property for a given instance of a body, but you must not rely on a particular choice of body splitting. parallel_reduce makes the choice of body splitting nondeterministically. The left-to-right property allows commutative operations to work, such as finding the first minimum number in a sequence along with its position, as shown later in Example 3-13.

When no worker threads are available, parallel_reduce executes sequentially from left to right in the same sense as for parallel_for. Sequential execution never invokes the splitting constructor or method join.

Example 3-11 uses the class defined in Example 3-10 to perform the reduction.

Example 3-11. Parallel reduction code

```
float ParallelSumFoo( const float a[], size_t n ) {
    SumFoo sf(a);
    parallel_reduce(blocked_range<size_t>(0,n,YouPickAGrainSize), sf );
    return sf.sum;
}
```

As with `parallel_for`, you must provide a reasonable grain size, with enough iterations to take at least 10,000 instructions. If you are not sure, it is best to err on the side of too large a grain size. You can also use a partitioner object to allow the runtime library to guide the chunking of the range.

`parallel_reduce` generalizes to any associative operation. In general, the splitting constructor does two things:

- Copies read-only information necessary to run the loop body
- Initializes the reduction variables to the identity element of the operations

The `join` method should do the corresponding merges. You can do more than one reduction at the same time: for instance, you can gather the `min` and `max` with a single `parallel_reduce`.

Advanced example

An example of a more advanced associative operation is to find the index containing the smallest element of an array. A serial version might look like Example 3-12.

Example 3-12. Original minimization code

```
long SerialMinIndexFoo( const float a[], size_t n ) {
    float value_of_min = FLT_MAX;        // FLT_MAX from <climits>
    long index_of_min = -1;
    for( size_t i=0; i<n; ++i ) {
        float value = Foo(a[i]);
        if( value<value_of_min ) {
            value_of_min = value;
            index_of_min = i;
        }
    }
    return index_of_min;
}
```

The loop works by keeping track of the minimum value found so far, and the index of this value. This is the only information carried between loop iterations. To convert the loop to use `parallel_reduce`, the function object must keep track of the information carried, and must be able to merge this information when iterations are spread across multiple threads. Also, the function object must record a pointer to a to provide context.

Example 3-13 shows the complete function object.

Example 3-13. Function object for minimization

```
class MinIndexFoo {
    const float *const my_a;
public:
    float value_of_min;
    long index_of_min;
    void operator()( const blocked_range<size_t>& r ) {
        const float *a = my_a;
        for( size_t i=r.begin(); i!=r.end(); ++i ) {
        float value = Foo(a[i]);
        if( value<value_of_min ) {
            value_of_min = value;
                index_of_min = i;
        }
        }
    }

    MinIndexFoo( MinIndexFoo& x, split ) :
        my_a(x.my_a),
        value_of_min(FLT_MAX),      // FLT_MAX from <climits>
        index_of_min(-1)
    {}

    void join( const SumFoo& y ) {
        if( y.value_of_min<value_of_min ) {
            value_of_min = y.value_of_min;
            index_of_min = y.index_of_min;
        }
    }

    MinIndexFoo( const float a[] ) :
        my_a(a),
        value_of_min(FLT_MAX),      // FLT_MAX from <climits>
        index_of_min(-1),
    {}
};
```

Now SerialMinIndex can be rewritten using parallel_reduce (see Example 3-14).

Example 3-14. Parallel minimization

```
long ParallelMinIndexFoo( float a[], size_t n ) {
    MinIndexFoo mif(a);
    parallel_reduce(blocked_range<size_t>(0,n,YouPickAGrainSize), mif );
    return mif.index_of_min;
}
```

Chapter 11 contains a prime number finder based on parallel_reduce.

Parallel_reduce with partitioner

Parallel_reduce has an optional third argument to specify a partitioner. See the section "Automatic grain size" for more information.

Example 3-15 extends Examples 3-10 and 3-11 by using an auto_partitioner.

Example 3-15. Parallel sum with partitioner

```
#include "tbb/parallel_reduce.h"
#include "tbb/blocked_range.h"

using namespace tbb;

struct Sum {
    float value;
    Sum() : value(0) {}
    Sum( Sum& s, split ) {value = 0;}
    void operator()( const blocked_range<float*>& range ) {
        float temp = value;
        for( float* a=range.begin(); a!=range.end(); ++a ) {
            temp += *a;
        }
        value = temp;
    }
    void join( Sum& rhs ) {value += rhs.value;}
};

float ParallelSum( float array[], size_t n ) {
    Sum total;
    parallel_reduce( blocked_range<float*>( array, array+n ),
                     total, auto_partitioner() );
    return total.value;
}
```

Two important changes from Example 3-11 should be noted:

- The call to parallel_reduce takes a third argument, an auto_partitioner object.
- The blocked_range constructor is not provided with a grainsize parameter.

Advanced Topic: Other Kinds of Iteration Spaces

The examples so far have used the class blocked_range<T> to specify ranges. This class is useful in many situations, but it does not fit every one. You can define your own iteration space objects to use with Intel Threading Building Blocks. The object must specify how it can be split into subspaces by providing two methods and a *splitting constructor*. You can see these simple definitions in the class blocked_range<T>.

If your class is called R, the methods and constructor could be as shown in Example 3-16.

Example 3-16. Define your own iteration space object

```
class R {
    // True if range is empty
    bool empty( ) const;
    // True if range can be split into nonempty subranges
    bool is_divisible( ) const;
    // Split r into subranges r and *this
    R( R& r, split );
    ...
};
```

The method `empty` must return `true` if the range is empty. The method `is_divisible` needs to return `true` if the range can be split into two nonempty subspaces, and such a split is worth the overhead. The splitting constructor needs to take two arguments:

- The first of type `R`
- The second of type `tbb::split`

The second argument is not used; it serves only to distinguish the constructor from an ordinary copy constructor.

The splitting constructor should attempt to split `r` into two halves of roughly the same size, update `r` to be the first half, and let the constructed object be the second half. The two halves should be nonempty. The parallel algorithm templates call the splitting constructor on `r` only if `r.is_divisible` is true.

The code in Example 3-17 defines a type `TrivialIntegerRange` that models the Range Concept. It represents a half-open interval [`lower`,`upper`) that is divisible down to a single integer.

Example 3-17. Trivial integer range

```
struct TrivialIntegerRange {
    int lower;
    int upper;
    bool empty( ) const {return lower==upper;}
    bool is_divisible( ) const {return upper>lower+1;}
    TrivialIntegerRange( TrivialIntegerRange& r, split ) {
        int m = (r.lower+r.upper)/2;
        lower = m;
        upper = r.upper;
        r.upper = m;
    }
};
```

`TrivialIntegerRange` is for demonstration and is not very practical because it lacks a grainsize parameter. Use the library class `blocked_range` instead. Example 3-18 shows the implementation of `blocked_range` in the Threading Building Blocks library. A full discussion of the class is beyond the scope of this book, but the code serves to show the relationships among the various methods of an iteration space and the use of the grain size.

Example 3-18. Implementation of blocked_range

```
class blocked_range {
public:
  typedef Value const_iterator;
  typedef size_t size_type;

  blocked_range() : my_begin(), my_end() {}

  blocked_range( Value begin, Value end, size_type grainsize ) :
    my_end(end), my_begin(begin), my_grainsize(grainsize)
  {
    __TBB_ASSERT( my_grainsize>0, "grainsize must be positive" );
  }

  const_iterator begin() const {return my_begin;}
  const_iterator end() const {return my_end;}

  size_type size() const {
    __TBB_ASSERT( !(end()<begin()), "size() unspecified if end()<begin()" );
    return size_type(my_end-my_begin);
  }

  size_type grainsize() const {return my_grainsize;}

  //------------------------------------------------------------------------
  // Methods that implement Range Concept
  //------------------------------------------------------------------------
  bool empty() const {return !(my_begin<my_end);}
  bool is_divisible() const {return my_grainsize<size();}

  blocked_range( blocked_range& r, split ) :
    my_end(r.my_end),
    my_begin(do_split(r)),
    my_grainsize(r.my_grainsize)
  {}

private:
  Value my_end;
  Value my_begin;
  size_type my_grainsize;

  static Value do_split( blocked_range& r ) {
    __TBB_ASSERT( r.is_divisible(), "cannot split blocked_range that is not divisible" );
    Value middle = r.my_begin + (r.my_end-r.my_begin)/2u;
    r.my_end = middle;
    return middle;
  }

  template<typename RowValue, typename ColValue>
  friend class blocked_range2d;
};
```

The iteration space does not have to be linear. Look at Example 3-19 (code from the header file *tbb/blocked_range2d.h*) for an example of a two-dimensional range. Its splitting constructor attempts to split the range along its longest axis. When used with parallel_for, it causes the loop to be *recursively blocked* in a way that improves cache usage. This nice cache behavior means that using parallel_for over a blocked_range2d<T> can make a loop run faster than the sequential equivalent, even on a single processor.

Example 3-19. A two-dimensional range

```
class blocked_range2d {
public:
    typedef blocked_range<RowValue> row_range_type;
    typedef blocked_range<ColValue> col_range_type;

private:
    row_range_type my_rows;
    col_range_type my_cols;

public:

    blocked_range2d( RowValue row_begin, RowValue row_end, typename row_range_type::size_
type row_grainsize,
                     ColValue col_begin, ColValue col_end, typename col_range_type::size_
type col_grainsize ) :
        my_rows(row_begin,row_end,row_grainsize),
        my_cols(col_begin,col_end,col_grainsize)
    {
    }

    bool empty( ) const {
        // Yes, it is a logical OR here, not AND.
        return my_rows.empty() || my_cols.empty( );
    }

    bool is_divisible( ) const {
        return my_rows.is_divisible() || my_cols.is_divisible( );
    }

    blocked_range2d( blocked_range2d& r, split ) :
        my_rows(r.my_rows),
        my_cols(r.my_cols)
    {
        if( my_rows.size()*double(my_cols.grainsize()) < my_cols.size( )*double(my_rows.
grainsize()) ) {
            my_cols.my_begin = col_range_type::do_split(r.my_cols);
        } else {
            my_rows.my_begin = row_range_type::do_split(r.my_rows);
        }
    }
```

Example 3-19. A two-dimensional range (continued)

```
    const row_range_type& rows( ) const {return my_rows;}

    const col_range_type& cols( ) const {return my_cols;}
};
```

Notes on blocked_range2d

The template class `blocked_range2d` is included in Threading Building Blocks because beneficial uses for it showed up in many common applications. Parallelizing over two dimensions instead of one often yields more parallelism and better cache behavior than parallelizing over only one dimension.

The idea of extending to three or more dimensions, and the idea of making the number of dimensions a parameter, were both considered but rejected because they added too much complexity with few practically motivating cases.

A constructor for `blocked_range2d` that takes two `blocked_range` arguments was considered as an alternative to the six-argument constructor, but so far, practice has shown that such a constructor just adds extra clutter.

parallel_scan

A `parallel_scan` computes a parallel prefix, also known as a parallel scan. This computation is an advanced concept in parallel computing that is sometimes useful in scenarios that appear to have inherently serial dependencies.

A mathematical definition of the parallel prefix is as follows. Let $\oplus$ be an associative operation $\oplus$ with left-identity element $id_\oplus$. The parallel prefix of $\oplus$ over a sequence $x_0, x_1, \dots x_{n-1}$ is a sequence $y_0, y_1, y_2, \dots y_{n-1}$ where:

- $y_0 = id_\oplus \oplus x_0$
- $y_i = y_{i-1} \oplus i$

For example, if $\oplus$ is addition, the parallel prefix corresponds to a running sum and the identity element is 0. A serial implementation of parallel prefix is:

```
    T temp = id⊕;
    for( int i=1; i<=n; ++i ) {
        temp = temp ⊕ x[i];
        y[i] = temp;
    }
```

Parallel prefix performs this in parallel by reassociating the application of $\oplus$ and using two passes. It may invoke $\oplus$ up to twice as many times as the serial prefix algorithm. But given the right grain size and sufficient hardware threads, it can outperform the serial prefix because—even though it does more work—it can distribute the work across more than one hardware thread.

Because `parallel_scan` needs two passes, systems with only two hardware threads tend to exhibit only a small speedup. `parallel_scan` is better suited for future systems with more than two cores. It shows how a problem that appears inherently sequential can be parallelized.

Example 3-20 demonstrates how to use `parallel_scan` in a way similar to the sequential example.

Example 3-20. parallel_scan

```
using namespace tbb;

class Body {
    T reduced_result;
    T* const y;
    const T* const x;
public:
    Body( T y_[], const T x_[] ) : reduced_result(0), x(x_), y(y_) {}
    T get_reduced_result() const {return reduced_result;}

    template<typename Tag>
    void operator()( const blocked_range<int>& r, Tag ) {
        T temp = reduced_result;
        for( int i=r.begin(); i<r.end(); ++i ) {
            temp = temp ⊕ x[i];
            if( Tag::is_final_scan() )
                y[i] = temp;
        }
        reduced_result = temp;
    }
    Body( Body& b, split ) : x(b.x), y(b.y), reduced_result(id⊕) {}
    void reverse_join( Body& a ) {
      reduced_result = a.reduced_result ⊕ reduced_result;
    }
    void assign( Body& b ) {reduced_result = b.reduced_result;}
};

float DoParallelScan( T y[], const T x[], int n) {
    Body body(y,x);
    parallel_scan( blocked_range<int>(0,n,1000), body );
    return body.get_reduced_result();
}
```

The definition of `operator()` demonstrates typical patterns when using `parallel_scan`:

- A single template defines both the first pass and the second pass versions. Doing so is not required, but it usually saves coding effort because the two versions are usually similar. The library defines static method `is_final_scan()` to enable differentiation among the versions.

- The prescan variant computes the ⊕ reduction, but does not update y. The prescan is used by parallel_scan to generate look-ahead partial reductions.
- The final scan variant computes the ⊕ reduction and updates y.

The operation reverse_join is similar to the operation join used by parallel_reduce, except that the arguments are reversed. In other words, this is the *right* argument of ⊕.

The template function parallel_scan decides whether and when to generate parallel work. It is thus crucial that ⊕ is associative and that the methods of Body faithfully represent it. Operations such as floating-point addition that are somewhat associative can be used, with the understanding that the results may be rounded differently depending upon the association used by parallel_scan. The reassociation may differ between runs, even on the same machine. However, if no worker threads are available, execution associates identically to the serial form shown at the beginning of this section.

Parallel_scan with partitioner

Parallel_scan has an optional third argument to specify a partitioner (Example 3-21). See the section "Automatic grain size" for more information.

Example 3-21. parallel_scan with partitioner argument

```
using namespace tbb;

class Body {
    T sum;
    T* const y;
    const T* const x;
public:
    Body( T y_[], const T x_[] ) : sum(0), x(x_), y(y_) {}
    T get_sum( ) const {return sum;}

    template<typename Tag>
    void operator( )( const blocked_range<int>& r, Tag ) {
        T temp = sum;
        for( int i=r.begin(); i<r.end( ); ++i ) {
            temp = temp ⊕ x[i];
            if( Tag::is_final_scan( ) )
                y[i] = temp;
        }
        sum = temp;
    }
    Body( Body& b, split ) : x(b.x), y(b.y), sum(id⊕) {}
    void reverse_join( Body& a ) { sum = a.sum ⊕ sum;}
    void assign( Body& b ) {sum = b.sum;}
};

float DoParallelScan( T y[], const T x[], int n) {
    Body body(y,x);
    parallel_scan( blocked_range<int>(0,n), body, auto_partitioner( ) );
    return body.get_sum( );
}
```

Two important changes from Example 3-20 should be noted:

- The call to `parallel_scan` takes a third argument, an `auto_partitioner` object.
- The `blocked_range` constructor is not provided with a `grainsize` parameter.

Recursive Range Specifications

Most algorithms provided by the Threading Building Blocks library are generic and operate on all types that model the necessary concepts. Recursive ranges define the space for the algorithm to operate upon and therefore are important to understand.

Splittable Concept

Requirements for a type whose instances can be split into two pieces. Table 3-1 lists the requirements for a splittable type X with instance x.

Table 3-1. Splittable Concept

Pseudosignature	Semantics
`X::X(X& x, split)`	Split x into two parts, one reassigned to x and the other to the newly constructed object.

Description

A type is splittable if it has a *splitting constructor* that allows an instance to be split into two pieces. The splitting constructor takes as arguments a reference to the original object, and a dummy argument of type `split`, which is defined by the library. The dummy argument distinguishes the splitting constructor from a copy constructor. After the constructor runs, x and the newly constructed object should represent the two pieces of the original x. The library uses splitting constructors in two contexts:

- *Partitioning* a range into two subranges that can be processed concurrently
- *Forking* a body (function object) into two bodies that can run concurrently

The following model types provide examples.

Model Types: Splittable Ranges

`blocked_range` and `blocked_range2d` represent splittable ranges. For each of these, splitting partitions the range into two subranges.

The bodies for `parallel_reduce`, `parallel_scan`, `simple_partitioner`, and `auto_partitioner` must be splittable. For each of these, splitting results in two bodies that can run concurrently.

split Class

Type for dummy argument of a splitting constructor.

```
#include "tbb/tbb_stddef.h"
```

```
class split;
```

Description

An argument of type split is used to distinguish a splitting constructor from a copy constructor.

Members

```
namespace tbb {
    class split {
    };
}
```

Range Concept

Requirements for a type representing a recursively divisible set of values. Table 3-2 lists the requirements for a Range type R.

Table 3-2. Range Concept

Pseudosignature	Semantics
R::R(const R&)	Copy constructor
R::~R( )	Destructor
bool R::empty( ) const	True if range is empty
bool R::is_divisible( ) const	True if range can be partitioned into two subranges
R::R(R& r, split)	Split r into two subranges

Description

A Range can be recursively subdivided into two parts. It is recommended that the division be into nearly equal parts, but it is not required. Splitting as evenly as possible typically yields the best parallelism. Ideally, a range is recursively splittable *until the parts represent portions of work that are more efficient to execute serially rather than split further*. This key limit to splitting is called the grain size. The amount of work represented by a Range typically depends upon higher-level context; hence, a typical type that models a Range should provide a way to control the degree of splitting. For example, the template class blocked_range has a grainsize parameter that specifies the biggest range considered indivisible.

The constructor that implements splitting is called a *splitting constructor*. If the set of values has a sense of direction, by convention the splitting constructor should construct the second part of the range and update the argument to refer to the first part of the range. Following this convention causes the parallel_for, parallel_reduce, and parallel_scan algorithms, when running sequentially, to work across a range in the increasing order typical of an ordinary sequential loop.

Model Types

blocked_range models a one-dimensional range.

blocked_range2d models a two-dimensional range.

blocked_range<Value> Template Class

Template class for a recursively divisible half-open interval.

```
#include "tbb/blocked_range.h"

template<typename Value> class blocked_range;
```

Description

A blocked_range<Value> represents a half-open range [i,j) that can be recursively split. The types i and j must model the requirements in Table 3-3. Because the requirements are pseudosignatures, signatures that differ in ways that can be implicitly converted are allowed. For example, a blocked_range<int> is allowed because the difference of two int values can be implicitly converted to a size_t. Examples that model the Value requirements are integral types, pointers, and STL random-access iterators whose difference can be implicitly converted to a size_t.

A blocked_range models the Range Concept.

Table 3-3. Value Concept for block_range

Pseudosignature	Semantics
Value::Value(const Value&)	Copy constructor
Value::~Value( )	Destructor
bool operator<(const Value& i, const Value& j)	Value i precedes value j
size_t operator-(const Value& i, const Value& j)	Number of values in range [i,j)
Value operator+(const Value& i, size_t k)	kth value after i

A blocked_range<Value> specifies a grainsize of type size_t. A blocked_range is splittable into two subranges if the size of the range exceeds grainsize. The ideal grain size depends upon the context of the blocked_range<Value>, which is typically the range argument to the loop templates parallel_for, parallel_reduce, and parallel_scan. Too small a grain size may cause scheduling overhead within the loop templates to swamp speedup gained from parallelism. Too large a grain size may unnecessarily limit parallelism. For example, if the grain size is so large that the range can be split only once, the maximum possible parallelism is two.

For a blocked_range [i,j) where j<i, not all methods have specified behavior. However, enough methods do have specified behavior that parallel_for, parallel_reduce, and parallel_scan iterate over the same iteration space as the serial loop for(Value index=i; index<j; ++index)..., even when j<i. If the debug macro TBB_DO_ASSERT is non-zero, methods with unspecified behavior raise an assertion failure. You should *not* use iteration spaces [i,j) with j<i.

Members

```
namespace tbb {
    template<typename Value>
    class blocked_range {
    public:
        // types
        typedef size_t size_type;
        typedef Value const_iterator;

        // constructors
        blocked_range( Value begin, Value end, size_type grainsize=1);
        blocked_range( blocked_range& r, split );

        // capacity
        size_type size( ) const;
        bool empty( ) const;

        // access
        size_type grainsize( ) const;
        bool is_divisible( ) const;

        // iterators
        const_iterator begin( ) const;
        const_iterator end( ) const;
    };
}
```

size_type
> Description: the type for measuring the size of a blocked_range. The type is always a size_t.

const_iterator
> Description: the type of a value in the range. Despite its name, the type const_iterator is not necessarily an STL iterator; it merely needs to meet the Value requirements in Table 3-3. However, it is convenient to call it const_iterator so that if it is a const_iterator, the blocked_range behaves like a read-only STL container.

blocked_range(Value begin, Value end, size_t grainsize=1)
> Effects: constructs a blocked_range representing the half-open interval [begin,end) with the given grainsize.

> Example: the statement blocked_range<int> r(5, 14, 2); constructs a range of int that contains the values 5 through 13 inclusive, with a grainsize of 2. (The begin parameter 5 is taken to be inclusive, and the end parameter 14 to be exclusive.) Afterward, r.begin( )==5 and r.end( )==14.

blocked_range(blocked_range& range, split)

Requirements: is_divisible( ) is true.

Effects: partitions range into two subranges. The newly constructed blocked_range is approximately the second half of the original range, and range is updated to be the remainder. Each subrange has the same grainsize as the original range.

Example: let i and j be integers that define a half-open interval [i,j] and let g specify a grainsize. The statement blocked_range<int> r(i,j,g) constructs a blocked_range<int> that represents [i,j) with grainsize g. Running the statement blocked_range<int> s(r,split); subsequently causes r to represent [i, i +(j -i)/2) and s to represent [i +(j -i)/2, j), both with grainsize g.

size_type size( ) const

Requirements: end()<begin( ) is false.

Effects: determines size of range.

Returns: end()-begin( ).

bool empty( ) const

Effects: determines whether the range is empty.

Returns: !(begin()<end( )).

size_type grainsize( ) const

Returns: grain size of range.

bool is_divisible( ) const

Requirements: !(end()<begin( )).

Effects: determines whether the range can be split into subranges.

Returns: true if size()>grainsize( ); false otherwise.

const_iterator begin( ) const

Returns: inclusive lower bound on the range.

const_iterator end( ) const

Returns: exclusive upper bound on the range.

blocked_range2d Template Class

Template class that represents a recursively divisible, two-dimensional, half-open interval.

```
#include "tbb/blocked_range2d.h"
template<typename RowValue, typename ColValue>
  class blocked_range2d;
```

Description

A blocked_range2d<RowValue,ColValue> represents a half-open, two-dimensional range [i0,j0)x[i1,j1). Each axis of the range has its own splitting threshold. The RowValue and ColValue must meet the requirements in Table 3-3. A blocked_range is splittable if either axis is splittable. A blocked_range models the Range Concept.

Members

```
namespace tbb {
template<typename RowValue, typename ColValue=RowValue>
    class blocked_range2d {
    public:
        // Types
        typedef blocked_range<RowValue> row_range_type;
        typedef blocked_range<ColValue> col_range_type;

        // Constructors
        blocked_range2d( RowValue row_begin, RowValue row_end,
                    typename row_range_type::size_type row_grainsize,
                    ColValue col_begin, ColValue col_end,
                    typename col_range_type::size_type col_grainsize);
        blocked_range2d( blocked_range2d& r, split );

        // Capacity
        bool empty( ) const;

        // Access
        bool is_divisible( ) const;
        const row_range_type& rows( ) const;
        const col_range_type& cols( ) const;
    };
}
```

row_range_type

> Description: a blocked_range<RowValue>. That is, the type of the row values.

col_range_type

> Description: a blocked_range<ColValue>. That is, the type of the column values.

blocked_range2d<RowValue,ColValue>(RowValue row_begin, RowValue row_end, typename row_range_type::size_type row_grainsize, ColValue col_begin, ColValue col_end, typename col_range_type::size_type col_grainsize)

> Effects: constructs a blocked_range2d representing a two-dimensional space of values. The space is the half-open Cartesian product [row_begin,row_end)x[col_begin,col_end), with the given grain sizes for the rows and columns.
>
> Example: the statement blocked_range2d<char,int> r('a', 'z'+1, 3, 0, 10, 2); constructs a two-dimensional space that contains all value pairs of the form (i, j), where i ranges from 'a' to 'z' with a grain size of 3, and j ranges from 0 to 9 with a grain size of 2.

blocked_range2d<RowValue,ColValue> (blocked_range2d& range, split)

> Effects: partitions a range into two subranges. The newly constructed blocked_range2d is approximately the second half of the original range, and range is updated to be the remainder. Each subrange has the same grain size as the original range. The split is either by rows or by columns. The choice of which axis to split is intended to cause, after repeated splitting, the subranges to approach the aspect ratio of the respective row and column grain sizes. For example, if the row_grainsize is twice the col_grainsize, the subranges will tend toward having twice as many rows as columns.

```
bool empty( ) const
```
Effects: determines whether the range is empty.

Returns: rows().empty()||cols().empty( ).
```
bool is_divisible( ) const
```
Effects: determines whether the range can be split into subranges.

Returns: rows().is_divisible()||cols().is_divisible( ).
```
const row_range_type& rows( ) const
```
Returns: range containing the rows of the value space.
```
const col_range_type& cols( ) const
```
Returns: range containing the columns of the value space.

Partitioner Concept

Requirements for a type that decides whether a range should be operated on by a task body or further split. Table 3-4 lists the requirements for a partitioner type P.

Table 3-4. Partitioner Concept

Pseudosignature	Semantics
P::~P( )	Destructor.
template <typename Range> bool P::should_execute_range(const Range &r, const task &t)	True if r should be passed to the body of t. False if r should instead be split.
P::P(P& p, split)	Split p into two partitioners.

Description

The partitioner implements rules for deciding when a given range should no longer be subdivided, but should be operated over as a whole by a task's body.

The default behavior of the algorithms parallel_for, parallel_reduce, and parallel_scan is to recursively split a range until no subrange remains that is divisible, as decided by the function is_divisible of the Range Concept. The Partitioner Concept models rules for the early termination of the recursive splitting of a range, providing the ability to change the default behavior. A Partitioner object's decision making is implemented using two functions: a splitting constructor and the function should_execute_range.

Within the parallel algorithms, each Range object is associated with a Partitioner object. Whenever a Range object is split using its splitting constructor to create two subranges, the associated Partitioner object is likewise split to create two matching Partitioner objects.

When a parallel_for, parallel_reduce, or parallel_scan algorithm needs to decide whether to further subdivide a range, it invokes the function should_execute_range for the Partitioner object associated with the range. If the function returns true for the given range and task, no further splits are performed on the range and the current task applies its body over the entire range.

Model Types: Partitioners

simple_partitioner models the default behavior of splitting a range until it cannot be further subdivided.

auto_partitioner models an adaptive behavior that monitors the work-stealing actions of the task_scheduler to reduce the number of splits performed.

simple_partitioner Class

A class that models the default range-splitting behavior of the parallel_for, parallel_reduce, and parallel_scan algorithms, where a range is recursively split until it cannot be further subdivided.

```
#include "tbb/partitioner.h"
```

```
class simple_partitioner;
```

Description

The class simple_partitioner models the default range-splitting behavior of the parallel_ for, parallel_reduce, and parallel_scan algorithms.

simple_partitioner( )
> An empty default constructor.

simple_partitioner(simple_partitioner &partitioner, split)
> An empty splitting constructor.

template<typename Range> bool should_execute_range (const Range &r, const task &t)
> A function that returns true when the provided range should be executed to completion by the given task. It returns !range.is_divisible( ).

auto_partitioner Class

A class that models an adaptive partitioner that monitors the work-stealing actions of the task_scheduler to manage the number of splits performed.

```
#include "tbb/partitioner.h"
```

```
class auto_partitioner;
```

Description

The class auto_partitioner models an adaptive partitioner that limits the number of splits needed for load balancing by reacting to work-stealing events.

The range is first divided into S_I subranges, where S_I is proportional to the number of threads created by the task scheduler. These subranges are executed to completion by tasks unless they are stolen. If a subrange is stolen by an idle thread, the auto_partitioner further subdivides the range to create additional subranges.

The auto_partitioner creates additional subranges only if threads are actively stealing work. If the load is well balanced, the use of only a few large initial subranges reduces the overheads incurred when splitting and joining ranges. However, if there is a load imbalance that results in work stealing, the auto_partitioner creates additional subranges that can be stolen to more finely balance the load.

The auto_partitioner therefore attempts to minimize the number of range splits, while providing ample opportunities for work stealing.

auto_partitioner( )
> An empty default constructor.

auto_partitioner(auto_partitioner &partitioner, split)
> A splitting constructor that divides the auto_partitioner partitioner into two partitioners.

template<typename Range> bool should_execute_range (const Range &r, const task &t)
> A function that returns true when the provided range should be operated on as a whole by the given task's body. This function may return true even if range.is_divisible( ) == true and always returns true if range.is_divisible( ) == false. That is, this function may decide that t should process an r that can be further subdivided, but it always decides that t should process an r that cannot be further subdivided.

Table 3-5 provides guidance for selecting between the simple_partitioner and auto_partitioner classes.

Table 3-5. Guidance for selecting a partitioner

Partitioner type	Discussion
simple_partitioner	Recursively splits a range until it is no longer divisible. The Range::is_divisible function is wholly responsible for deciding when recursive splitting halts. When used with classes such as blocked_range and blocked_range2d, the selection of an appropriate grain size is therefore critical to allow concurrency while limiting overhead.
auto_partitioner	Guides splitting decisions based on the work-stealing behavior of the task scheduler. When used with classes such as blocked_range and blocked_range2d, the selection of an appropriate grain size is less important. Subranges that are larger than the grain size are used unless load imbalances are detected. Therefore, acceptable performance may often be achieved by simply using the default grain size of 1.

 Ranges larger than the grain size may be passed to the body when using an auto_partitioner. The body should therefore not use the value of grainsize as an upper bound on the size of the range (for allocating temporary storage, for example).

parallel_for<Range,Body> Template Function

```
#include "tbb/parallel_for.h"

template<typename Range, typename Body>

void parallel_for( const Range& range, const Body& body );

template<typename Range, typename Body, typename Partitioner>

  void parallel_for( const Range& range, const Body& body,

                    Partitioner &partitioner );
```

Description

A parallel_for<Range,Body> represents parallel execution of Body over each value in Range. Type Range must model the Range Concept. The body must model the requirements in Table 3-6.

Table 3-6. Requirements for parallel_for body

Pseudosignature	Semantics
Body::Body(const Body&)	Copy constructor
Body::~Body( )	Destructor
void Body::operator( )(Range& range) const	Apply body to range

A parallel_for recursively splits the range into subranges to the point where is_divisible( ) returns false for each subrange, and makes copies of the body for each of these subranges. For each such body/subrange pair, it invokes Body::operator( ). The invocations are interleaved with the recursive splitting in order to minimize space overhead and efficiently use the cache.

Some of the copies of the range and body may be destroyed after parallel_for returns. This late destruction is not an issue in typical usage, but it is something to be aware of when looking at execution traces or writing range or body objects with complex side effects.

When worker threads are available, parallel_for executes iterations in nondeterministic order. Do not rely upon any particular execution order for correctness. However, due to efficiency concerns, parallel_for tends to operate on consecutive runs of values.

When no worker threads are available, parallel_for executes iterations from left to right in the following sense. Imagine drawing a binary tree that represents the recursive splitting. Each nonleaf node represents splitting a subrange r by invoking the splitting constructor Range(r,split( )). The left child represents the updated value of r. The right child represents the newly constructed object. Each leaf in the tree represents an indivisible subrange. The method Body::operator( ) is invoked on each leaf subrange, from left to right.

Complexity

If the range and body take O(1) space, and the range splits into nearly equal pieces, the space complexity is O(p log n), where p is the number of threads and n is the size of the range.

---

parallel_reduce<Range,Body> Template Function

Computes reduction over a range of values.

```
#include "tbb/parallel_reduce.h"

template<typename Range, typename Body>

void parallel_reduce( const Range& range, Body& body );

template<typename Range, typename Body, typename Partitioner>

  void parallel_reduce( const Range& range, Body& body,

                        Partitioner &partitioner );
```

Description

A `parallel_reduce<Range,Body>` performs parallel reduction of Body over each value in Range. Type Range must model the Range Concept. The body must model the requirements in Table 3-7.

Table 3-7. Requirements for parallel_reduce body

Pseudosignature	Semantics
Body::Body(Body&, split);	Splitting constructor. Must be able to run the operator( ) and join methods concurrently.
Body::~Body( )	Destructor.
void Body::operator( )(Range& range);	Accumulate results for the subrange.
void Body::join(Body& rhs);	Join results. The result in rhs should be merged into the result of this.

A `parallel_reduce` recursively splits the range into subranges to the point where is_divisible( ) returns false for each subrange. A `parallel_reduce` uses the splitting constructor to make one or more copies of the body for each thread. It may copy a body while the body's operator( ) or join method runs concurrently. You are responsible for ensuring the safety of such concurrency. In typical usage, the safety requires no extra effort.

When worker threads are available, `parallel_reduce` invokes the splitting constructor for the body. For each such split, it invokes the join method after processing in order to merge the results from the bodies.

Complexity

If the range and body take O(1) space, and the range splits into nearly equal pieces, the space complexity is O(p log n), where p is the number of threads and n is the size of the range.

---

parallel_scan<Range,Body> Template Function

Template function that computes parallel prefix.

```
#include "tbb/parallel_scan.h"
template<typename Range, typename Body>
  void parallel_scan( const Range& range, Body& body );
template<typename Range, typename Body, typename Partitioner>
    void parallel_scan( const Range& range, Body& body,
                              Partitioner &partitioner );
```

Description

A parallel_scan<Range,Body> computes a parallel prefix, also known as a parallel scan. This can be useful in scenarios that appear to have inherently serial dependencies. Given an associative operation $\oplus$ with left-identity element $id_\oplus$, the parallel prefix of $\oplus$ over a sequence x_0, x_1, ... x_{n-1} is a sequence y_0, y_1, y_2, ... y_{n-1}, where $y_0 = id_\oplus \oplus x_0$ and $y_i = y_{i-1} \oplus x_i$.

The template parallel_scan<Range,Body> implements a parallel prefix generically. The body must model the requirements in Table 3-8.

Table 3-8. parallel_scan requirements

Pseudosignature	Semantics
void Body::operator( )(const Range& r, pre_scan_tag)	Preprocess iterations for range r.
void Body::operator( )(const Range& r, final_scan_tag)	Do final processing for iterations of range r.
Body::Body(Body& b, split)	Split b so that this and b can accumulate separately.
Void Body::reverse_join(Body& a)	Merge preprocessing state of a into this, where a was created earlier from b by b's splitting constructor.
Void Body::assign(Body& b)	Assign state of b to this.

pre_scan_tag and final_scan_tag Classes

Types that distinguish the phases of parallel_scan.

```
#include "tbb/parallel_scan.h"
struct pre_scan_tag;
struct final_scan_tag;
```

Description

The types pre_scan_tag and final_scan_tag are dummy types used in conjunction with parallel_scan.

Members

```
namespace tbb {

    struct pre_scan_tag {
        static bool is_final_scan();
    };

    struct final_scan_tag {
        static bool is_final_scan();
    };

}
bool is_final_scan()
```
    Returns: true for a final_scan_tag; false otherwise.

Summary of Loops

The high-level loop templates in Intel Threading Building Blocks give you efficient, scalable ways to exploit the power of multi-core chips without having to start from scratch. They let you design your software at a concurrent task level and not worry about low-level manipulation of threads. Because they are generic, you can customize them to your specific needs. Although algorithms in this chapter can unlock the power of multi-core processing for many applications, sometimes you will require more complex algorithms. The next chapter takes the models shown in this chapter to a higher level.

CHAPTER 4

Advanced Algorithms

Algorithm templates are the keys to using Intel Threading Building Blocks. This chapter presents some relatively complex algorithms that build on the foundation laid in Chapter 3, so you should understand Chapter 3 before jumping into this chapter. This chapter covers Threading Building Blocks' support for the following types of generic parallel algorithms.

Parallel algorithms for streams:

parallel_while
> Use for an unstructured stream or pile of work. Offers the ability to add additional work to the pile while running.

pipeline
> Use when you have a linear sequence of stages. Specify the maximum number of items that can be in transit. Each stage can be serial or parallel. This uses the cache efficiently because each worker thread takes an item through as many stages as possible, and the algorithm is biased toward finishing old items before tackling new ones.

Parallel sort:

parallel_sort
> A comparison sort with an average time complexity not to exceed $O(n \log n)$ on a single processor and approaching $O(N)$ as more processors are used. When worker threads are available, parallel_sort creates subtasks that may be executed concurrently.

Parallel Algorithms for Streams

You can successfully parallelize many applications using only the constructs discussed thus far. However, some situations call for other parallel patterns. This section describes the support for some of these alternative patterns:

parallel_while

> Use for an unstructured stream or pile of work. Offers the ability to add additional work to the pile while running.

pipeline

> Use when you have a linear pipeline of stages. Specify the maximum number of items that can be in flight. Each stage can be serial or parallel. This uses the cache efficiently because each worker thread handles an item through as many stages as possible, and the algorithm is biased toward finishing old items before tackling new ones.

Cook Until Done: parallel_while

For some loops, the end of the iteration space is not known in advance, or the loop body may add more iterations to do before the loop exits. You can deal with both situations using the template class tbb::parallel_while.

A linked list is an example of an iteration space that is not known in advance. In parallel programming, it is usually better to use dynamic arrays instead of linked lists because accessing items in a linked list is inherently serial. But if you are limited to linked lists, if the items can be safely processed in parallel, and if processing each item takes at least a few thousand instructions, you can use parallel_while in a situation where the serial form is as shown in Example 4-1.

Example 4-1. Original list processing code

```
void SerialApplyFooToList( Item*root ) {
    for( Item* ptr=root; ptr!=NULL; ptr=ptr->next )
        Foo(pointer->data);
}
```

If Foo takes at least a few thousand instructions to run, you can get parallel speedup by converting the loop to use parallel_while. Unlike the templates described earlier, parallel_while is a class, not a function, and it requires *two* user-defined objects. The first object defines the stream of items. The object must have a method, pop_if_present, such that when bool b = pop_if_present(v) is invoked, it sets v to the next iteration value if there is one and returns true. If there are no more iterations, it returns false. Example 4-2 shows a typical implementation of pop_if_present.

Example 4-2. pop_if_present for a parallel_while

```
class ItemStream {
    Item* my_ptr;
public:
    bool pop_if_present( Item*& item ) {
        if( my_ptr ) {
            item = my_ptr;
            my_ptr = my_ptr->next;
            return true;
```

Example 4-2. pop_if_present for a parallel_while (continued)

```
    } else {
        return false;
    }
};
ItemStream( Item* root ) : my_ptr(root) {}
}
```

The second object defines the loop body, and must define an operator( ) const and an argument_type member type. This is similar to a C++ function object from the C++ standard header, <functional>, except that it must be const (see Example 4-3).

Example 4-3. Use of parallel_while

```
class ApplyFoo {
public:
    void operator()( Item* item ) const {
        Foo(item->data);
    }
    typedef Item* argument_type;
};
```

Given the stream and body classes, the new code is as shown in Example 4-4.

Example 4-4. ParallelApplyFooToList

```
void ParallelApplyFooToList( Item*root ) {
    parallel_while<ApplyFoo> w;
    ItemStream stream;
    ApplyFoo body;
    w.run( stream, body );
}
```

The pop_if_present method does not have to be thread-safe for a given stream because parallel_while never calls it concurrently for the same stream. Notice that this convenience makes parallel_while nonscalable because the fetching is serialized. But in many situations, you still get useful speedup over doing things sequentially.

> parallel_while may concurrently invoke pop_if_present on the same object, but only if the object is in different streams.

There is a second way that parallel_while can acquire work, and this is the way it can become scalable. The body of a parallel_while w, if given a reference to w when it is constructed, can add more work by calling w.add(item), where item is of type Body::argument_type.

For example, perhaps processing a node in a tree is a prerequisite to processing its descendants. With parallel_while, after processing a node, you could use parallel_while::add to add the descendant nodes. The instance of parallel_while does not terminate until all items have been processed.

Notes on parallel_while scaling

Use of parallel_while usually does not provide scalable parallelism if the add method is not used because the input stream typically acts as a bottleneck. However, this bottleneck is broken if the stream is used to get things started and further items come from prior items invoking the add method.

Even in the nonscalable case, parallel_while covers a commonly desired idiom of walking a sequential structure (e.g., a linked list) and dispatching concurrent work for each item in the structure.

parallel_while Template Class   Template class that processes work items.

```
#include "tbb/parallel_while.h"

template<typename Body> class parallel_while;
```

Description

A parallel_while<Body> performs parallel iteration over items. The processing to be performed on each item is defined by a function object of type Body. The items are specified in two ways:

- An initial stream of items
- Additional items that are added while the stream is being processed

Table 4-1 shows the requirements on the stream and body.

Table 4-1. Requirements for parallel_while stream and body

Pseudosignature	Semantics
bool S::pop_if_present(B::argument_type& item)	Get next stream item. parallel_while does not concurrently invoke the method on the same object.
B::operator( )(B::argument_type& item) const	Process item. parallel_while may concurrently invoke the operator for the same object but a different item.
B::argument_type( )	Default constructor.
B::argument_type(const B::argument_type&)	Copy constructor.
~B::argument_type( )	Destructor.

For example, a unary function object, as defined in Section 20.3 of the C++ standard, models the requirements for B. A concurrent_queue models the requirements for S.

To achieve speedup, the grain size of B::operator( ) needs to be on the order of 10,000 instructions to execute. Otherwise, the internal overheads of parallel_while swamp the useful work. The parallelism in parallel_while is not scalable if all the items come from the input stream. To achieve scaling, design your algorithm such that the add method often adds more than one piece of work.

Members

```
namespace tbb {
    template<typename Body>
    class parallel_while {
    public:
        parallel_while( );
        ~parallel_while( );

        typedef typename Body::argument_type value_type;

        template<typename Stream>
        void run( Stream& stream, const Body& body );

        void add( const value_type& item );
    };
}
```

parallel_while<Body>( )

> Effects: constructs a parallel_while that is not yet running.

~parallel_while<Body>( )

> Effects: destroys a parallel_while.

Template <typename Stream> void run(Stream& stream, const Body& body)

> Effects: applies body to each item in stream and any other items that are added by the method add. Terminates when both of the following conditions become true:
>
> - stream.pop_if_present returns false
> - body(x) has returned for all items x generated from the stream or the add method

void add(const value_type& item)

> Requirements: must be called from a call to body.operator( ) by parallel_while. Otherwise, the termination semantics of the run method are undefined.
>
> Effects: adds item to collection of items to be processed.

Working on the Assembly Line: Pipeline

Pipelining is a common parallel pattern that mimics a traditional manufacturing assembly line. Data flows through a series of pipeline stages and each stage processes the data in some way. Given an incoming stream of data, some of these stages can operate in parallel, and others cannot. For example, in video processing, some operations on frames do not depend on other frames and so can be done on multiple frames at the same time. On the other hand, some operations on frames require processing prior frames first.

Pipelined processing is common in multimedia and signal processing applications. A classical thread-per-stage implementation suffers two problems:

- The speedup is limited to the number of stages.
- When a thread finishes a stage, it must pass its data to *another* thread.

Eliminating these problems is desirable. To do so, you specify whether a stage is serial or parallel. A serial stage processes items one at a time, in order. A parallel stage may process items out of order or concurrently. By allowing some stages to be run concurrently, you make available more opportunities for load balancing and concurrency. Given sufficient processor cores and concurrent opportunities, the throughput of the pipeline is limited to the throughput of the slowest serial filter.

The `pipeline` and `filter` classes implement the pipeline pattern. Here we'll look at a simple text-processing problem to demonstrate the usage of `pipeline` and `filter`. The problem is to read a text file, capitalize the first letter of each word, and write the modified text to a new file. Figure 4-1 illustrates the pipeline.

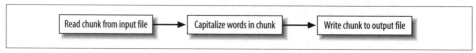

Figure 4-1. Pipeline

Assume that the file I/O is sequential. However, the capitalization stage can be done in parallel. That is, if you can serially read *n* chunks very quickly, you can capitalize the *n* chunks in parallel, as long as they are written in the proper order to the output file.

To decide whether to capitalize a letter, inspect whether the *preceding* character is a blank. For the first letter in each chunk, you must inspect the last letter of the preceding chunk. But doing so would introduce a complicated dependency in the middle stage.

The solution is to have each chunk also store the last character of the preceding chunk. The chunks overlap by one character. This *overlapping window* strategy is quite common to pipeline-processing problems. In the example, the window is represented by an instance of the `MyBuffer` class. It looks like a typical Standard Template Library (STL) container for characters, except that `begin( )[-1]` is legal and holds the last character of the preceding chunk (see Example 4-5).

Example 4-5. Use of pipeline class

```
// Buffer that holds block of characters and last character of preceding buffer.
class MyBuffer {
    static const size_t buffer_size = 10000;
    char* my_end;
    // storage[0] holds the last character of the preceding buffer.
    char storage[1+buffer_size];
public:
    // Pointer to first character in the buffer
```

Example 4-5. Use of pipeline class (continued)

```
    char* begin( ) {return storage+1;}
    const char* begin( ) const {return storage+1;}
    // Pointer to one past last character in the buffer
    char* end( ) const {return my_end;}
    // Set end of buffer.
    void set_end( char* new_ptr ) {my_end=new_ptr;}
    // Number of bytes a buffer can hold
    size_t max_size( ) const {return buffer_size;}
    // Number of bytes in buffer.
    size_t size() const {return my_end-begin();}
};
// Below is the top-level code for building and running the pipeline
    // Create the pipeline
    tbb::pipeline pipeline;

    // Create file-reading stage and add it to the pipeline
    MyInputFilter input_filter( input_file );
    pipeline.add_filter( input_filter );

    // Create capitalization stage and add it to the pipeline
    MyTransformFilter transform_filter;
    pipeline.add_filter( transform_filter );

    // Create file-writing stage and add it to the pipeline
    MyOutputFilter output_filter( output_file );
    pipeline.add_filter( output_filter );

    // Run the pipeline
    pipeline.run( MyInputFilter::n_buffer );

    // Remove filters from pipeline before they are implicitly destroyed.
    pipeline.clear( );
```

The parameter passed to the pipeline::run method controls the level of parallelism. Conceptually, *tokens* flow through the pipeline. A serial stage must process each token one at a time, in order. A parallel stage can process multiple tokens in parallel.

If the number of tokens were unlimited, there might be a problem where the unordered stage in the middle keeps gaining tokens because the output stage cannot keep up. This situation typically leads to undesirable resource consumption by the middle stage. The parameter to the pipeline::run method specifies the maximum number of tokens that can be in flight. Once this limit is reached, the pipeline class doesn't create a new token at the input stage until another token is destroyed at the output stage.

This top-level code also shows the clear method that removes all stages from the pipeline. This call is required if the filters have to be destroyed before the pipeline. The pipeline is a container that holds filters, and as with most containers in C++, it is illegal to destroy an item while it is in the container.

Now look in detail at how the stages are defined. Each stage is derived from the filter class. First let's consider the output stage because it is the simplest (see Example 4-6).

Example 4-6. Output stage for pipeline

```
// Filter that writes each buffer to a file.
class MyOutputFilter: public tbb::filter {
    FILE* my_output_file;
public:
    MyOutputFilter( FILE* output_file );
    /*override*/void* operator()( void* item );
};

MyOutputFilter::MyOutputFilter( FILE* output_file ) :
    tbb::filter(/*is_serial=*/true),
    my_output_file(output_file)
{
}

void* MyOutputFilter::operator()( void* item ) {
    MyBuffer& b = *static_cast<MyBuffer*>(item);
    fwrite( b.begin(), 1, b.size(), my_output_file );
    return NULL;
}
```

The class is derived from the `filter` class. When its constructor calls the base class constructor for `filter`, it specifies that this is a serial filter. The class overrides the virtual method `filter::operator()`, which is the method invoked by the pipeline to process an item. The parameter `item` points to the item to be processed. The value returned points to the item to be processed by the next filter. Because this is the last filter, the return value is ignored, and thus can be `NULL`.

The middle stage is similar. Its `operator()` returns a pointer to the item to be sent to the next stage (see Example 4-7).

Example 4-7. Middle stage for pipeline

```
// Filter that changes the first letter of each word
// from lowercase to uppercase.
class MyTransformFilter: public tbb::filter {
public:
    MyTransformFilter();
    /*override*/void* operator()( void* item );
};

MyTransformFilter::MyTransformFilter() :
    tbb::filter(/*serial=*/false)
{}

/*override*/void* MyTransformFilter::operator()( void* item ) {
    MyBuffer& b = *static_cast<MyBuffer*>(item);
    bool prev_char_is_space = b.begin()[-1]==' ';
```

Example 4-7. Middle stage for pipeline (continued)

```
    for( char* s=b.begin(); s!=b.end( ); ++s ) {
        if( prev_char_is_space && islower(*s) )
            *s = toupper(*s);
        prev_char_is_space = isspace(*s);
    }
    return &b;
}
```

The middle stage operates on purely local data. Thus, any number of invocations on operator( ) can run concurrently on the same instance of MyTransformFilter. The class communicates this fact to the pipeline by constructing its base class, filter, with the <serial> parameter set to false.

The input filter is the most complicated because it has to decide when the end of the input is reached and it must allocate buffers (see Example 4-8).

Example 4-8. Input stage for pipeline

```
class MyInputFilter: public tbb::filter {
public:
    static const size_t n_buffer = 4;
    MyInputFilter( FILE* input_file_ );
private:
    FILE* input_file;
    size_t next_buffer;
    char last_char_of_previous_buffer;
    MyBuffer buffer[n_buffer];
    /*override*/ void* operator( )(void*);
};

MyInputFilter::MyInputFilter( FILE* input_file_ ) :
    filter(/*is_serial=*/true),
    next_buffer(0),
    input_file(input_file_),
    last_char_of_previous_buffer(' ')
{
}

void* MyInputFilter::operator( )(void*) {
    MyBuffer& b = buffer[next_buffer];
    next_buffer = (next_buffer+1) % n_buffer;
    size_t n = fread( b.begin(), 1, b.max_size(), input_file );
    if( !n ) {
        // end of file
        return NULL;
    } else {
        b.begin( )[-1] = last_char_of_previous_buffer;
        last_char_of_previous_buffer = b.begin( )[n-1];
        b.set_end( b.begin( )+n );
        return &b;
    }
}
```

The input filter is serial because it is reading from a sequential file. The override of operator( ) ignores its parameter because it is generating a stream, not transforming it. It remembers the last character of the preceding chunk so that it can properly overlap windows.

The buffers are allocated from a circular queue of size n_buffer. This might seem risky because after the initial n_buffer input operations, buffers are recycled without any obvious checks as to whether they are still in use. But the recycling is indeed safe because of two constraints:

- The pipeline received n_buffer tokens when pipeline::run was called. Therefore, no more than n_buffer buffers are ever in flight simultaneously.

- The last stage is serial. Therefore, the buffers are retired by the last stage in the order they were allocated by the first stage.

Notice that if the last stage were *not* serial, you would have to keep track of which buffers are currently in use because buffers might be retired out of order.

The directory *examples/pipeline/text_filter* that comes with Threading Building Blocks contains the complete code for the text filter.

Throughput of pipeline

The throughput of a pipeline is the rate at which tokens flow through it, and it is limited by two constraints. First, if a pipeline is run with *n* tokens, there obviously cannot be more than *n* operations running in parallel. Selecting the right value of *n* may involve some experimentation. Too low a value limits parallelism; too high a value may demand too many resources (for example, more buffers).

Second, the throughput of a pipeline is limited by the throughput of the slowest sequential stage. This is true even for a pipeline with no parallel stages. No matter how fast the other stages are, the slowest sequential stage is the bottleneck. So in general, you should try to keep the sequential stages fast and, when possible, shift work to the parallel stages.

The text-processing example has relatively poor speedup because the serial stages are limited by the I/O speed of the system. Indeed, even when files are on a local disk, you are unlikely to see a speedup of much more than 2X. To really benefit from a pipeline, the parallel stages need to be doing more substantial work compared to the serial stages.

The window size, or subproblem size for each token, can also limit throughput. Making windows too small may cause overheads to dominate the useful work. Making windows too large may cause them to spill out of cache. A good guideline is to try for a large window size that still fits in cache. You may have to experiment a bit to find a good window size.

Nonlinear pipelines

The pipeline template supports only linear pipelines. It does not directly handle more baroque plumbing, such as in Figure 4-2.

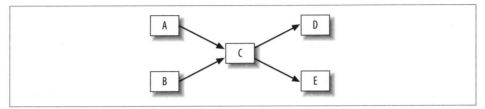

Figure 4-2. Nonlinear pipeline

However, you can still use pipeline for this. One solution is to topologically sort the stages into a linear order, as in Figure 4-3. Another solution, which injects dummy stages to get lower latency, is provided in Chapter 11 in the section titled "Two Mouths: Feeding Two from the Same Task in a Pipeline."

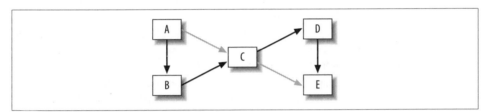

Figure 4-3. Topologically sorted pipeline

In the topological sorting of the stages (Figure 4-3), the light gray arrows are the original arrows that are now implied by transitive closure of the other arrows. It might seem that a lot of parallelism is lost by forcing a linear order on the stages, but in fact, the only loss is in the *latency* of the pipeline, not the throughput. The latency is the time it takes a token to flow from the beginning to the end of the pipeline. Given a sufficient number of processors, the latency of the original nonlinear pipeline is three stages. This is because stages A and B could process the token concurrently, and likewise, stages D and E could process the token concurrently. In the linear pipeline, the latency is five stages. The behavior of stages A, B, D, and E may need to be modified to properly handle objects that don't need to be acted upon by the stage, other than to be passed along to the next stage in the pipeline.

The throughput remains the same because, regardless of the topology, the throughput is still limited by the throughput of the slowest serial stage. If pipeline supported nonlinear pipelines, it would add a lot of programming complexity, and would not improve throughput. The linear limitation of pipeline is a good trade-off of gain versus pain.

pipeline Class

```
#include "tbb/pipeline.h"
```

```
class pipeline;
```

Description

A pipeline represents the pipelined application of a series of filters to a stream of items. Each filter is parallel or serial. See the filter class for details.

A pipeline contains one or more filters, denoted here as f_i, where i denotes the position of the filter in the pipeline. The pipeline starts with filter f_0, followed by f_1, f_2, and so on. The following steps describe how to use the class:

1. Derive f_i classes from filter. The constructor for f_i specifies whether it is serial via the Boolean parameter to the constructor for the base class filter.

2. Override the virtual method filter::operator( ) to perform the filter's action on the item, and return a pointer to the item to be processed by the next filter. The first filter, f_0, generates the stream. It should return NULL if there are no more items in the stream. The return value for the last filter is ignored.

3. Create an instance of class pipeline.

4. Create instances of the f_i filters and add them to the pipeline in order from first to last. An instance of a filter can be added once, at most, to a pipeline. A filter should never be a member of more than one pipeline at a time.

5. Call the method pipeline::run. The parameter max_number_of_live_tokens puts an upper bound on the number of stages that will be run concurrently. Higher values may increase concurrency at the expense of more memory consumption from having more items in flight.

Given sufficient processors and tokens, the throughput of the pipeline is limited to the throughput of the slowest serial filter.

A filter must be removed from the pipeline before destroying it. You can accomplish this by destroying the pipeline first, or by calling pipeline::clear( ).

Members

```
namespace tbb {
    class pipeline {
    public:
        pipeline( );
        virtual ~pipeline( );
        void add_filter( filter& f );
        void run( size_t max_number_of_live_tokens );
        void clear( );
    };
}
```

pipeline( )
    Effects: constructs a pipeline with no filters.

~pipeline( )
    Effects: removes all filters from the pipeline and destroys the pipeline.

```
void add_filter( filter& f )
```
Effects: appends filter f to the sequence of filters in the pipeline. The filter f must not already be in a pipeline.

```
void run( size_t max_number_of_live_tokens )
```
Effects: runs the pipeline until the first filter returns NULL and each subsequent filter has processed all items from its predecessor. The number of items processed in parallel depends upon the structure of the pipeline and the number of available threads. At most, max_number_of_live_tokens are in flight at any given time.

```
void clear( )
```
Effects: removes all filters from the pipeline.

filter Class

Abstract base class that represents a filter in a pipeline.

```
#include "tbb/pipeline.h"

class filter;
```

Description

A filter represents a filter in a pipeline. A filter is parallel or serial. A parallel filter can process multiple items in parallel and possibly out of order. A serial filter processes items one at a time in the original stream order. Parallel filters are preferred when viable because they permit parallel speedup. Whether the filter is serial or parallel is specified by an argument to the constructor.

The filter class should be used only in conjunction with pipeline.

Members

```
namespace tbb {
    class filter {
    protected:
        filter( bool is_serial );
    public:
        bool is_serial( ) const;
        virtual void* operator()( void* item ) = 0;
        virtual ~filter( );
    };
}
```

```
filter( bool is_serial )
```
Effects: constructs a serial filter if is_serial is true, or a parallel filter if is_serial is false.

```
~filter( )
```
Effects: destroys the filter. The filter must not be in a pipeline; otherwise, memory might be corrupted. The debug version of the library raises an assertion failure if the filter is in a pipeline. Always clear or destroy the containing pipeline first. A way to remember this is that a pipeline acts like a container of filters, and a C++ container usually does not allow one to destroy an item while it is in the container.

```
bool is_serial( ) const
```
   Returns: true if filter is serial; false if filter is parallel.
```
virtual void* operator( )( void * item )
```
   Effects: the derived filter should override this method to process an item and return a pointer to item to be processed by the next filter. The item parameter is NULL for the first filter in the pipeline.

   Returns: the first filter in a pipeline should return NULL if there are no more items to process. The result of the last filter in a pipeline is ignored.

parallel_sort

parallel_sort is a comparison sort with an average time complexity $O(n \log n)$. When worker threads are available, parallel_sort creates subtasks that may be executed concurrently. This sort provides an *unstable* sort of the sequence [begin1, end1). Being an unstable sort means that it might not preserve the relative ordering of elements with equal keys.

The sort is deterministic; sorting the same sequence will produce the same result each time. The requirements on the iterator and sequence are the same as for std::sort.

A call to parallel_sort(i,j,comp) sorts the sequence [i,j) using the third argument comp to determine relative orderings. If comp(x,y) returns true, x appears before y in the sorted sequence. A call to parallel_sort(i,j) is equivalent to parallel_sort(i,j,std::less<T>).

Example 4-9 shows two sorts. The sort of array a uses the default comparison, which sorts in ascending order. The sort of array b sorts in descending order by using std::greater<float> for comparison.

Example 4-9. Two sorts
```
#include "tbb/parallel_sort.h"
#include <math.h>

using namespace tbb;

const int N = 100000;
float a[N];
float b[N];

void SortExample( ) {
    for( int i = 0; i < N; i++ ) {
        a[i] = sin((double)i);
        b[i] = cos((double)i);
    }
    parallel_sort(a, a + N);
    parallel_sort(b, b + N, std::greater<float>( ));
}
```

parallel_sort<RandomAccessIterator, Compare> Template Function

Sorts a sequence.

```
#include "tbb/parallel_sort.h"
template<typename RandomAccessIterator>
  void parallel_sort(RandomAccessIterator begin,
                     RandomAccessIterator end);
template<typename RandomAccessIterator, typename Compare>
  void parallel_sort(RandomAccessIterator begin,
                     RandomAccessIterator end,
                     const Compare& comp );
```

Description

Performs an *unstable* sort of the sequence [begin1, end1). The requirements on the iterator and sequence are the same as for std::sort. Specifically, RandomAccessIterator must be a random access iterator, and its value type T must model the requirements in Table 4-2.

Table 4-2. Requirements on value type T of RandomAccessIterator for parallel_sort

Pseudosignature	Semantics
void swap(T& x, T& y)	Swaps x and y.
bool Compare::operator( )(const T& x, const T& y)	True if x comes before y; false otherwise.

Complexity ·

parallel_sort is a comparison sort with an average time complexity of $O(n \log n)$ on a single-processor core, where n is the number of elements in the sequence. Complexity reduces to $O(N)$ as the number of processors increases. When worker threads are available, parallel_sort creates subtasks that may be executed concurrently, leading to improved execution times.

CHAPTER 5
Containers

Intel Threading Building Blocks provides *highly concurrent* containers that permit multiple threads to invoke a method simultaneously on the same container. At this time, a concurrent queue, vector, and hash map are provided. All of these highly concurrent containers can be used with this library, OpenMP, or raw threads.

Highly concurrent containers are very important because Standard Template Library (STL) containers generally are not concurrency-friendly, and attempts to modify them concurrently can easily corrupt the containers. As a result, it is standard practice to wrap a lock (mutex) around STL containers to make them safe for concurrent access, by letting only one thread operate on the container at a time. But that approach eliminates concurrency, and thus is not conducive to multi-core parallelism.

As much as possible, the interfaces of the Threading Building Blocks containers are similar to STL, but they do not match completely because some STL interfaces are inherently not thread-safe. The Threading Building Blocks containers provide fine-grained locking or lock-free implementations, and sometimes both.

Fine-grained locking
> Multiple threads operate on the container by locking only those portions they really need to lock. As long as different threads access different portions, they can proceed concurrently.

Lock-free algorithms
> Different threads proceed straight through the operation without locks, accounting for and correcting the effects of other interfering threads. There is inevitably some waiting at the end, but the contention over locks can be avoided during the operations.

 Locks are worth avoiding because they limit concurrency, and mistakes create problems that are difficult to debug. Threading Building Blocks avoids the need for locks, but does not guarantee you freedom from locks.

Highly concurrent containers come at a cost. They typically have higher overhead than regular STL containers, and so operations on highly concurrent containers may take longer than for STL containers. Therefore, you should use highly concurrent containers when the speedup from the additional concurrency that they enable outweighs their slower sequential performance.

Unlike STL, the Intel Threading Building Blocks containers are not templated with an allocator argument. The library retains control over memory allocation.

Why Do Containers Not Use an Allocator Argument?

An allocator argument is not supported for two reasons. First, it would lead to code bloat because much more of the container class code would be in the headers. Second, there is an advantage in having detailed control over memory allocation, so trade-offs can be made between cache-aligned memory and packed memory to avoid always paying for alignment.

The containers use a mix of cache_aligned_allocator and the default operator, new. The cache_aligned_allocator uses the scalable allocator (Chapter 6) if it is present. There are places for improvement; for instance, the concurrent_hash_map should use the scalable_allocator in a future version to enhance its scalability.

There is no requirement to link in the scalable allocator, as it will default to using malloc. Performance will likely be better if you link with the scalable allocator.

If you have your own scalable memory allocator which you prefer, you will have to work a little to force Threading Building Blocks containers to use it. The only recourse currently is to have your allocator connected using the same interface as the Threading Building Blocks scalable_allocator (the four C routines prototyped in *tbb/scalable_allocator.h*). Perhaps a future version will address this area.

---

concurrent_queue

The template class concurrent_queue<T> implements a concurrent queue with values of type T. Multiple threads may simultaneously push and pop elements from the queue.

In a single-threaded program, a queue is a first-in first-out structure. But if multiple threads are pushing and popping concurrently, the definition of *first* is uncertain. The only guarantee of ordering offered by concurrent_queue is that if a thread pushes multiple values, and another thread pops those same values, they will be popped in the same order that they were pushed.

Pushing is provided by the push method. There are blocking and nonblocking flavors of pop:

pop_if_present

> This method is nonblocking: it attempts to pop a value, and if it cannot because the queue is empty, it returns anyway.

pop

> This method blocks until it pops a value. If a thread must wait for an item to become available and it has nothing else to do, it should use pop(item) and not while(!pop_if_present(item)) continue; because pop uses processor resources more efficiently than the loop.

Unlike most STL containers, concurrent_queue::size_type is a *signed* integral type, not unsigned. This is because concurrent_queue::size() is defined as the number of push operations started minus the number of pop operations started. If pops outnumber pushes, size() becomes negative. For example, if a concurrent_queue is empty and there are n pending pop operations, size() returns −n. This provides an easy way for producers to know how many consumers are waiting on the queue. In particular, consumers may find the empty() method useful; it is defined to be true if and only if size() is not positive.

By default, a concurrent_queue<T> is unbounded. It may hold any number of values until memory runs out. It can be bounded by setting the queue capacity with the set_capacity method. Setting the capacity causes push to block until there is room in the queue. Bounded queues are slower than unbounded queues, so if there is a constraint elsewhere in your program that prevents the queue from becoming too large, it is better not to set the capacity.

Iterating over a concurrent_queue for Debugging

The template class concurrent_queue supports STL-style iteration. This support is intended only for debugging, when you need to dump a queue. It provides iterator and const_iterator types. Both follow the usual STL conventions for forward iterators. The iterators go in the forward direction only and are too slow to be very useful in production code. The iteration order is from least recently pushed item to most recently pushed item. If a queue is modified, all iterators pointing to it become invalid and unsafe to use. The snippet of code in Example 5-1 dumps a queue. The operator << is defined for a Foo.

Example 5-1. Concurrent queue listing dump program

```
concurrent_queue<Foo> q;
...
for(concurrent_queue<Foo>::const_iterator i(q.begin()); i!=q.end(); ++i ) {
    cout << *i;
}
```

The iterators are relatively slow. You should use them *only* for debugging.

When Not to Use Queues

Queues are widely used in parallel programs to buffer consumers from producers. Before using an explicit queue, however, consider using parallel_while or pipeline instead. These options are often more efficient than queues for the following reasons:

- A queue is inherently a bottleneck because it must maintain first-in first-out order.
- A thread that is popping a value may have to wait idly until the value is pushed.
- A queue is a passive data structure. If a thread pushes an item and another thread pops it, the item must be moved to the other processor. Even if the original thread pops the item, enough time could elapse between the push and the pop for the item (and whatever it references) to be discarded from the cache.

In contrast, parallel_while and pipeline avoid these bottlenecks. Because their threading is implicit, they optimize the use of worker threads so that they do other work until a value shows up. They also try to keep items hot in the cache. For example, when another work item is added to a parallel_while, it is kept local to the thread that added it, unless another idle thread can steal it before the "hot" thread processes it. By applying this selectivity in pulling from another queue, items are more often processed by the hot thread.

concurrent_queue Template Class
Template class for queue with concurrent operations.

```
#include "tbb/concurrent_queue.h"

template<typename T> class concurrent_queue;
```

Description

A concurrent_queue is a bounded data structure that permits multiple threads to concurrently push and pop items. Its behavior is first-in first-out in reference to any items pushed by a single thread and popped by a single thread. The default bounds are large enough to make the queue practically unbounded, subject to memory limitations on the target machine.

The interface is different from that of an STL std::queue because concurrent_queue is designed for concurrent operations. See Table 5-1 for the differences.

Table 5-1. std::queue versus tbb::concurrent_queue

Feature	STL std::queue	tbb::concurrent_queue
Access to front and back	`front` and `back` methods	Not present. They would be unsafe while concurrent operations are in progress.
`size_type`	Unsigned integral type	Signed integral type.
`size()`	Returns the number of items in the queue	Returns the number of pushes minus the number of pops. Waiting push or pop operations are included in the difference. The size is negative if there are pops waiting for corresponding pushes.
Copy and pop item from queue q	`x=q.front()` `q.pop()`	`q.pop(x)` waits for the object indefinitely. For an immediate return, use `pop_if_present`.

Copy and pop item unless queue q is empty	`bool b=!q.empty();`
	`if(b) {`
	    `x=q.front();`
	     `q.pop();`
	`}`
		`q.pop_if_present(x)` returns `true`, with the object in x, if an object is available; otherwise returns `false` immediately (no waiting).

Pop of empty queue	Not allowed	Waits until an item becomes available.

If the push or pop operation blocks, it blocks using a user-space lock, which can waste processor resources when the blocking time is long. The concurrent_queue class is designed for situations where the blocking time is typically short relative to the rest of the application time.

Members

```
namespace tbb {
    template<typename T>
    class concurrent_queue {
    public:
        // types
        typedef T value_type;
        typedef T& reference;
        typedef const T& const_reference;
        typedef std::ptrdiff_t size_type;
        typedef std::ptrdiff_t difference_type;

        concurrent_queue() {}
        ~concurrent_queue();

        void push( const T& source );
        void pop( T& destination );
        bool pop_if_present( T& destination );
        size_type size() const {return internal_size();}
        bool empty() const;
        size_t capacity();
        void set_capacity( size_type capacity );

        typedef implementation-defined iterator;
        typedef implementation-defined const_iterator;

        // iterators (these are slow and intended only for debugging)
```

```
        iterator begin( );
        iterator end( );
        const_iterator begin( ) const;
        const_iterator end( ) const;
    };
}
```
concurrent_queue( )
> Effects: constructs an empty queue.

~concurrent_queue( )
> Effects: destroys all items in the queue.

void push(const T& source)
> Effects: waits until size( )<capacity, then pushes a copy of source onto the back of the queue.

void pop(T& destination)
> Effects: waits until a value becomes available and pops it from the queue. Assigns it to destination. Destroys the original value.

bool pop_if_present(T& destination)
> Effects: if a value is available, pops it from the queue, assigns it to destination, and destroys the original value. Otherwise, does nothing.
>
> Returns: true if value was popped; false otherwise.

size_type size( ) const
> Returns: number of pushes minus number of pops. The result is negative if there are pop operations waiting for corresponding pushes.

bool empty( ) const
> Returns: size( )== 0.
>
> This does not mean the queue is really empty. Because size is the difference between pushes and pops, empty( ) can return true when there is work in flight.

size_type capacity( ) const
> Returns: maximum number of values that the queue can hold.

void set_capacity(size_type capacity)
> Effects: sets the maximum number of values that the queue can hold.

Example

Example 5-2 builds a queue with the integers 0...9, and then dumps the queue to standard output. Its overall effect is to print 0 1 2 3 4 5 6 7 8 9.

Example 5-2. Concurrent queue count

```
#include "tbb/concurrent_queue.h"
#include <iostream>

using namespace std;
using namespace tbb;

int main( ) {
    concurrent_queue<int> queue;
    for( int i=0; i<10; ++i )
```

Example 5-2. Concurrent queue count (continued)

```
        queue.push(i);
    for( concurrent_queue<int>::const_iterator i(queue.begin()); i!=queue.end(); ++i )
        cout << *i << " ";
    cout << endl;
    return 0;

}
```

`iterator begin( )`
>   Returns: iterator pointing to the beginning of the queue.

`iterator end( )`
>   Returns: iterator pointing to the end of the queue.

`const_iterator begin( ) const`
>   Returns: const_iterator pointing to the beginning of the queue.

`const_iterator end( ) const`
>   Returns: const_iterator pointing to the end of the queue.

concurrent_vector

A concurrent_vector<T> is a dynamically growable array of items of type T for which it is safe to simultaneously access elements in the vector while growing it. However, be careful not to let another task access an element that is under construction or is otherwise being modified. For safe concurrent growing, concurrent_vector has two methods for resizing that support common uses of dynamic arrays: grow_by and grow_to_at_least. The index of the first element is 0. The method grow_by(n) enables you to safely append n consecutive elements to a vector, and returns the index of the first appended element. Each element is initialized with T( ). So for instance, Example 5-3 safely appends a C string to a shared vector.

Example 5-3. Concurrent vector
```
void Append( concurrent_vector<char>& vector, const char* string ) {
    size_t n = strlen(string)+1;
    memcpy( &vector[vector.grow_by(n)], string, n+1 );
}
```

The related method grow_to_at_least(n) grows a vector to size n if it is shorter. Concurrent calls to grow_by and grow_to_at_least do not necessarily return in the order that elements are appended to the vector.

The size( ) method returns the number of elements in the vector, which may include elements that are still undergoing concurrent construction by grow_by and grow_to_at_least. Also, it is safe to use iterators while the concurrent_vector is being grown, as long as the iterators never go past the current value of end( ). However, the iterator may reference an element undergoing concurrent construction. You must synchronize construction and access of an element.

A concurrent_vector<T> never moves an element until the array is cleared, which can be an advantage over the STL std::vector (which can move elements to resize the vector), even for single-threaded code. However, concurrent_vector does have more overhead than std::vector. Use concurrent_vector only if you really need to dynamically resize it while other accesses are (or might be) in flight, or if you require that an element never move.

 Operations on concurrent_vector are concurrency-safe with respect to growing, but are not safe for clearing or destroying a vector. Never invoke clear( ) if other operations are in process on the concurrent_vector.

concurrent_vector Template Class

Template class for vector that can be concurrently grown and accessed.

```
#include "tbb/concurrent_vector.h"
```

```
template<typename T> class concurrent_vector;
```

Members

```
namespace tbb {
    template<typename T>
    class concurrent_vector {
    public:
        typedef size_t size_type;
        typedef T value_type;
        typedef ptrdiff_t difference_type;
        typedef T& reference;
        typedef const T& const_reference;

        // whole vector operations
        concurrent_vector( ) {}
        concurrent_vector( const concurrent_vector& );
        concurrent_vector& operator=( const concurrent_vector&);
        ~concurrent_vector( );
        void clear( );

        // concurrent operations
        size_type grow_by( size_type delta );
        void grow_to_at_least( size_type new_size );
        size_type push_back( const_reference value );
        reference operator[]( size_type index );
        const_reference operator[]( size_type index ) const;

        // parallel iteration
        typedef implementation-defined iterator;
        typedef implementation-defined const_iterator;
        typedef generic_range_type<iterator> range_type;
        typedef generic_range_type<const_iterator> const_range_type;
```

```
range_type range( size_t grainsize );
const_range_type range( size_t grainsize ) const;

// capacity
size_type size( ) const;
bool empty( ) const;
size_type capacity( ) const;
void reserve( size_type n );
size_type max_size( ) const;

// STL support
iterator begin( );
iterator end( );
const_iterator begin( ) const;
const_iterator end( ) const;

typedef implementation-defined reverse_iterator;
typedef implementation-defined const_reverse_iterator;
iterator rbegin( );
iterator rend( );
const_iterator rbegin( ) const;
const_iterator rend( ) const;
    };
}
```

Whole Vector Operations

These operations are *not* thread-safe on the same instance:

concurrent_vector( )
    Effects: constructs an empty vector.

concurrent_vector(const concurrent_vector& src)
    Effects: constructs a copy of src.

concurrent_vector& operator=(const concurrent_vector& src)
    Effects: assigns contents of src to *this.

    Returns: reference to lefthand side.

~concurrent_vector( )
    Effects: erases all elements and destroys the vector.

void clear( )
    Effects: erases all elements. Afterward, size( )==0.

Concurrent Operations

The methods described in this section safely execute on the same instance of a concurrent_vector<T>:

```
size_type grow_by( size_type delta )
```
> Effects: atomically appends delta elements to the end of the vector. The new elements are initialized with T( ), where T is the type of the values in the vector.
>
> Returns: old size of the vector. If it returns *k*, the new elements are at the half-open index range [*k*...*k+delta*).

```
void grow_to_at_least( size_type n )
```
> Effects: grows the vector until it has at least n elements. The new elements are initialized with T( ), where T is the type of the values in the vector.

```
size_t push_back( const_reference value );
```
> Effects: atomically appends a copy of value to the end of the vector.
>
> Returns: index of the copy.

```
reference operator[]( size_type index )
```
> Returns: reference to the element with the specified index.

```
const_reference operator[]( size_type index ) const;
```
> Returns: const reference to the element with the specified index.

Parallel Iteration

The types const_range_type and range_type model the Range Concept and provide the methods in Table 5-2 to access the bounds of the range. The types differ only in that the bounds for a const_range_type are of type const_iterator, whereas the bounds for a range_type are of type iterator.

Use the range types in conjunction with parallel_for, parallel_reduce, and parallel_scan to iterate over pairs in a concurrent_vector.

Table 5-2. Concept for concurrent_vector range R

Pseudosignature	Semantics
R::iterator R::begin( ) const	First item in range
R::iterator R::end( ) const	One past last item in range

```
range_type range( size_t grainsize )
```
> Returns: range over an entire concurrent_vector that permits read-write access.

```
const_range_type range( size_t grainsize ) const
```
> Returns: range over an entire concurrent_vector that permits read-only access.

Capacity

```
size_type size( ) const
```
> Returns: number of elements in the vector. The result may include elements that are under construction by concurrent calls to the grow_by or grow_to_at_least method.

```
bool empty( ) const
```
Returns: size( )==0.

```
size_type capacity( ) const
```
Returns: maximum size the vector can grow to without allocating more memory.

```
void reserve( size_type n )
```
Returns: reserve space for at least n elements.

Throws: `std::length_error` if n>max_size( ).

```
size_type max_size( ) const
```
Returns: highest size vector that might be representable.

 max_size( ) is a requirement on STL containers. The C++ standard defines it as "size( ) of the largest possible container," which is vague. Threading Building Blocks does what most STL libraries do and computes max_size( ) on the *very* optimistic assumption that the machine's address space is fully populated with usable memory, and that the container is the only object in this space. In practice, if you allocate a container of size max_size( ), you will most likely get an out-of-memory exception. In the freak event that you succeed, the next request will surely run out of memory.

Iterators

The template class concurrent_vector<T> supports random access iterators as defined in Section 24.1.4 of the ISO C++ standard. Unlike an std::vector, the iterators are not raw pointers. A concurrent_vector<T> meets the reversible container requirements in Table 66 of the ISO C++ standard.

```
iterator begin( )
```
Returns: iterator pointing to the beginning of the vector.

```
iterator end( )
```
Returns: iterator pointing to the end of the vector.

```
const_iterator begin( ) const
```
Returns: const_iterator pointing to the beginning of the vector.

```
const_iterator end( ) const
```
Returns: const_iterator pointing to the end of the vector.

```
iterator rbegin( )
```
Returns: const_reverse_iterator(end( )).

```
iterator rend( )
```
Returns: const_reverse_iterator(begin( )).

```
const_reverse_iterator rbegin( ) const
```
Returns: const_reverse_iterator(end( )).

```
const_ reverse_iterator rend( ) const
```
Returns: const_reverse_iterator(begin( )).

concurrent_hash_map

A concurrent_hash_map<Key,T,HashCompare> is a hash table that permits concurrent accesses. The table is a map from a key to a type T. The HashCompare traits type defines how to hash a key and how to compare two keys.

Example 5-4 builds a concurrent_hash_map in which the keys are strings and the corresponding data is the number of times each string occurs in the array Data.

Example 5-4. Concurrent hash map

```
#include "tbb/concurrent_hash_map.h"
#include "tbb/blocked_range.h"
#include "tbb/parallel_for.h"
#include <string>

using namespace tbb;
using namespace std;

// Structure that defines hashing and comparison operations for user's type.
struct MyHashCompare {
    static size_t hash( const string& x ) {
        size_t h = 0;
        for( const char* s = x.c_str(); *s; ++s )
            h = (h*17)^*s;
        return h;
    }
    //! True if strings are equal
    static bool equal( const string& x, const string& y ) {
        return x==y;
    }
};

// A concurrent hash table that maps strings to ints.
typedef concurrent_hash_map<string,int,MyHashCompare> StringTable;

// Function object for counting occurrences of strings.
struct Tally {
    StringTable& table;
    Tally( StringTable& table_ ) : table(table_) {}
    void operator()( const blocked_range<string*> range ) const {
        for( string* p=range.begin(); p!=range.end(); ++p ) {
            StringTable::accessor a;
            table.insert( a, *p );
            a->second += 1;
        }
    }
};

const size_t N = 1000000;

string Data[N];
```

Example 5-4. Concurrent hash map (continued)

```
void CountOccurrences( ) {
    // Construct empty table.
    StringTable table;

    // Put occurrences into the table
    parallel_for( blocked_range<string*>( Data, Data+N, 100 ),
                                     Tally(table) );

    // Display the occurrences
    for( StringTable::iterator i=table.begin(); i!=table.end( ); ++i )
        printf("%s %d\n",i->first.c_str( ),i->second);
}
```

A concurrent_hash_map acts as a container of elements of type std::pair<const Key,T>. Typically, when accessing a container element, you are interested in either updating it or reading it. The template class concurrent_hash_map supports these two operations with the accessor and const_accessor classes, respectively, which act as smart pointers.

An accessor represents *update* (*write*) access. As long as it points to an element, all other attempts to look up that key in the table block until the accessor is done. A const_accessor is similar, except that it represents *read-only* access. Therefore, multiple const_accessors can point to the same element at the same time. This feature can greatly improve concurrency in situations where elements are frequently read and infrequently updated.

The find and insert methods take an accessor or const_accessor as an argument. The choice tells concurrent_hash_map whether you are asking for update or read-only access, respectively. Once the method returns, the access lasts until the accessor or const_accessor is destroyed.

Because having access to an element can block other threads, try to shorten the lifetime of the accessor or const_accessor. To do so, declare it in the innermost block possible. To release access even sooner than the end of the block, use the release method.

Example 5-5 is a rework of the loop body that uses release instead of waiting for the destruction of the accessor for the lock to be released.

Example 5-5. Use of release method

```
StringTable accessor a;
for( string* p=range.begin(); p!=range.end( ); ++p ) {
    table.insert( a, *p );
    a->second += 1;
    a.release( );
}
```

The method remove(key) can also operate concurrently. It implicitly requests write access. Therefore, before removing the key, it waits on any other extant accesses on the key.

More on HashCompare

In general, the definition of HashCompare must provide two signatures:

- A hash method that maps a Key to a size_t
- An equal method that determines whether two keys are equal

The signatures fall naturally in a single class because *if two keys are equal, they must hash to the same value*. Otherwise, the hash table might not work. You could trivially meet this requirement by always hashing to 0, but that would cause tremendous inefficiency. Ideally, each key should hash to a different value, or at least the probability of two distinct keys hashing to the same value should be kept low.

The methods of HashCompare should be static unless you need to have them behave differently for different instances. If so, construct the concurrent_hash_map using the constructor that takes a HashCompare as a parameter. Example 5-6 is a variation on an earlier example that uses instance-dependent methods. The instance performs either case-sensitive or case-insensitive hashing and comparison, depending upon an internal flag, ignore_case.

Example 5-6. Hash compare

```
// Structure that defines hashing and comparison operations
class VariantHashCompare {
    // If true, then case of letters is ignored.
    bool ignore_case;
public:
    size_t hash( const string& x ) {
        size_t h = 0;
        for( const char* s = x.c_str(); *s; s++ )
            h = (h*17)^*(ignore_case?tolower(*s):*s);
        return h;
    }
    // True if strings are equal
    bool equal( const string& x, const string& y ) {
        if( ignore_case )
            strcasecmp( x.c_str(), y.c_str() )==0;
        else
            return x==y;
    }
    VariantHashCompare( bool ignore_case_ ) : ignore_case() {}
};

typedef concurrent_hash_map<string,int, VariantHashCompare>
        VariantStringTable;
VariantStringTable CaseSensitiveTable(VariantHashCompare(false));
VariantStringTable CaseInsensitiveTable(VariantHashCompare(true));
```

The directory *examples/concurrent_hash_map/count_strings* contains a complete example that uses concurrent_hash_map to enable multiple processors to cooperatively build a histogram.

concurrent_hash_map<Key,T,HashCompare> Template Class   Template class for associative container with concurrent access.

```
#include "tbb/concurrent_hash_map.h"

template<typename Key, typename T, typename HashCompare> class concurrent_hash_map;
```

Description

A concurrent_hash_map maps keys to values in a way that permits multiple threads to concurrently access values. The keys are unordered. The interface resembles typical STL associative containers, but with some differences that are critical to supporting concurrent access.

The Key and T types must model the CopyConstructible Concept.

The HashCompare type specifies how keys are hashed and compared for equality. It must model the HashCompare Concept defined in Table 5-3.

Table 5-3. HashCompare Concept

Pseudosignature	Semantics
HashCompare::HashCompare(const HashCompare &)	Copy constructor
HashCompare::~HashCompare ( )	Destructor
bool HashCompare::equal(const Key& j, const Key& k) const	True if keys are equal
size_t HashCompare::hash(const Key& k)	Hash code for key

As for most hash tables, if two keys are equal, they must hash to the same hash code. That is, for a given HashCompare h and any two keys j and k, the following assertion must hold: !h.equal(j,k) || h.hash(j)==h.hash(k). The importance of this property is the reason that concurrent_hash_map places key equality and hashing in a single object instead of keeping them as separate objects.

Members

```
namespace tbb {
    template<typename Key, typename T, typename HashCompare>
    class concurrent_hash_map {
    public:
        // types
        typedef Key key_type;
        typedef T mapped_type;
        typedef std::pair<const Key,T> value_type;
        typedef size_t size_type;
        typedef ptrdiff_t difference_type;

        // whole-table operations
        concurrent_hash_map();
        concurrent_hash_map( const concurrent_hash_map& );
        ~concurrent_hash_map();
        concurrent_hash_map operator=( const concurrent_hash_map& );
        void clear();
```

```
// concurrent access
class const_accessor;
class accessor;

// concurrent operations on a table
bool find( const_accessor& result, const Key& key ) const;
bool find( accessor& result, const Key& key );
bool insert( const_accessor& result, const Key& key );
bool insert( accessor& result, const Key& key );
bool erase( const Key& key );

// parallel iteration
typedef implementation defined range_type;
typedef implementation defined const_range_type;
range_type range( size_t grainsize );
const_range_type range( size_t grainsize ) const;

// Capacity
size_type size( ) const;
bool empty( ) const;
size_type max_size( ) const;

// Iterators
typedef implementation defined iterator;
typedef implementation defined const_iterator;
iterator begin( );
iterator end( );
const_iterator begin( ) const;
const_iterator end( ) const;
};
}
```

Whole-Table Operations

These operations affect an entire table. Do not concurrently invoke them on the same table.

concurrent_hash_map( )
> Effects: constructs an empty table.

concurrent_hash_map(const concurrent_hash_map& table)
> Effects: copies a table. The table being copied may have map operations running on it concurrently.

~concurrent_hash_map( )
> Effects: removes all items from the table and destroys it. This method is not safe to execute concurrently with other methods on the same concurrent_hash_map.

```
concurrent_hash_map& operator= ( concurrent_hash_map& source )
```
> Effects: if the source table and destination table (this) are distinct, clear the destination table and copy all key-value pairs from the source table to the destination table. Otherwise, do nothing.

> Returns: reference to the destination table.

```
void clear( )
```
> Effects: erases all key-value pairs from the table.

Concurrent Access

The member classes const_accessor and accessor are called *accessors*. Accessors allow multiple threads to concurrently access pairs in a shared concurrent_hash_map. An accessor acts as a smart pointer to a pair in a concurrent_hash_map. It holds an implicit lock on a pair until the instance is destroyed or the release method is called on the accessor.

The const_accessor and accessor classes differ in the kind of access they permit, as shown in Table 5-4.

Table 5-4. Differences between const_accessor and accessor

Class	value_type	Implied lock on pair
const_accessor	const std::pair<const Key,T>	Reader lock: permits shared access with other readers
accessor	std::pair<const Key,T>	Writer lock: blocks access by other threads

Accessors cannot be assigned or copy-constructed because allowing that would greatly complicate the locking semantics.

---

const_accessor   Provides read-only access to a pair in a concurrent_hash_map.

```
#include "tbb/concurrent_hash_map.h"
```

```
template<typename Key, typename T, typename HashCompare> class concurrent_hash_
map<Key,T,HashCompare>::const_accessor;
```

Description

A const_accessor permits read-only access to a key-value pair in a concurrent_hash_map.

Members

```
namespace tbb {
    template<typename Key, typename T, typename HashCompare>
    class concurrent_hash_map<Key,T,HashCompare>::const_accessor {
    public:
        // types
        typedef const std::pair<const Key,T> value_type;
```

```
        // construction and destruction
        const_accessor();
        ~const_accessor();

        // inspection
        bool empty() const;
        const value_type& operator*() const;
        const value_type* operator->() const;

        // early release
        void release();
    };
}
```

bool empty() const
> Returns: true if the instance points to nothing; false if the instance points to a key-value pair.

void release()
> Effects: if the instance contains a key-value pair, releases the implied lock on the pair and sets the instance to point to nothing. Otherwise, does nothing.

const value_type& operator*() const
> Effects: raises an assertion failure if empty() is true and TBB_DO_ASSERT is defined as nonzero.
>
> Returns: const reference to a key-value pair.

const value_type* operator->() const
> Returns: &operator*().

const_accessor()
> Effects: constructs a const_accessor that points to nothing.

~const_accessor
> Effects: if pointing to a key-value pair, releases the implied lock on the pair.

accessor class
Class that provides read and write access to a pair in a concurrent_hash_map.

#include "tbb/concurrent_hash_map.h"

template<typename Key, typename T, typename HashCompare>

class concurrent_hash_map<Key,T,HashCompare>::accessor;

Description

An accessor permits read and write access to a key-value pair in a concurrent_hash_map. It is derived from a const_accessor, and thus can be implicitly cast to a const_accessor.

Members

```
namespace tbb {
    template<typename Key, typename T, typename HashCompare>
    class concurrent_hash_map<Key,T,HashCompare>::accessor:
        concurrent_hash_map<Key,T,HashCompare>::const_accessor {
    public:
```

```
        typedef std::pair<const Key,T> value_type;
        value_type& operator*( ) const;
        value_type* operator->( ) const;
    };
}
```
value_type& operator*( ) const
> Effects: raises an assertion failure if empty( ) is true and TBB_DO_ASSERT is defined as nonzero.

> Returns: reference to a key-value pair.

value_type* operator->( ) const
> Returns: &operator*( ).

Concurrent Operations: find, insert, erase

The operations find, insert, and erase are the only operations that may be concurrently invoked on the same concurrent_hash_map. These operations search the table for a key-value pair that matches a given key. The find and insert methods each have two variants. One takes a const_accessor argument and provides read-only access to the desired key-value pair. The other takes an accessor argument and provides write access.

 If the non-const variant succeeds in finding the key, the consequent write access blocks any other thread from accessing the key until the accessor object is destroyed. Where possible, use the const variant to improve concurrency.

The result of the map operation is true if the operation succeeds.

bool find(const_accessor& result, const Key& key) const
> Effects: searches a table for a pair with the given key. If the key is found, provides read-only access to the matching pair.

> Returns: true if the key is found; false if the key is not found.

bool find(accessor& result, const Key& key)
> Effects: searches a table for a pair with the given key. If the key is found, provides write access to the matching pair.

> Returns: true if the key is found; false if the key is not found.

bool insert(const_accessor& result, const Key& key)
> Effects: searches a table for a pair with the given key. If not present, inserts a new pair into the table. The new pair is initialized with pair(key,T( )). Provides read-only access to the matching pair.

> Returns: true if a new pair is inserted; false if the key is already in the map.

```
bool insert( accessor& result, const Key& key )
```
Effects: searches a table for a pair with the given key. If not present, inserts a new pair into the table. The new pair is initialized with `pair(key,T( ))`. Provides write access to the matching pair.

Returns: `true` if a new pair is inserted; `false` if the key is already in the map.

```
bool erase( const Key& key )
```
Effects: searches a table for a pair with the given key. Removes the matching pair if it exists.

Returns: `true` if the pair is removed; `false` if the key is not in the map.

Parallel Iteration

The types `const_range_type` and `range_type` model the Range Concept and provide methods to access the bounds of the range, as shown in Table 5-5. The types differ only in that the bounds for a `const_range_type` are of type `const_iterator`, whereas the bounds for a `range_type` are of type `iterator`.

Use the range types in conjunction with `parallel_for`, `parallel_reduce`, and `parallel_scan` to iterate over pairs in a `concurrent_hash_map`.

Table 5-5. Concept for concurrent_hash_map range R

Pseudosignature	Semantics
`R::iterator R::begin( ) const`	First item in range
`R::iterator R::end( ) const`	One past last item in range

```
const_range_type range( size_t grainsize ) const
```
Effects: constructs a `const_range_type` representing all keys in the table. The grainsize parameter is in units of hash table slots. Each slot typically has only one key-value pair.

Returns: a `const_range_type` object for the table.

```
range_type range( size_t grainsize )
```
Returns: like `const_range_type`, but returns a `range_type` object for the table.

Capacity

```
size_type size( ) const
```
Returns: number of key-value pairs in the table.

This method takes constant time, but it is slower than the corresponding method in most STL containers.

```
bool empty( ) const
```
Returns: size( )==0.

This method takes constant time, but it is slower than the corresponding method in most STL containers.

```
size_type max_size( ) const
```
Returns: inclusive upper bound on the number of key-value pairs that the table can hold.

Iterators

The template class concurrent_hash_map supports forward iterators; that is, iterators that can advance only forward across the table. Reverse iterators are not supported. All elements will be visited in a walk from begin to end, but there is no guarantee on the order of the walk.

```
iterator begin( )
```
Returns: iterator pointing to the beginning of the key-value sequence.

```
iterator end( )
```
Returns: iterator pointing to the end of the key-value sequence.

```
const_iterator begin( ) const
```
Returns: const_iterator pointing to the beginning of the key-value sequence.

```
const_iterator end( ) const
```
Returns: const_iterator pointing to the end of the key-value sequence.

CHAPTER 6

Scalable Memory Allocation

Making sure your memory allocation is handled by a *scalable* shared memory allocator is very important. This chapter explains why and introduces a solution included with Intel Threading Building Blocks.

Allocating memory is not only one of the most basic programming tasks, it's also one of the most challenging to do efficiently in multithreaded programs on multiprocessor systems. Solutions necessarily depend on the operating system and C++ compiler in use; a totally portable solution would not offer adequate performance.

Because memory allocation is such an essential requirement for programs, C++ offers several ways to plug in new memory allocators. Threading Building Blocks comes with a scalable allocator that supports the same signatures as std::allocator.

Limitations

The scalable memory allocator is cleanly separate from the rest of Threading Building Blocks so that your choice of memory allocator for concurrent usage is independent of your choice of parallel algorithm and container templates.

Every memory allocator has its merits. The Threading Building Blocks scalable allocator is built for scalability and speed. In some situations, this comes at a cost of wasted virtual space. Specifically, it wastes a lot of space when allocating blocks in the 9K to 12K range. It is also not yet terribly sophisticated about paging issues.

Threading Building Blocks does not define malloc; if you want to replace malloc, it is up to you to provide one to fit your particular needs.

Problems in Memory Allocation

When ordinary, nonthreaded allocators are used, memory allocation becomes a serious bottleneck in a multithreaded program because each thread competes for a global lock for each allocation and deallocation of memory from a single global heap.

Programs that run this way are not scalable. In fact, because of this contention, programs that make intensive use of memory allocation may actually *slow down* as the number of processor cores increases! Programs utilizing the Standard Template Library (STL) may be more memory-intensive than is obvious because the memory allocation is hidden from view.

Another serious issue for concurrent programs is called *false sharing*. False sharing occurs when multiple threads use memory locations that are close together, even if they are not actually using the same memory locations. Because processor cores fetch and hold memory in chunks called *cache lines*, any memory accesses within the same cache line should be done only by the same thread. Otherwise, accesses to memory on the same cache line will cause unnecessary contention and swapping of cache lines back and forth, resulting in slowdowns which can easily be a hundred times worse for the affected memory accesses.

False Sharing

To illustrate why false sharing carries such a performance penalty, we can look at the extra overhead imposed on the caches and operating system when two threads access memory near each other. We'll assume for the sake of this example that a cache line contains 64 bytes, two threads are running on processors that share the cache, and your program defines two arrays containing one thousand 4-byte elements:

```
float A_array[1000];
float B_array[1000];
```

The end of A_array and the beginning of B_array probably lie at least partly within the same cache line because the compiler allocates them in sequence. Consider program activity as follows:

Thread A writes to A_array[999]. The processor reads the 64 bytes including this element into the cache.

Thread B writes to B_array[0].

Extra overhead: the processor must flush the cache line so that A_array[0] is saved to memory, and the operating system must invalidate the cache for thread A.

Continuing its work, thread A writes to A_array[1].

Extra overhead: the processor must flush the cache line so that B_array[0] is saved to memory, and the operating system must reload the cache for thread A while invalidating the cache for thread B.

You can see that a tremendous overhead can easily be imposed from false sharing of data, even if thread A uses only A_array and thread B uses only B_array. The solution is to align the arrays to cache-line boundaries so that there is no false sharing.

Memory Allocators

The solution to the challenges of concurrent memory allocation is to use a scalable memory allocator, either in Intel Threading Building Blocks or in another third-party solution. The Threading Building Blocks scalable memory allocator utilizes a memory management algorithm divided on a per-thread basis to minimize contention associated with allocation from a single global heap.

Threading Building Blocks offers two choices, both similar to the STL template class, std::allocator:

scalable_allocator
: This template offers just scalability, but it does not completely protect against false sharing. Memory is returned to each thread from a separate pool, which helps protect against false sharing if the memory is not shared with other threads.

cache_aligned_allocator
: This template offers both scalability and protection against false sharing. It addresses false sharing by making sure each allocation is done on a cache line.

Note that protection against false sharing between two objects is guaranteed only if both are allocated with cache_aligned_allocator. For instance, if one object is allocated by cache_aligned_allocator<T> and another object is allocated some other way, there is no guarantee against false sharing.

The functionality of cache_aligned_allocator comes at some cost in space because it allocates in multiples of cache-line-size memory chunks, even for a small object. The padding is typically 128 bytes. Hence, allocating many small objects with cache_aligned_allocator may increase memory usage.

Use cache_aligned_allocator only if false sharing is likely to be a real problem. Trying both allocators and measuring the resulting performance for a particular program is a good idea.

Although you do not need to use this scalable memory allocator, it is unwise to ignore the problem of scalable memory allocation. You are advised to use a scalable solution for concurrency because the default memory allocation routines are not yet ready for efficient concurrent use.

The following subsections describe the basic use of these templates, which involves linking the proper library and specifying the use of the allocator in templates. These tasks are the first step toward reducing memory contention, but in general, you will need to think about all memory allocation in your program to make sure no memory allocations which are created or used concurrently will cause performance issues. Later sections of this chapter discuss what you need to do in order to cover all memory allocations and thereby improve performance.

Which Library to Link into Your Application

Both the debug and release versions for Threading Building Blocks are divided into two dynamic shared libraries, one with general support and the other with a scalable memory allocator. The latter is distinguished by malloc in its name (although it does *not* define a routine actually called malloc). For example, the release versions for Windows are *tbb.dll* and *tbbmalloc.dll*, respectively.

Therefore, applications have a variety of choices. The scalable_allocator template requires the scalable memory allocator library and does not require the general library. The cache_aligned_allocator<T> template uses the scalable allocator library if it is present, and otherwise reverts to using malloc and free. Thus, cache_aligned_allocator<T> can be used without the memory allocator library, but the resulting allocators will likely not scale. The rest of Threading Building Blocks can be used with or without the scalable memory allocator library.

Using the Allocator Argument to C++ STL Template Classes

The interface to scalable_allocator and cache_aligned_allocator is identical to std::allocator and conforms to the relevant requirements in the ISO C++ standard, so you can use either as the allocator argument to STL template classes. The following code shows how to declare an STL vector that uses cache_aligned_allocator for allocation:

```
std::vector< int, cache_aligned_allocator<int> >;
```

Replacing malloc, new, and delete

As emphasized earlier in this chapter, the Threading Building Blocks containers are not likely to provide adequate performance when used with general C++ memory routines. A production-quality solution to memory allocation requires some custom memory-allocation functions that reflect your operating system and C++ compiler. You can make the replacement in one of the following ways:

- Replace malloc/free and related memory routines (C programs).
- Replace global new and delete operators (C++ programs).

Replace malloc, free, realloc, and calloc

Four simple interfaces to allow for malloc, free, realloc, and calloc exist:

```
#include "tbb\scalable_allocator.h"
void * scalable_malloc (size_t size);
void   scalable_free (void* ptr);
void * scalable_realloc (void* ptr, size_t size);
void * scalable_calloc (size_t nobj, size_t size);
```

These can be used to replace the C language malloc, free, realloc, and calloc memory functions by calling them instead. In general, that is the safest and easiest choice. Be sure that memory from scalable_malloc is freed using scalable_free, and memory from malloc is freed using free. Mixing these up can have results which are difficult to debug. Therefore, Threading Building Blocks does not attempt to replace malloc, free, realloc, and calloc for you. If you are diligent and make sure you are not maxing malloc/free and scalable_malloc/scalable_free (including if you use a module compiled to use the standard malloc to obtain objects you later free), you can also override the definitions using extern statements and macros. Code to do that is shown in Chapter 11 in Example 11-52 ("Replacing malloc, calloc, realloc, and free").

Note: You do not want to make malloc a call to scalable_allocator because scalable_malloc(n) returns a pointer with sufficient alignment for any type, whereas scalable_allocator<char>( ).allocate(n) is guaranteed only to return a pointer with sufficient alignment for type char.

> For the moment, in some cases scalable_malloc and scalable_free make calls to malloc and free, so replacing them by linking in routines with these names which in turn call the scalable allocator would cause a big problem. This may change in a future implementation, but for now you should not redefine malloc or free in a way which would have malloc or free call the scalable allocator.

Replace new and delete

The C++ standard provides eight signatures, which you can replace with functions using the Threading Building Blocks scalable memory allocator. There are four pairs of new/delete operators, which provide throw/no-throw versions of each as well as scalar and array forms. Example 6-1 shows the complete list of signatures.

Example 6-1. ISO 14882 C++ new/delete
```
void* operator new(std::size_t size) throw(std::bad_alloc);
void* operator new(std::size_t size, const std::nothrow_t&) throw( );
void* operator new[](std::size_t size) throw(std::bad_alloc);
void* operator new[](std::size_t size, const std::nothrow_t&) throw( );
void  operator delete(void* ptr) throw( );
void  operator delete(void* ptr, const std::nothrow_t&) throw( );
void  operator delete[](void* ptr) throw( );
void  operator delete[](void* ptr, const std::nothrow_t&) throw( );
```

Replacing all eight signatures is the only way to ensure portability. Some implementations may simply implement the array forms in terms of the scalar forms, but relying on that could lead to more problems than it is worth if that assumption proves not to be true in the future.

The replacements you write for new and delete have to go in the right place (before any use of new or delete).

Actual code to do new/delete replacement can be found in Chapter 11 in Example 11-50 ("Replacement of new and delete functions, demonstration").

 Consult your C++ compiler documentation carefully to understand limitations and other issues. Understanding the particulars of your environment is important.

Allocator Concept

The Allocator Concept for allocators in Intel Threading Building Blocks is similar to the allocator requirements in Table 32 of the ISO C++ standard, but with further guarantees required by the ISO C++ standard (Section 20.1.5, paragraph 4) for use with ISO C++ containers. Table 6-1 summarizes the Allocator Concept. Here, A and B represent instances of the allocator class.

Table 6-1. Allocator Concept

Pseudosignature	Semantics
`typedef T* A::pointer`	Pointer to T
`typedef const T* A::const_pointer`	Pointer to const T
`typedef T& A::reference`	Reference to T
`typedef const T& A::const_reference`	Reference to const T
`typedef T A::value_type`	Type of value to be allocated
`typedef size_t A::size_type`	Type for representing number of values
`typedef ptrdiff_t A::difference_type`	Type for representing pointer difference

`template<typename U> struct rebind {`
`  typedef A<U> A::other;`
`};`
	Rebind to a different type U

`A( ) throw( )`	Default constructor
`A( const A& ) throw( )`	Copy constructor
`template<typename U> A( const A& )`	Rebinding constructor
`~A( ) throw( )`	Destructor
`T* A::address( T& x ) const`	Return address
`const T* A::const_address( const T& x ) const`	Take const address
`T* A::allocate( size_type n, void* hint=0 )`	Allocate space for n values
`void A::deallocate( T* p, size_t n )`	Deallocate n values
`size_type A::max_size( ) const throw( )`	Maximum plausible argument permitted to the method allocate
`void A::construct( T* p, const T& value )`	new(p) T(value)
`void A::destroy( T* p )`	p->T::~T( )
`bool operator==( const A&, const B& )`	Return true
`bool operator!=( const A&, const B& )`	Return false

Model Types

Both template classes, scalable_allocator<T> and cached_aligned_allocator<T>, model the Allocator Concept.

scalable_allocator<T> Template Class

Template class for scalable memory allocation.

```
#include "tbb/scalable_allocator.h"

template<typename T> class scalable_allocator;
```

Description

A scalable_allocator allocates and frees memory in a way that scales with the number of processors. Memory allocated by a scalable_allocator function should be freed by a scalable_allocator function, not by an std::allocator function.

Members

See Allocator Concept.

cache_aligned_allocator<T> Template Class

Template class for allocating memory in way that avoids false sharing.

```
#include "tbb/cache_aligned_allocator.h"

template<typename T> class cache_aligned_allocator;
```

Description

A cache_aligned_allocator allocates memory on cache-line boundaries to avoid false sharing. False sharing is when logically distinct items occupy the same cache line, which can hurt performance if multiple threads attempt to access the different items simultaneously.

A cache_aligned_allocator models the allocator requirements. It can be used to replace an std::allocator.

Members

```
namespace tbb {

    template<typename T>
    class NFS_Allocator {
    public:
        typedef T* pointer;
        typedef const T* const_pointer;
        typedef T& reference;
        typedef const T& const_reference;
        typedef T value_type;
        typedef size_t size_type;
        typedef ptrdiff_t difference_type;
        template<typename U> struct rebind {
```

```
        typedef cache_aligned_allocator<U> other;
    };

#if _WIN64
    char* _Charalloc( size_type size );
#endif /* _WIN64 */

    cache_aligned_allocator() throw();
    cache_aligned_allocator( const cache_aligned_allocator& ) throw();
    template<typename U>
    cache_aligned_allocator( const cache_aligned_allocator<U>& ) throw();
    ~cache_aligned_allocator();

    pointer address(reference x) const;
    const_pointer address(const_reference x) const;

    pointer allocate( size_type n, void* hint=0 );
    void deallocate( pointer p, size_type );
    size_type max_size() const throw();

    void construct( pointer p, const T& value );
    void destroy( pointer p );
};

template<>
class cache_aligned_allocator<void> {
public:
    typedef void* pointer;
    typedef const void* const_pointer;
    typedef void value_type;
    template<typename U> struct rebind {
        typedef cache_aligned_allocator<U> other;
    };
};

template<typename T, typename U>
bool operator==( const cache_aligned_allocator<T>&,
                 const cache_aligned_allocator<U>& );

template<typename T, typename U>
bool operator!=( const cache_aligned_allocator<T>&,
                 const cache_aligned_allocator<U>& );

}
```

 For the sake of brevity, the following list describes only those methods that differ significantly from the corresponding methods of std::allocator.

pointer allocate(size_type n, void* hint=0)
   Effects: allocates size bytes of memory on a cache-line boundary. The allocation may include extra hidden padding.

Returns: pointer to the allocated memory.

`void deallocate( pointer p, size_type n )`

Requirements: the pointer p must be the result of the method allocate(n). The memory must not have been already deallocated.

Effects: deallocates memory pointed to by p, and also deallocates any extra hidden padding.

`char* _Charalloc( size_type size )`

This method is provided only on 64-bit Windows platforms. It is a non-ISO method that exists for backward compatibility with versions of Windows containers that seem to require it. Please do not use it directly.

aligned_space Template Class
Uninitialized memory space.

`template<typename T, size_t N> class aligned_space;`

`#include "tbb/aligned_space.h"`

Description

An `aligned_space` occupies enough memory to hold an array T[N]. The calling code is responsible for initializing or destroying the objects. An `aligned_space` is typically used as a local variable or field in scenarios where a block of fixed-length uninitialized memory is needed.

Members

```
namespace tbb {
    template<typename T, size_t N>
    class aligned_space {
    public:
        aligned_space( );
        ~aligned_space( );
        T* begin( );
        T* end( );
    };
}
```

`aligned_space( )`

Effects: none. Does not invoke constructors.

`~aligned_space( )`

Effects: none. Does not invoke destructors.

`T* begin( )`

Returns: pointer to the beginning of storage.

`T* end( )`

Returns: begin( )+N.

CHAPTER 7
Mutual Exclusion

One of the key advantages of threading is the capability of tasks to share data and other resources, such as open files, network connections, and the user interface. But concurrency creates some uncertainty over when each task reads or writes resources, leading to the need for mutual exclusion.

The Threading Building Blocks algorithms encourage code that does not make extensive use of concurrent accesses to the same objects. Threading Building Blocks also provides concurrent containers, which greatly reduce the difficulty of using key data structures concurrently.

Explicit synchronization is still sometimes necessary, but you are encouraged to exploit implicit task synchronization where possible. For occasions when you need to provide your own locking, the mutual exclusions methods described in this chapter prove to be much better in common multithreading applications than other synchronization objects (such as Windows synchronization objects).

Chapter 2 introduced mutual exclusion and locks, explained deadlock and race conditions, and pointed out what to look for to have thread-safe programs. If you are unfamiliar with these terms, you should read the appropriate sections in Chapter 2. This chapter describes atomic operations, which are preferred, and locks. When it is not possible to use an atomic operation, locks need to be used to obtain mutual exclusion.

Because you program in terms of tasks, not threads, you will probably think of mutual exclusion of tasks. This leads to task-safe code, but because it is normally referred to as *thread-safe* code, we will use that name as well. Otherwise, all discussion of mutual exclusion will be in terms of tasks. Mutual exclusion of tasks will lead to mutual exclusion of the corresponding threads upon which Threading Building Blocks maps your tasks.

When to Use Mutual Exclusion

To prevent race conditions and other nondeterministic and undesirable behavior, no two tasks should invoke a method or function concurrently on the *same* objects.

In other words, you need to provide your own locking. When planning the program's division of labor, try to stick to *intuitively obvious* locking. Threading Building Blocks provides a lot of help, but it cannot always hide the necessary locking.

Leaving the control to you in parallel programming is important because locking more often creates overhead, which will often lead to poor scalability. In general, you should work to divide data among tasks so tasks implicitly have exclusive access to individual objects and thereby avoid any chance of concurrent updates. When you cannot do so, use fine-grained locking so that you hold a lock for as little time as possible.

When can intuition fail us, and the intuitively obvious not be obvious enough? When reads are not what they seem and actually modify some state. It is okay for concurrent uses of objects if all uses are strictly for reading and do not modify any state. Here are two cases where something *seems* like a read but is not and must be controlled by mutual exclusion:

Objects that share internal state
> An example is string structures that have different string objects point to a shared string buffer if the actual string values are the same or overlap. The objects in these cases must protect themselves internally to prevent the creation of race conditions due to lack of control.

Structures where reads track usage
> Beware of any exotic objects you might design or use that modify state when used. An example is a self-balancing binary search tree structure (splay tree) where a read access can cause internal modifications of the data structure.

Descriptions of the classes in this book note any departures from the need for synchronization. For example, the concurrent containers are more liberal. By their nature, they permit concurrent operations on the same container object.

This chapter assumes that you understand the importance of mutual exclusion and when it is needed. This chapter will define a few concepts as it goes along to show how Intel Threading Building Blocks fits the requirements, but it won't spend time on tutorials about locking.

Threading Building Blocks offers two kinds of mutual exclusion:

Mutexes
> These will be familiar to anyone who has used locks in other environments, and they include common variants such as reader-writer locks.

Atomic operations

These are based on atomic operations offered by hardware processors, and they provide a solution that is simpler and faster than mutexes in a limited set of situations. These should be preferred when the circumstances make their use possible.

Mutexes

A *mutex* is a global variable that multiple tasks can access. Before entering code that you do not want to execute concurrently, a task should request a lock on the mutex. If the mutex is already locked, the task is stalled waiting. Once the lock is granted, the task can proceed. The task should proceed quickly and release the lock on the mutex promptly to avoid unnecessary stalls in other tasks.

If a mutex creates a lot of lock requests, it is considered highly contested. Highly contested locks will result in many tasks being stalled and a sharp reduction in program scalability. Avoiding highly contested locks through careful program design is important.

A mutex, used properly, ensures that no task reads or writes a variable or other resource when another task is writing it. Intel Threading Building Blocks mutexes work with generic programming in C++, even in the presence of exceptions. Meeting all these requirements is no small feat and takes some consideration to ensure their proper usage.

In Threading Building Blocks, mutual exclusion is implemented by classes known as *mutexes* and *locks*. A mutex is an object on which a task can acquire a lock. Only one task at a time can have a lock on a mutex; other tasks have to wait their turn.

Mutual exclusion controls how many tasks can simultaneously run a region of code. In general, you protect a region of code from concurrency when that code reads or writes a small amount of memory, which is generally interrelated by a particular operation you want to effect.

Consider a simple way to write code to allocate a node from a list of available nodes:

```
Node* AllocateNode( ) {
    Node* n;
    FreeListMutexType::scoped_lock lock;
    lock.acquire(FreeListMutex);
    n = FreeList;
    if( n )
        FreeList = n->next;
    lock.release( );
    if( !n )
        n = new Node( );
    return n;
}
```

The acquire method waits until it can acquire a lock on the mutex FreeListMutex; the release method releases the lock. It is recommended that you add extra braces where possible, to clarify for future maintainers which code is protected by the lock:

```
Node* AllocateNode( ) {
    Node* n;
    FreeListMutexType::scoped_lock lock;
  {
    lock.acquire(FreeListMutex);
    n = FreeList;
    if( n )
        FreeList = n->next;
    lock.release( );
  }
    if( !n )
        n = new Node( );
    return n;
}
```

If you are familiar with C interfaces for locks, you may be wondering why Threading Building Blocks does not simply acquire and release methods on the mutex object itself. The reason is that the C interface would not be exception-safe because, if the protected region threw an exception, control would skip over the release. With the object-oriented interface, destruction of the scoped_lock object causes the lock to be released, no matter whether the protected region was exited by normal control flow or an exception. In the version of AllocateNode that uses acquire and release, the explicit release causes the lock to be released before its scope ends, so when the scope ends and the destructor runs, it sees that the lock was released and does nothing.

All mutexes in Threading Building Blocks have a similar interface, which not only makes them easier to learn, but also enables generic programming. For example, all of the mutexes have a nested scoped_lock type, so given a mutex of type M, the corresponding lock type is M::scoped_lock.

 It is recommended that you always use a typedef for the mutex type, as shown in the next example. That way, you can change the type of the lock later without having to edit the rest of the code. In the example, you could replace the typedef with typedef queuing_mutex FreeListMutexType, and the code would still be correct.

The simplest mutex is the spin_mutex. A task trying to acquire a lock on a busy spin_mutex waits until it can acquire the lock. A spin_mutex is appropriate when the lock is held for only a few instructions.

For instance, the code in Example 7-1 uses a mutex that ensures only one task has access at a time. Five lines of code were added in Example 7-1 to the sequential code to provide the proper mutual exclusion to make this code thread-safe: lines 1, 3, 4, 9, and 20.

Example 7-1. SpinMutex example

```
1  #include "tbb/spin_mutex.h"
2  Node* FreeList;
3  typedef spin_mutex FreeListMutexType;
4  FreeListMutexType FreeListMutex;
5
6  Node* AllocateNode( ) {
7      Node* n;
8      {
9          FreeListMutexType::scoped_lock mylock(FreeListMutex);
10         n = FreeList;
11         if( n )
12             FreeList = n->next;
13     }
14     if( !n )
15         n = new Node( );
16     return n;
17 }
18
19 void FreeNode( Node* n ) {
20     FreeListMutexType::scoped_lock mylock(FreeListMutex);
21     n->next = FreeList;
22     FreeList = n;
23 }
```

The *this constructor for scoped_lock waits until there are no other locks on the FreeListMutex mutex. The destructor releases the lock. The destructor runs at the closing brace, which terminates the scope of the lock; hence the name *scoped lock*. This interaction with the compiler also explains the unusual braces inside the AllocateNode routine. Their role is to keep the lifetime of the lock as short as possible so that other waiting tasks can get their chance as soon as possible. Without the extra braces, the scope of the lock in this example would be the entire routine.

Be sure to name the lock object; otherwise, it will be destroyed too soon because C++ compilers are allowed to eliminate unnamed objects. For example, if the creation of the scoped_lock object in the example is changed to:

```
FreeListMutexType::scoped_lock (FreeListMutex);
```

the scoped_lock is destroyed when execution reaches the semicolon, which releases the lock *before* FreeList is accessed.

Mutex Flavors

Connoisseurs distinguish various attributes of mutexes. It helps to know some of these, because they involve trade-offs between generality and efficiency. Picking the right one often helps performance. Mutexes can be described by the following qualities, also summarized in Table 7-1.

Table 7-1. *Traits and behavior of mutexes*

Mutex	Scalable	Fair	Reentrant	Sleeps	Size
mutex	OS-dependent	OS-dependent	No	Yes	Three or more words
spin_mutex	No	No	No	No	One byte
queuing_mutex	Yes	Yes	No	No	One word
spin_rw_mutex	No	No	No	No	One word
queuing_rw_mutex	Yes	Yes	No	No	One word

Scalable

Some mutexes are called *scalable*. In a strict sense, this is not an accurate name because a mutex limits execution to one task at a time and is therefore necessarily a drag on scalability. A *scalable mutex* is rather one that does *no worse* than forcing single-threaded performance. A mutex actually can do worse than serialize execution if the waiting tasks consume excessive processor cycles and memory bandwidth, reducing the speed of tasks trying to do real work. Scalable mutexes are often slower than nonscalable mutexes under light contention, so a nonscalable mutex may be better. When in doubt, use a scalable mutex.

Fair

Mutexes can be *fair* or *unfair*. A fair mutex lets tasks through in the order they arrive. Fair mutexes avoid starving tasks. Each task gets its turn. However, unfair mutexes can be faster because they let tasks that are running go through first, instead of the task that is next in line, which may be sleeping because of an interrupt.

Reentrant

Mutexes can be *reentrant* or *nonreentrant*. A reentrant mutex allows a task that is already holding a lock on the mutex to acquire another lock on it. This is useful in some recursive algorithms, but it typically adds overhead to the lock implementation.

Sleep or spin

Mutexes can cause a task to *spin in user space* or *sleep* while it is waiting. For short waits, spinning in user space is fastest because putting a task to sleep takes cycles. But for long waits, sleeping is better because it causes the task to give up its processor to some task that needs it. Spinning is also undesirable in processors with multiple-task support in a single core, such as Intel processors with hyperthreading technology.

The following is a summary of mutex behaviors:

- A spin_mutex is nonscalable, unfair, nonreentrant, and spins in user space. It would seem to be the worst of all possible worlds, except that it is *very fast* in *lightly contended* situations. If you can design your program so that contention is somehow spread out among many spin mutexes, you can improve performance over other kinds of mutexes. If a mutex is heavily contended, your algorithm will not scale anyway. Consider redesigning the algorithm instead of looking for a more efficient lock.

- A queuing_mutex is scalable, fair, nonreentrant, and spins in user space. Use it when scalability and fairness are important.

- A spin_rw_mutex and a queuing_rw_mutex are similar to spin_mutex and queuing_ mutex, but they additionally support *reader* locks.

> spin_mutex is *very fast* in lightly contended situations; use it if you need to protect a small section of code.

- A mutex is a wrapper around the system's native mutual exclusion mechanism. On Windows systems, it is implemented on top of a CRITICAL_SECTION. On Linux systems, it is implemented on top of a pthread mutex. The advantages of using the wrapper are that it adds an exception-safe interface and provides an interface identical to the other mutexes in Threading Building Blocks, which makes it easy to swap in a different kind of mutex later if warranted by performance measurements.

> Future versions of Threading Building Blocks may be able to put tasks to sleep more often, which can be very desirable.

Reader-Writer Mutexes

Mutual exclusion is necessary when at least one task *writes* to a shared variable. But it does no harm to permit multiple readers into a protected region. The reader-writer variants of the mutexes, denoted by _rw_ in the class names, enable multiple readers by distinguishing *reader locks* from *writer locks*. There can be more than one reader lock on a given mutex.

Requests for a reader lock are distinguished from requests for a writer lock via an extra Boolean parameter in the constructor for scoped_lock. The parameter is false to request a reader lock and true to request a writer lock. It defaults to true so that when it is omitted, a spin_rw_mutex or queuing_rw_mutex behaves like its non-_rw_ counterpart. The next section shows an example where the parameter is explicitly false in order to obtain a reader lock.

Upgrade/Downgrade

It is possible to upgrade a reader lock to a writer lock by using the method upgrade_ to_writer. Here is an example:

```
std::vector<string> MyVector;
typedef spin_rw_mutex MyVectorMutexType;
MyVectorMutexType MyVectorMutex;

void AddKeyIfMissing( const string& key ) {
    // Obtain a reader lock on MyVectorMutex
    MyVectorMutexType::scoped_lock lock(MyVectorMutex,/*is_writer=*/false);
    size_t n = MyVector.size();
    for( size_t i=0; i<n; ++i )
        if( MyVector[i]==key ) return;
    if( !MyVectorMutex.upgrade_to_writer() )
        // Check if key was added while lock was temporarily released
        for( int i=n; i<MyVector.size(); ++i )
            if(MyVector[i]==key ) return;
    vector.push_back(key);
}
```

Note that after obtaining a lock on the vector, the routine must sometimes search the vector again. This is necessary because upgrade_to_writer might have to temporarily release the lock before it can upgrade. Otherwise, deadlock might ensue. The upgrade_to_writer method returns a bool that is true if it successfully upgrades the lock without releasing it, and false if the lock is released temporarily. Thus, when upgrade_to_writer returns false, the code must rerun the search to check that the key was not inserted by another writer. The example presumes that keys are always added to the end of the vector, and that keys are never removed. Because of these assumptions, it does not have to re-search the entire vector, but only the elements beyond those originally searched. The critical point to remember is that when upgrade_to_writer returns false, any assumptions established while holding a reader lock may have been invalidated and must be rechecked.

For symmetry, there is a corresponding method, downgrade_to_reader, though in practice there are few reasons to use it.

Lock Pathologies

Locks can introduce performance and correctness problems. If you are new to locking, here are some of the problems to avoid.

Deadlock

Deadlock happens when tasks are trying to acquire more than one lock, and each holds some of the locks the other tasks need in order to proceed. More precisely, deadlock happens when:

- There is a cycle of tasks.
- Each task holds at least one lock on a mutex, and is waiting on a mutex for which the *next* task in the cycle already has a lock.
- No task is willing to give up its lock.

Think of classic gridlock at an intersection. Each car has "acquired" part of the road, but it needs to acquire the road under another car to get through. There are three common ways to avoid deadlock:

- Avoid needing to hold two locks at the same time. Break your program into small actions, each of which can be accomplished while holding a single lock.

- Always acquire locks in the same order. For example, if you have *outer container* and *inner container* mutexes, and you need to acquire a lock on one of each, you could always acquire the *outer sanctum* one first. Another example is to acquire locks in alphabetical order, in a situation where the locks have names. Or if the locks are unnamed, acquire locks in order of the numerical addresses for the mutex.

- Use atomic operations instead of locks, as discussed later in this chapter.

Convoying and priority inversion

Convoying is a problem that comes up between threads of the same priority and is a concern when using locks and Threading Building Blocks. Convoying occurs when the operating system interrupts a task that is holding a lock. All other tasks must wait until the interrupted task resumes and releases the lock. Fair mutexes can make the situation even worse because if a waiting task is interrupted, all the tasks behind it must wait for it to resume.

To avoid convoying, use atomic operations instead of locks where possible.

Convoying is similar to priority inversion. Priority inversion describes a general case where a lower-priority task holds a shared resource that is required by a higher-priority task. The higher-priority task is therefore blocked until the lower-priority task has released the resource, effectively *inverting* the relative priorities of the two tasks.

To minimize convoying and priority inversion, use atomic operations if possible. Otherwise, hold *any* lock as briefly as possible. Precompute whatever you can before acquiring the lock.

Mutexes

Mutexes provide mutual exclusion of tasks from sections of code.

In general, strive for designs that minimize the use of explicit locking, because it can lead to serial bottlenecks. If explicit locking is necessary, try to spread it out so that multiple tasks usually do not contend to lock the same mutex.

Mutex Concept

The mutexes and locks here have simple interfaces that are designed for high performance. The interfaces enforce the *scoped locking pattern*, which is widely used in C++ libraries because:

- It does not require the programmer to remember to release the lock.
- It releases the lock if an exception is thrown out of the mutual exclusion region protected by the lock.

There are two parts to the pattern: a *mutex* and a *lock*. The constructor of the lock object acquires the lock, and the destructor of the lock object releases the lock. Here's an example:

```
{
    // Construction of myLock acquires lock on myMutex
    M::scoped_lock myLock( myMutex );
    ... actions to be performed while holding the lock ...
    // Destruction of myLock releases lock on myMutex
}
```

If the actions throw an exception, the lock is automatically released as the block is exited.

Table 7-2 summarizes the classes that model the Mutex Concept.

Table 7-2. Mutex Concept

Pseudosignature	Semantics
M( )	Construct unlocked mutex.
~M( )	Destroy unlocked mutex.
M::scoped_lock( )	Construct lock without acquiring mutex.
M::scoped_lock(M&)	Construct lock and acquire lock on mutex.
M::~scoped_lock( )	Release lock (if acquired).
M::scoped_lock::acquire(M&)	Acquire lock on mutex.
M::scoped_lock::release( )	Release lock.

mutex Class   Class that models the Mutex Concept using underlying OS locks.

```
#include "tbb/mutex.h"class mutex;
```

Description

A mutex models the Mutex Concept. It is a wrapper around OS calls that provide mutual exclusion. Here are the advantages of using a mutex instead of the OS calls:

- The mutex class is portable across all operating systems supported by Intel Threading Building Blocks.
- The mutex releases the lock if an exception is thrown from the protected region of code.

Members

See Table 7-2.

---

spin_mutex Class
Class that models the Mutex Concept using a spin lock.

```
#include "tbb/spin_mutex.h"

class spin_mutex;
```

Description

A `spin_mutex` models the Mutex Concept. A `spin_mutex` is not scalable, fair, or reentrant. It is ideal when the lock is lightly contended and is held for only a few machine instructions. If a task cannot acquire a `spin_mutex` when the class is created, it busy-waits, which can degrade system performance if the wait is long. However, if the wait is typically short, a `spin_mutex` significantly improves performance compared to other mutexes.

Members

See Table 7-2.

---

queuing_mutex Class
Class that models the Mutex Concept that is fair and scalable.

```
#include "tbb/queuing_mutex.h"

class queuing_mutex;
```

Description

A `queuing_mutex` models the Mutex Concept. A `queuing_mutex` is scalable, in the sense that if a task has to wait to acquire the mutex, it spins on its own local cache line. A `queuing_mutex` is fair, in that tasks acquire the lock in the order they requested it, even if they are later suspended. A `queuing_mutex` is not reentrant.

The current implementation does busy-waiting, so using a `queuing_mutex` may degrade system performance if the wait is long.

Members

See Table 7-2.

ReaderWriterMutex Concept

The ReaderWriterMutex Concept extends the Mutex Concept to include the notion of reader-writer locks. It introduces a Boolean parameter, `write`, that specifies whether a writer lock (`write = true`) or reader lock (`write = false`) is being requested. Multiple reader locks can be held simultaneously on a `ReaderWriterMutex` if it does not have a writer lock on it. A writer lock on a `ReaderWriterMutex` excludes all other tasks from holding a lock on the mutex at the same time.

Table 7-3 shows the requirements for `ReaderWriterMutex RW`.

Table 7-3. ReaderWriterMutex Concept

Pseudosignature	Semantics
RW( )	Construct an unlocked mutex.
~*RW*( )	Destroy an unlocked mutex.
RW::scoped_lock::acquire(*RW*&, bool write=true)	Acquire lock on mutex.
RW::scoped_lock::release( )	Release lock.
bool *RW*::scoped_lock::upgrade_to_writer( )	Change reader lock to writer lock.
bool *RW*::scoped_lock::downgrade_to_reader( )	Change writer lock to reader lock.

The following sections explain the semantics of the ReaderWriterMutex Concept in detail.

Model Types

`spin_rw_mutex` and `queuing_rw_mutex` model the ReaderWriterMutex Concept.

`ReaderWriterMutex( )`
> Effect: constructs an unlocked `ReaderWriterMutex`.

`~ReaderWriterMutex( )`
> Effect: destroys an unlocked `ReaderWriterMutex`. The effect of destroying a locked `ReaderWriterMutex` is undefined.

`ReaderWriterMutex::scoped_lock( )`
> Effect: constructs a `scoped_lock` object that does not hold a lock on any mutex.

`ReaderWriterMutex::scoped_lock( ReaderWriterMutex& rw, bool write=true)`
> Effect: constructs a `scoped_lock` object that acquires a lock on mutex `rw`. The lock is a writer lock if `write` is true; it is a reader lock otherwise.

`ReaderWriterMutex::~scoped_lock( )`
> Effect: if the object is holding a lock on a `ReaderWriterMutex`, releases the lock.

`void ReaderWriterMutex:: scoped_lock:: acquire( ReaderWriterMutex& rw, bool write=true )`
> Effect: acquires a lock on mutex `rw`. The lock is a writer lock if `write` is true; it is a reader lock otherwise.

`bool ReaderWriterMutex:: scoped_lock::try_acquire( ReaderWriterMutex& rw, bool write=true )`
> Effect: attempts to acquire a lock on mutex `rw`. The lock is a writer lock if `write` is true; it is a reader lock otherwise.
>
> Returns: true if the lock is acquired, false otherwise.

`void ReaderWriterMutex:: scoped_lock::release( )`
> Effect: releases the lock. The effect is undefined if no lock is held.

`bool ReaderWriterMutex:: scoped_lock::upgrade_to_writer( )`
> Effect: changes a reader lock to a writer lock. The effect is undefined if the object does not already hold a reader lock.
>
> Returns: false if the lock is released and reacquired; true otherwise.

```
bool ReaderWriterMutex:: scoped_lock::downgrade_to_reader( )
```

> Effect: changes a writer lock to a reader lock. The effect is undefined if the object does not already hold a writer lock.

> Returns: `false` if the lock is released and reacquired; `true` otherwise.

Intel's current implementations for `spin_rw_mutex` and `queuing_rw_mutex` always return `true`. Different implementations might sometimes return `false`.

---

spin_rw_mutex Class   Class that models ReaderWriterMutex Concept that is unfair and not scalable.

```
#include "tbb/spin_rw_mutex.h"
```

```
class spin_rw_mutex;
```

Description

A `spin_rw_mutex` models the ReaderWriterMutex Concept. A `spin_rw_mutex` is not scalable, fair, or reentrant. It is ideal when the lock is lightly contended and is held for only a few machine instructions. If a task cannot acquire a `spin_rw_mutex` when the class is created, it busy-waits, which can degrade system performance if the wait is long. However, if the wait is typically short, a `spin_rw_mutex` significantly improves performance compared to other ReaderWriterMutex mutexes.

Members

See Table 7-3.

---

queuing_rw_mutex Class   Class that models ReaderWriterMutex Concept that is fair and scalable.

```
#include "tbb/queuing_rw_mutex.h"
```

```
class queuing_rw_mutex;
```

Description

A `queuing_rw_mutex` models the ReaderWriterMutex Concept. A `queuing_rw_mutex` is scalable, in the sense that if a task has to wait to acquire the mutex, it spins on its own local cache line. A `queuing_rw_mutex` is fair, in that tasks acquire the lock in the order they requested it, even if they later are suspended. A `queuing_rw_mutex` is not reentrant.

Members

See Table 7-3.

Atomic Operations

Atomic operations are a fast and relatively easy alternative to mutexes. They do not suffer from the deadlock and convoying problems described earlier, in the section "Lock Pathologies." The main limitation of atomic operations is that they are limited in current computer systems to fairly small data sizes: the largest is usually the size of the largest scalar, often a double-precision floating-point number.

Atomic operations are also limited to a small set of operations supported by the underlying hardware processor. But sophisticated algorithms can accomplish a lot with these operations; this section shows a couple of examples. You should not pass up an opportunity to use an atomic operation in place of mutual exclusion.

The class atomic<T> implements atomic operations with C++ style.

A classic use of atomic operations is for thread-safe reference counting. Suppose x is a reference count of type int and the program needs to take some action when the reference count becomes zero. In single-threaded code, you could use a plain int for x, and write --x; if(x==0) action( ). But this method might fail for multithreaded code because two tasks might interleave their operations, as shown in Figure 7-1, where t_a and t_b represent machine registers and time progresses downward.

Task A	Task B
$t_a = x$	$t_b = x$
$x = t_a - 1$	$x = t_b - 1$
if (x==0)	if (x==0)

Figure 7-1. Interleaving of machine instructions

The problem shown in Figure 7-1 is a classic race condition. Although the code intends x to be decremented twice, x ends up being only one less than its original value. Also, another problem results because the test of x is separate from the decrement: if x starts out as 2, and both tasks decrement x before either task evaluates the if condition, *both* tasks will call action( ).

Note that simply writing if(--x==0) action( ) does not solve the problem—as long as x is a conventional variable—because at the machine code level, the decrement is still a separate instruction from the compare. Two tasks can still interleave their operations.

To correct this problem, you need to ensure that only one task at a time does the decrement *and* that the value checked by the if is the result of the decrement. You can do this by introducing a mutex, but it is much faster and simpler to declare x as atomic<int> and write if(--x==0) action( ). The method atomic<int>::operator-- acts atomically; no other task can interfere.

atomic<T> supports atomic operations on type T, which must be an integral or pointer type. Five fundamental operations are supported, with additional interfaces in the form of overloaded operators for syntactic convenience. For example, ++, --, -=, and += operations on atomic<T> are all forms of the fundamental operation *fetch-and-add*. Table 7-4 shows the five fundamental operations on a variable x of type atomic<T>.

Table 7-4. Fundamental operations on a variable x of type atomic<T>

Operation	Description
= x	Read the value of x.
x =	Write the value of x, and return it.
x.fetch_and_store(y)	Execute y=x and return the old value of x.
x.fetch_and_add(y)	Execute x+=y and return the old value of x.
x.compare_and_swap(y,z)	If x equals z, execute x=y.
	In either case, return the old value of x.

Because these operations happen atomically, they can be used safely without mutual exclusion. Consider Example 7-2.

Example 7-2. GetUniqueInteger atomic example

```
atomic<unsigned> counter;

unsigned GetUniqueInteger( ) {
    return counter.fetch_and_add(1);
}
```

The routine GetUniqueInteger returns a different integer each time it is called, until the counter wraps around. This is true no matter how many tasks call GetUniqueInteger simultaneously.

The operation compare_and_swap is fundamental to many nonblocking algorithms. A problem with mutual exclusion is that if a task holding a lock is suspended, all other tasks are blocked until the holding task resumes. Nonblocking algorithms avoid this problem by using atomic operations instead of locking. They are generally complicated and require sophisticated analysis to verify. However, the idiom in Example 7-3 is straightforward and worth knowing. It updates a shared variable, globalx, in a way that is somehow based on its old value:

Example 7-3. compare_and_swap atomically

```
atomic<int> globalx;

int UpdateX( ) {     // Update x and return old value of x.
    do {
        // Read globalx
        oldx = globalx;
        // Compute new value
        newx = ...expression involving oldx....
        // Store new value if another task has not changed globalX.
    } while( globalx.compare_and_swap(newx,oldx)!=oldx );
    return oldx;
}
```

In some OS implementations, `compare_and_swap` can cause tasks to iterate the loop until *no* other task interferes, and this may seem less efficient in highly contended situations because of the repetition. But typically, if the update takes only a few instructions, the idiom is faster than the corresponding mutual-exclusion solution, so you should use `compare_and_swap`.

The update idiom (`compare_and_swap`) is inappropriate if the A-B-A problem (see sidebar) thwarts your intent. It is a frequent problem when trying to design a non-blocking algorithm for linked data structures.

A-B-A Problem

The A-B-A problem occurs when a thread checks a location to be sure the value is *A*, and proceeds with an update only if it is *A*. The question arises whether it is a problem if other tasks change the same location in a way that the first task does not detect:

A task reads a value *A* from `globalx`.

Other tasks change `globalx` from *A* to *B* and then back to *A*.

At the same time, the original task does its `compare_and_swap`, reading *A* and thus not detecting the intervening change to *B*.

If the task erroneously proceeds under an assumption that the location has not changed since the task first read it, the task may proceed to corrupt the object or otherwise get the wrong result.

Consider an example with linked lists. Assume a linked list $W(1) \rightarrow X(9) \rightarrow Y(7) \rightarrow Z(4)$, where the letters are the node locations and the numbers are the values in the nodes. Assume a task transverses the list to find a node X to dequeue. The task fetches the next pointer, `X.next` (which is Y), with the intent to put it in `W.next`. But before the swap is done, the task is suspended for some time.

During the suspension, other tasks are busy. They dequeue X and then happen to reuse that same memory and queue a new version of node X as well as dequeuing Y and adding Q at some point in time. Now the list is $W(1) \rightarrow X(2) \rightarrow Q(3) \rightarrow Z(4)$.

Once the original task finally wakes up, it finds that `W.next` still points to X, so it swaps out `W.next` to become Y, thereby making a complete mess out of the linked list.

Atomic operations are the way to go if they embody enough protection for your algorithm. If the A-B-A problem can ruin your day, find a more complex solution.

Why atomic<T> Has No Constructors

The template class `atomic<T>` deliberately has no constructors because examples such as `GetUniqueInteger` are commonly required to work correctly even before all file-scope constructors have been called. If `atomic<T>` had constructors, a file-scope instance might be initialized after it had been referenced.

You can rely on zero initialization to initialize an atomic<T> to 0. To create an atomic<T> with a specific value, default-construct it first, and afterward assign a value to it. For example:

```
atomic<int> x;
x = 2048;
```

Memory Consistency and Fences

A processor may reorder memory reads and writes so they occur in an order that is inconsistent with the original program. *Memory consistency* is a term used to describe how inconsistent the processor's actual memory accessing can be relative to the original program. Obviously, two accesses to a single location need to happen in an order which preserves the intent of the original program. It is not okay to reorder a read of a variable that occurs after a write of the same variable. What is less clear is whether the order of reads and writes of different variables (different addresses) matters. In a multithreaded environment, it may matter a great deal how reads and writes are ordered because multiple threads can view the state of memory. The stronger memory consistency is, the less challenging it is for programmers, but the more limiting it is for hardware efficiency.

Some processor architectures, such as the Intel Itanium, IBM POWER and PowerPC, and Alpha processors, have *weak memory consistency*, in which memory operations on different addresses may be reordered by the hardware for the sake of efficiency. For Sun SPARC processors, the ordering is different under Solaris (which uses total-store order or TSO) and Linux (which uses relaxed-memory order or RMO). Therefore, Sun SPARC has *weak memory consistency* under Linux but not under Solaris.

The subject is complex, and the interested reader should consult other works on the subject. If you are programming only IA-32 and Intel 64/AMD64 processor platforms, you can skip this section. These platforms have the strongest memory consistency models.

To constrain reordering, the processor may invoke *fences*, which prevent reordering that could risk corrupting results. Table 7-5 describes the different types of fences. Each kind of fence stops the hardware from moving any other operation past the atomic operation.

Table 7-5. Types of fences

Kind	Description	Default for
Acquire	Operations after the fence never move over it.	Read
Release	Operations before the fence never move over it.	Write
Full	Operations on either side of the fence never move over it.	fetch_and_store fetch_and_add compare_and_swap

The rightmost column lists the operations that default to a particular kind. Normally, you should leave the defaults in place to avoid unexpected surprises. For read and write, the defaults are the only kinds of fences available. However, if you are familiar with weak memory consistency, you might want to change the full fences to lesser fences. To do this, use variants that take a template argument. The argument can be acquire or release, which are values of the enum type memory_semantics.

For example, suppose various tasks are producing parts of a data structure, and you want to signal a consuming task when the data structure is ready. One way to do this is to initialize an atomic counter with the number of busy producers; as each producer finishes, it decrements the count by executing:

```
refcount.fetch_and_add<release>(-1);
```

The argument release guarantees that the producer's work (which involves writing to shared memory) occurs before refcount is decremented. By default, the fetch_and_add fence would block instruction reordering in both directions, but that's not required in this particular situation, so you can safely allow instructions to be moved before the decrement.

Similarly, when the consumer checks refcount, the consumer must use an acquire fence, which is the default for reads. So the consumer's reads of the data structure do not happen until after the consumer sees refcount become 0.

atomic<T> Template Class

Template class for atomic operations.

```
#include "tbb/atomic.h"

template<typename T> atomic;
```

Description

An atomic<T> supports atomic read, write, fetch-and-add, fetch-and-store, and compare-and-swap. Type T may be an integral type or a pointer type. When T is a pointer type, arithmetic operations are interpreted as pointer arithmetic. For example, if x has type atomic<float*> and a float occupies four bytes, ++x advances x by four bytes. The specialization atomic<void*> does not allow pointer arithmetic.

Some of the methods offer two method variants, one of which is a templated form that permits more selective memory fencing using memory_semantics. For instance, the first of the following fetch_and_add calls is templated to specify a release fence, whereas the second call is not templated:

```
refcount.fetch_and_add<release>(-1);
refcount.fetch_and_add(1);
```

On IA-32 and Intel 64 processors, the templated calls have the same effect as the nontemplated variants because the processors do not support weaker memory consistency. On processors with *weak memory consistency*, the templated calls may improve performance by allowing the memory subsystem more latitude on the orders of reads and writes; therefore, using them may improve performance. Table 7-5 shows the fencing defaults (nontemplated form).

The template class atomic<T> does not have any nontrivial constructors because such constructors could lead to accidental introduction of compiler temporaries that would subvert the purpose of atomic<T>. See the section "Why atomic<T> Has No Constructors," earlier in this chapter.

Members

```
namespace tbb {
    enum memory_semantics {
        acquire,
        release
    };
    struct atomic<T> {
        typedef T value_type;

        template<memory_semantics M>
        value_type fetch_and_add( value_type addend );

        value_type fetch_and_add( value_type addend );

        template<memory_semantics M>
        value_type fetch_and_increment( );

        value_type fetch_and_increment( );

        template<memory_semantics M>
        value_type fetch_and_decrement( );

        value_type fetch_and_decrement( );

        template<memory_semantics M>
        value_type compare_and_swap( value_type new_value,
                                     value_type comparand );

        value_type compare_and_swap( value_type new_value,
                                     value_type comparand );

        template<memory_semantics M>
        value_type fetch_and_store( value_type new_value );

        value_type fetch_and_store( value_type new_value );

        operator value_type( ) const;

        value_type operator=( value_type new_value );

        value_type operator+=(value_type);
        value_type operator-=(value_type);
        value_type operator++( );
        value_type operator++(int);
        value_type operator--( );
        value_type operator--(int);
    };
}
```

enum memory_semantics

Description: defines values used to select the template variants that permit more selective memory fencing (see Table 7-5).

value_type fetch_and_add(*value_type* addend)

Effect: atomically adds addend to the variable (*this) that invoked the method.

Returns: original value (*this).

value_type fetch_and_increment( )

Effect: atomically increments the variable (*this) that invoked the method.

Returns: original value (*this).

value_type fetch_and_decrement( )

Effect: atomically decrements the variable (*this) that invoked the method.

Returns: original value (*this).

value_type compare_and_swap(*value_type* new_value, *value_type* comparand)

Effect: atomically compares the variable (*this) that invoked the method with comparand, and if they are equal, sets the variable (*this) to new_value.

Returns: original value (*this).

value_type fetch_and_store(*value_type* new_value)

Effect: atomically exchanges the variable (*this) that invoked the method with new_value.

Returns: original value (*this).

CHAPTER 8
Timing

Intel Threading Building Blocks provides a thread-safe and portable method to compute elapsed time.

Many operating systems provide a fine-grained method to track the accounting of central processing unit (CPU) time, and most provide a way to track elapsed/wall-clock time. The method of extracting an elapsed measurement with subsecond accuracy varies a great deal.

The class tick_count in Threading Building Blocks provides a simple interface for measuring wall-clock time, as shown in Example 8-1.

Example 8-1. Using tick_count to measure elapsed time

```
#include "tbb/tick_count.h"
using namespace tbb;
...
tick_count t0 = tick_count::now( );
... do some work ...
tick_count t1 = tick_count::now( );
printf("work took %g seconds\n",(t1-t0).seconds( ));
```

This is guaranteed to work even if the processor core running a task changes while the work is being done, and therefore the tick_count calls run on different processors.

 Unlike some timing interfaces, tick_count is guaranteed to be safe to use across threads. It is based on a common or global clock. It is valid to subtract tick_count values that were created by different threads to compute elapsed time.

A tick_count value obtained from the static method tick_count::now( ) represents the current absolute time. This value has no meaning other than for use in comparisons with other tick_count values. Subtracting two tick_count values yields a relative time in tick_count::interval_t, as shown in Example 8-1. Relative time is expressed in seconds as a double in order to allow fractional values in keeping with the resolution available on the operating system.

The resolution of tick_count corresponds to the highest-resolution timing service on the platform that is valid across threads in the same process. The routines are wrappers around operating system services that have been verified as safe to use across threads.

 Because the highest-resolution counters—the CPU timer registers—are *not* valid across threads on some platforms, the resolution of tick_count cannot be guaranteed to be consistent from platform to platform. The library seeks to do the best that the platform can supply.

tick_count Class

Class for computing wall-clock times.

```
#include "tbb/tick_count.h"
```

```
class tick_count;
```

Description

A tick_count is an absolute timestamp. One tick_count object may be subtracted from another to compute a relative time tick_count::interval_t, which can be converted to seconds.

Example

```
#include "tbb/tick_count.h"
using namespace tbb;

void Foo( ) {
    tick_count t0 = tick_count::now( );
    ...action being timed...
    tick_count t1 = tick_count::now( );
    printf("time for action = %g seconds\n", (t1-t0).seconds( ) );
}
```

Members

```
namespace tbb {

    class tick_count {
    public:
        class interval_t;
        static tick_count now( );
    };

    tick_count::interval_t  operator-( const tick_count& t1,
                                       const tick_count& t0 );
} // tbb
```

static tick_count tick_count::now( )
    Returns: current wall-clock timestamp.

tick_count::interval_t operator-;(const tick_count& t1, const tick_count& t0)
    Returns: relative time that t1 occurred after t0.

tick_count::interval_t Class

Class for relative wall-clock time.

```
#include "tbb/tick_count.h"
```

```
class tick_count::interval_t;
```

Description

A `tick_count::interval_t` represents relative wall-clock time or duration.

Members provide for the accumulation and reduction of intervals by other `interval_t` values, and for the conversion of `interval_t` values into seconds.

Members

```
namespace tbb {

    class tick_count::interval_t {
    public:
        interval_t();
        double seconds() const;
        interval_t operator+=( const interval_t& i );
        interval_t operator-=( const interval_t& i );
    };

    tick_count::interval_t  operator+( const tick_count::interval_t& i,
                                       const tick_count::interval_t& j );
    tick_count::interval_t  operator-( const tick_count::interval_t& i,
                                       const tick_count::interval_t& j );

} // tbb
```

interval_t( )
    Effects: constructs an `interval_t` representing a zero time duration.

double seconds( ) const
    Returns: a time interval measured in seconds (can have noninteger values).

interval_t operator+=(const interval_t& i)
    Effects: *this = *this + i.

    Returns: a reference to *this after the addition.

interval_t operator-=(const interval_t& i)
    Effects: *this = *this - i.

    Returns: a reference to *this after the subtraction.

interval_t operator+ (const interval_t& i, const interval_t& j)
    Returns: an `interval_t` representing the sum of intervals i and j.

interval_t operator- (const interval_t& i, const interval_t& j)
    Returns: an `interval_t` representing the difference between intervals i and j.

CHAPTER 9

Task Scheduler

This chapter introduces the Intel Threading Building Blocks *task scheduler*. The task scheduler is the heart of Threading Building Blocks, but generally it is not used directly after you initialize it by constructing a tbb::task_scheduler_init.

The task scheduler is the engine that powers the loop templates. When practical, you should use the loop templates instead of the task scheduler because the templates hide the complexity of the scheduler. However, if you have an algorithm that does not naturally map onto one of the high-level templates, use the task scheduler. All of the scheduler functionality used by the high-level templates is available for you to use directly, so you can build new high-level templates that are just as powerful as the existing ones.

When Task-Based Programming Is Inappropriate

Using the task scheduler is usually the best approach to threading for performance, but there are cases when the built-in task scheduler is not the most appropriate solution. The task scheduler is intended for high-performance algorithms composed of nonblocking tasks. It still works if the tasks block occasionally. However, if threads block frequently, there is a performance loss when using the task scheduler because the processor is not doing any work while the task is blocked.

Blocking typically occurs while waiting for I/O or mutexes for long periods. If threads hold mutexes for long periods, your code is not likely to perform well anyway, no matter how many threads it has. If you have blocking tasks, it is best to use full-blown threads for those. The task scheduler is designed so that you can safely mix your own threads with Threading Building Blocks tasks.

Much Better Than Raw Native Threads

The task scheduler manages a thread pool and hides the complexity of native threads. The parallel algorithms (covered in Chapter 3) are all based on the task scheduler interface. The task scheduler is designed to address common performance issues of parallel programming with native threads, specifically those issues listed in Table 9-1. The following subsections of this chapter offer details on each item in the table.

Table 9-1. Problems with raw threads

Problem	Intel Threading Building Blocks approach
Oversubscription	One scheduler thread per hardware thread.
Choice of scheduling policy	Nonpreemptive unfair scheduling.
High coding overhead	Programmer specifies tasks, not threads.
Load imbalances	Work stealing balances load.
Portability	No code changes should be needed to use with any C++ compiler on any operating system.

Oversubscription

Getting the number of threads right is difficult. The threads you would create with a threading package are *logical threads*, which map onto the *physical threads* of the hardware. For computations that do not wait on external devices, the highest efficiency usually occurs when there is exactly one running logical thread per physical thread. Otherwise, there can be inefficiencies from any mismatch.

If there are not enough running logical threads to keep the physical threads working, the result is undersubscription or inefficiency. If there are more running logical threads than physical threads, this oversubscription usually leads to *time-sliced* execution of logical threads, which incurs overhead.

The Threading Building Blocks task scheduler avoids undersubscription and oversubscription by selecting the number of logical threads that will likely make the most efficient use of the underlying hardware. It maps tasks to logical threads in a way that tolerates interference by other threads from the same or other processes.

Nested parallelism makes oversubscription more likely because a nested subroutine has to do something very elaborate to check whether it is running within a parallel operation on a higher level. Coordinating the creation of new threads within independent threads is also complex.

It is important to try to take advantage of parallelism at all levels of nesting to avoid undersubscription. Unfortunately, with raw threads this is nontrivial. Threading Building Blocks avoids this problem by having you create tasks instead of threads.

The task scheduler tries to avoid oversubscription by having one logical thread per physical thread regardless of the number of tasks.

The key advantage of tasks versus logical threads is that tasks are much lighter in weight than logical threads. On Linux systems, starting and terminating a task is about 18 times faster than starting and terminating a thread. On Windows systems, the ratio is more than 100-fold. This is because a thread has its own copy of a lot of resources, such as register state and a stack. On Linux, a thread even has its own process ID. A task in Threading Building Blocks, in contrast, is typically a small routine and cannot be preempted at the task level by the scheduler (although its associated logical thread can be preempted by the operating system).

Fair Scheduling

Most general-purpose operating systems use a scheduler based on the idea of *fair scheduling*. You might be asking yourself, "With a name like *fair scheduling*, how could it be bad?"

It's bad because *fair*, when speaking of thread scheduling, means balancing time. Thread schedulers typically distribute time slices in a round-robin fashion. The distribution is called *fair* because each logical thread gets an equal share of time. Thread schedulers are typically fair because it is the safest strategy to undertake without understanding the higher-level organization of a program.

Preempting a thread in the name of fairness is often done out of concern that some very large tasks will dominate others. But Threading Building Blocks takes care of the difference in task loads by monitoring processors and starting new tasks on idle processors. It also offers some assurance that tasks are "right-sized," thanks to recursive splitting. This works very well in combination with the dynamic load balancing that Threading Building Blocks implements through task stealing.

In short, Threading Building Blocks does not need the inefficiencies of so-called fair scheduling. Preempting a task, in the name of fairness, would generally slow the completion of the overall task. It is better to let tasks complete.

In task-based programming, the task scheduler does have some of the higher-level information that is unavailable to the operating system, so the Threading Building Blocks task scheduler can sacrifice fairness for efficiency. Indeed, the scheduler often delays starting a task until the task can make useful progress. This chapter explains more about how this works and how it saves both time and space.

The result is that tasks are more efficient *because* the task scheduler is unfair.

High Coding Overhead

Raw threads, such as POSIX threads (pthreads) or Windows threads, expose the control of parallelism at its lowest level. They represent the *assembly languages of parallelism*. As such, they offer maximum flexibility at a high cost.

When using raw threads, programmers find basic work to be difficult and tedious to write correctly and efficiently. Code often becomes very dependent on the particular threading facilities of an operating system. Raw thread-level programming is too low-level to be intuitive and seldom results in code designed for scalable performance. Furthermore, the programming model does not encourage nested parallelism, which turns out to be very important.

With thread-based programming, you are forced to think at the low level of physical threads to get good efficiency because you want to maintain one logical thread per physical thread—and make sure that the logical thread is not blocked for long periods of time—to avoid undersubscription or oversubscription. You also have to deal with the relatively coarse grain of threads.

The main advantage of using tasks instead of threads is that they let you think at a higher, task-based level. You can concentrate on dependencies among tasks and leave efficient scheduling to the scheduler.

Load Imbalance

The task scheduler does load balancing. With thread-based programming, you are often stuck dealing with load balancing yourself, which can be tricky to get right. By breaking your program into many small tasks, the Threading Building Blocks scheduler assigns tasks to threads in a way that spreads out the work evenly.

Threading Building Blocks emphasizes scalable, data-parallel programming. Breaking up a program into separate functional blocks and assigning a separate thread to each block often doesn't scale well because the number of functional blocks is typically fixed. In contrast, the flexible data-parallel programming technique in Threading Building Blocks enables multiple threads to work on different parts of a collection. Data-parallel programming scales well to larger numbers of processors because it divides the collection (continually and recursively, if necessary) into smaller pieces. This scalability protects you from having to rewrite an application every time a new chip with more processor cores ships.

In addition to using the right number of threads, it is important to distribute work evenly across those threads. As long as you break your program into enough small tasks, the scheduler usually does a good job of assigning tasks to threads in order to balance the load on different processors.

Portability

Using the Threading Building Blocks interfaces makes your program portable. All standard-conforming C++ compilers should work with Threading Building Blocks. Intel released the first version of the library with Windows, Linux, and Mac OS X support on 32-bit x86 processors and 64-bit Itanium processors, and it worked with Intel, Microsoft, and GNU compilers. Intel has since added 64-bit support for Intel 64 and AMD64. More processor and operating-system support is becoming available. Porting to a new platform requires only a C++ compiler and a little additional work to implement key locks efficiently.

Initializing the Library Is Your Job

Each thread must initialize the Threading Building Blocks library using tbb::task_scheduler_init before using an algorithm template or the task scheduler. If you use the default task scheduler for the whole program and just define tasks using algorithm templates as shown in the earlier chapters of this book, it is enough to define tbb::task_scheduler_init once, in your main program. However, if you create your own tasks as shown in this chapter, each task has to initialize the scheduler as well.

Refer to the section "Initializing and Terminating the Library" in Chapter 3 for more information on the proper initialization and optional parameters to tbb::task_scheduler_init.

The section "Mixing with Other Threading Packages" in Chapter 10 explains how to construct task_scheduler_init objects if your program creates threads itself using another interface.

Example Program for Fibonacci Numbers

This section uses the computation of the Fibonacci numbers as an example to illustrate the direct use of the Intel Threading Building Blocks task scheduler. A Fibonacci number in the Fibonacci series F is defined as the sum of the previous two terms:

$$F_n = F_{n-1} + F_{n-2}$$

Therefore, the seventh Fibonacci number of the series beginning with $F_0 = 0$, $F_1 = 1$ is 8 ($F_6 = 8$). This example uses an inefficient method to compute Fibonacci numbers, but it demonstrates the basics of a task library using a simple recursive pattern.

To get scalable speedup out of task-based programming, you need to specify a lot of tasks. This is typically done in Threading Building Blocks with a recursive task pattern.

Example 9-1 shows a traditional, serial solution using recursion.

Example 9-1. Fibonacci serial version

```
long SerialFib( long n ) {
    if( n<2 )
        return n;
    else
        return SerialFib(n-1)+SerialFib(n-2);
}
```

The top-level code for the parallel task-based version is in Example 9-2.

Example 9-2. Fibonacci recursive parallel version

```
long ParallelFib( long n ) {
    long sum;
    FibTask& a = *new(task::allocate_root()) FibTask(n,&sum);
    task::spawn_root_and_wait(a);
    return sum;
}
```

This code uses a task of type FibTask to do the real work. It involves the following distinct steps:

1. Allocate space for the task. Tasks must be allocated by special methods so that the space can be efficiently recycled when the task completes. Allocation is done by a special *overloaded* new and task::allocate_root method. The _root suffix in the name denotes the fact that the task created has no parent. It is the root of a task tree.

2. Construct the task with the constructor FibTask(n,&sum), invoked by new. When the task is run in step 3, it computes the nth Fibonacci number and stores it into *sum.

3. Run the task to completion with task::spawn_root_and_wait.

The real work is done inside struct FibTask. Example 9-3 shows its definition.

Example 9-3. Fibonacci task

```
const int CutOff = 16;

class FibTask: public task {
public:
    const long n;
    long* const sum;
    FibTask( long n_, long* sum_ ) :
        n(n_), sum(sum_)
    {}
    task* execute() {          // Overrides virtual function task::execute
        if( n < CutOff ) {
            *sum = SerialFib(n);
        } else {
            long x, y;
            FibTask& a = *new( allocate_child() ) FibTask(n-1,&x);
            FibTask& b = *new( allocate_child() ) FibTask(n-2,&y);
            // Set ref_count to "two children plus one for the wait".
            set_ref_count(3);
            // Start b running.
            spawn( b );
            // Start a running and wait for all children (a and b).
            spawn_and_wait_for_all( a );
            // Do the sum
            *sum = x+y;
        }
        return NULL;
    }
};
```

This is a relatively large piece of code, compared to SerialFib, because it expresses parallelism without the help of any extensions to standard C++.

Like all tasks scheduled by Threading Building Blocks, FibTask is derived from the class task, which is defined by Threading Building Blocks. The fields n and sum hold the input value and the pointer to the output, respectively. These are copies of the arguments passed to the constructor for FibTask.

The execute method does the actual computation. Every task must provide a definition of execute that overrides the pure virtual method task::execute. The definition should do the work of the task and return either NULL or a pointer to the next task to run. In this simple example, it returns NULL.

The method FibTask::execute() does the following:

1. Checks whether n is so small that serial execution would be faster. Finding the right value of CutOff requires some experimentation. A value of at least 16 works well in practice for getting the greatest possible speedup out of this example. Resorting to a sequential algorithm when the problem size becomes small is characteristic of most divide-and-conquer patterns for parallelism. Finding the point at which to switch requires experimentation, so be sure to write your code in a way that allows you to experiment.

2. If the `else` branch is taken, the code creates and runs two child tasks that compute the (n-1)th and (n-2)th Fibonacci numbers. Here, the inherited method `allocate_child( )` is used to allocate space for the task. Remember that the top-level routine `ParallelFib` used `allocate_root( )` to allocate space for a task. The difference is that here the task is creating *child* tasks. This relationship is indicated by the choice of allocation method.

3. Calls `set_ref_count(3)`. The number 3 represents the two children and an additional implicit reference that is required by the method `spawn_and_wait_for_all`. Make sure to call `set_reference_count(3)` before spawning any children. Failure to do so results in undefined behavior. The debug version of the library usually detects and reports this type of error.

4. Spawns two child tasks. Spawning a task indicates to the scheduler that it can run the task whenever it chooses, possibly in parallel with executing other tasks. The first spawning, by the `spawn` method, returns immediately without waiting for the child task to start executing. The second spawning, by the method `spawn_and_wait_for_all`, causes the parent to wait until all currently allocated child tasks are finished.

5. After the two child tasks complete, the parent computes x+y and stores it in `*sum`.

At first glance, the parallelism might appear to be limited because the task creates only two child tasks. The trick here is *recursive parallelism*. The two child tasks each create two child tasks, and so on, until `n<Cutoff`. This chain reaction creates a lot of potential parallelism. The advantage of the task scheduler is that it turns this potential parallelism into real parallelism in a very efficient way, because it chooses tasks to run that keep physical threads busy with relatively little context switching.

Task Scheduling Overview

The library provides a task scheduler, which is the engine that drives the algorithm templates. You may also call it directly. This is worth considering if your application meets the criteria described earlier that make the default task scheduler inefficient.

Tasks are logical units of computation. The scheduler maps these onto physical threads. The mapping is non-preemptive. Each thread has an execute( ) method. Once a thread starts running execute( ), the task is bound to that thread until execute( ) returns. During that time, the thread services other tasks only when it waits on child tasks, at which time it may run the child tasks or—if there are no pending child tasks—service tasks created by other threads.

The task scheduler is intended for parallelizing computationally intensive work. Since task objects are not scheduled preemptively, they should not make calls that might block for long periods because, meanwhile, the blocked thread (and its associated processor) are precluded from servicing other tasks.

There is no guarantee that *potentially* parallel tasks *actually* execute in parallel, because the scheduler adjusts actual parallelism to fit available worker threads. For example, when given a single worker thread, the scheduler obviously cannot create parallelism. Furthermore, it is unsafe to use tasks in a producer/consumer relationship if the consumer needs to do some initialization or other work before the producer task completes, because there is no guarantee that the consumer will do this work (or even that it will run at all) while the producer is running. The pipeline algorithm in Threading Building Blocks, for instance, is designed not to require tasks to run in parallel.

Potential parallelism is typically generated by a split/join pattern. Two basic patterns of split/join are supported. The most efficient is *continuation passing*, in which the programmer constructs an explicit "continuation" task rather than leaving it to the default scheduler to determine the next task. The steps are shown in Figure 9-1, and the running tasks (that is, the tasks whose execute methods are active) at each step are shaded.

In step A, the parent is created. In step B, the parent task spawns off child tasks and specifies a continuation task to be executed when the children complete. The continuation inherits the parent's ancestor. The parent task then exits; in other words, it does not block on its children. In step C, the children run. In step D, after the children (or their continuations) finish, the continuation task starts running.

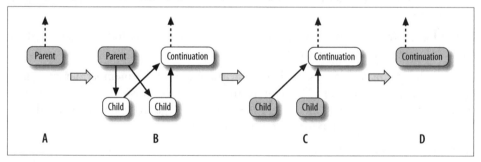

Figure 9-1. Continuation-passing style

Explicit continuation passing is efficient because it decouples the thread's stack from the tasks. However, it is more difficult to program. A second pattern is *blocking style*, which uses implicit continuations. It is sometimes less efficient in performance, but more convenient to program. In this pattern, the parent task blocks until its children complete, as shown in step C of Figure 9-2.

The convenience comes with a price. Because the parent blocks, its thread's stack cannot be popped yet. The thread must be careful about what work it takes on because continual stealing and blocking could cause the stack to grow without bound. To solve this problem, the scheduler constrains a blocked thread such that it never executes a task that is less deep than its deepest blocked task. This constraint may impact performance because it limits available parallelism and tends to cause threads to select smaller (deeper) subtrees than they would otherwise choose.

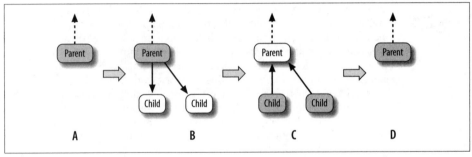

Figure 9-2. Blocking style

How Task Scheduling Works

The scheduler evaluates a *task graph*. The graph is a directed graph in which nodes are tasks, and each points to its parent, which is either NULL for the root task or another task that is waiting for it to complete. The task::parent( ) method gives you read-only access to the parent pointer.

Each task has a refcount that counts the number of tasks that have it as a parent. Each task also has a depth, which is usually one more than the depth of its parent. Figure 9-3 shows a task graph for the Fibonacci example shown earlier in Examples 9-2 and 9-3.

In the figure, the tasks with nonzero reference counts (A, B, and C) wait for their child tasks. The leaf tasks are running or are ready to run.

The scheduler runs tasks in a way that tends to minimize both memory demands and cross-thread communication. To achieve this, a balance must be reached between depth-first and breadth-first execution. Assuming that the tree is finite, depth-first is best for sequential execution for the following reasons:

Strike when the cache is hot

> The deepest tasks are the most recently created tasks and, therefore, the hottest in the cache. Also, if they can complete, task C can continue executing; although it's not the hottest in the cache, it's still warmer than the older tasks above it.

Minimize space

> Executing a shallow task in breadth-first fashion unfolds the tree under it and makes all those tasks take up space while they wait for threads. This creates a potentially exponential growth of nodes that coexist simultaneously. In contrast, depth-first execution creates the same number of nodes, but only a linear number have to exist at the same time because it stacks the other ready tasks (E, F, and G in the figure).

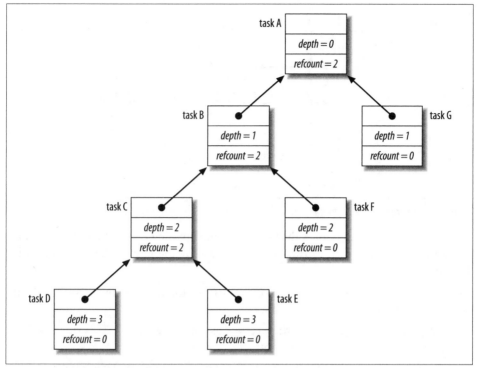

Figure 9-3. Fibonacci task graph

Though breadth-first execution has a severe problem with memory consumption, it does maximize parallelism if you have an infinite number of physical threads. Because physical threads are limited, it is better to use only enough breadth-first execution to keep the available processors busy. The scheduler implements breadth-first execution as follows:

- Each thread has its own ready pool, which is an array of lists of tasks.
- A task goes into each pool when it is deemed ready to run.
- Each thread steals tasks from other pools when necessary.

Figure 9-4 shows a snapshot of a pool that corresponds to the task graph in Figure 9-3.

The pool comprises an array of lists. The array is subscripted by the task's depth, and the lists are treated as stacks. Tasks are pushed onto the left side of a list and are popped from the left side. There are two intertwined actions on each ready pool: putting tasks into the pool, and getting tasks out of the pools to run them.

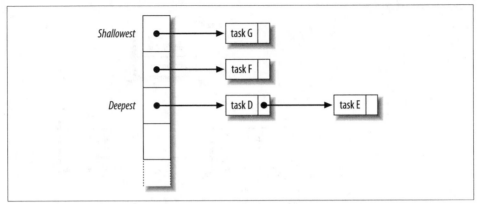

Figure 9-4. A thread's ready pool for the Fibonacci task graph in Figure 9-3

The rule for getting tasks out is that when a thread participates in task graph evaluation and needs a new task to run, it gets the task by the first of the following rules that applies:

- Use the task returned by the execute method for the previous task. This rule does not apply if execute returns NULL.
- Take the task at the front of the deepest list of its own pool. This rule does not apply if all lists in its pool are empty.
- Steal from the front of the shallowest list of another randomly chosen pool. If the chosen pool is empty, the thread tries this rule again until it succeeds.

Getting a task is always automatic; it just happens as part of task graph evaluation. Putting a task can be explicit or automatic.

When a task is put into a ready pool, it always goes into the pool of the putting thread. Stealing from another pool is allowed; donating to another pool is not.

There are three ways that a task can be put into a ready pool:

- The task is explicitly spawned—for example, by the spawn method.
- A task has been marked for reexecution by the task::recycle_to_reexecute method.
- The task's reference count becomes 0 after being implicitly decremented when a child task completes. This does not always happen when the last child task completes because sometimes a fictitious guard reference is added, in scenarios where automatic spawning of a task is not wanted.

To summarize, the task scheduler's fundamental strategy is *breadth-first theft and depth-first work*. The breadth-first theft rule raises parallelism sufficiently to keep threads busy. The depth-first work rule keeps each thread operating efficiently once it has sufficient work to do.

Recommended Task Recurrence Patterns

This section catalogues three recommended task recurrence patterns. In each pattern, the class T is assumed to be derived from the class task. Subtasks are labeled t_1, t_2, ... t_k. The subscripts indicate the order in which the subtasks execute if no parallelism is available. If parallelism is available, the subtask execution order is nondeterministic, except that t_1 is guaranteed to be executed by the spawning thread.

Blocking Style with Children

Example 9-4 shows the recommended style for a recursive task of type T where each level spawns *k* children.

Example 9-4. Blocking style with children

```
task* T::execute( ) {
    if( not recursing any further ) {
        ...
    } else {
        set_ref_count(k+1);
        task& t_k = new( allocate_child( ) ) T(...);  t_k.spawn( );
        task& t_k-1= new( allocate_child( ) ) T(...); t_k-1.spawn( );
        ...
        task& t_1 = new( allocate_child( ) ) T(...);  t_1.spawn_and_wait(t_1);
    }
    return NULL;
}
```

Child construction and spawning may be reordered if convenient, as long as a task is constructed before it is spawned.

The key points of the pattern are:

- The call to set_ref_count uses k+1 as its argument. The extra 1 is critical.
- Each task is allocated by allocate_child.

Continuation-Passing Style with Children

There are two recommended styles. They differ in terms of whether it is more convenient to recycle the parent as the continuation or as a child. The decision should be based on whether the continuation or the child acts more like the parent.

Recycling the parent as the continuation

This style is useful when the continuation needs to inherit much of the parent's state and the child does not need the state. The continuation must have the same type as the parent. Example 9-5 illustrates the model.

Example 9-5. Recycling parent as continuation

```
task* T::execute( ) {
    if( not recursing any further ) {
        ...
        return NULL;
    } else {
        set_ref_count(k);
        recycle_as_continuation();
        task& t_k   = new( allocate_child() ) T(...); t_k.spawn( );
        task& t_{k-1} = new( allocate_child() ) T(...); t_{k-1}.spawn( );
        ...
        task& t_1 = new( c.allocate_child() ) T(...);  t_1.spawn( );
        return &t_1;
    }
}
```

Here are the key points of the pattern:

- The call to set_ref_count uses k as its argument. There is no extra 1, as there is in blocking style.
- Each child task is allocated by allocate_child.
- The continuation is recycled from the parent, and hence gets the parent's state without doing copy operations.

Recycling the parent as a child

This style is useful when the child inherits much of its state from a parent and the continuation does not need the parent's state. The child must have the parent's type. In Example 9-6, C is the type of the continuation, and it must derive from the class task. If C does nothing but wait for all children to complete, C can be the class empty_task.

Example 9-6. Recycling parent as a child

```
task* T::execute( ) {
    if( not recursing any further ) {
        ...
        return NULL;
    } else {
        set_ref_count(k);
        // Construct continuation
        C& c = allocate_continuation( );
        // Recycle self as first child
        task& t_k   = new( c.allocate_child() ) T(...); t_k.spawn( );
        task& t_{k-1} = new( c.allocate_child() ) T(...); t_{k-1}.spawn( );
        ...
        task& t_2 = new( c.allocate_child() ) T(...);  t_2.spawn( );
        // task t_1 is our recycled self.
        recycle_as_child_of(c);
        ... update fields of *this to state subproblem to be solved by t_1
        return this;
    }
}
```

Here are the key points of the pattern:

- The call to set_ref_count uses k as its argument. There is no extra 1, as there is in blocking style.
- Each child task except for t_1 is allocated by c.allocate_child. It is critical to use c.allocate_child and not (*this).allocate_child; otherwise, the task graph will be wrong.
- Task t_1 is recycled from the parent, and hence gets the parent's state without performing copy operations. Do not forget to update the state to represent a child subproblem; otherwise, infinite recursion will occur.

Making Best Use of the Scheduler

This section explains useful programming techniques for scheduling tasks.

Recursive Chain Reaction

The scheduler works best with tree-structured task graphs, because that is where the strategy of breadth-first theft and depth-first work applies very well. Also, tree-structured task graphs allow fast creation of many tasks. For example, if a master task tries to create n children directly, it will take $O(n)$ steps. But with tree-structured forking, it takes only $O(\log n)$ steps because some of the tasks created can go on to create subtasks.

Often, domains are not obviously tree-structured, but you can easily map them to trees. For example, parallel_for works over an iteration space such as a sequence of integers. The template function parallel_for uses that definition to recursively map the iteration space onto a binary tree.

Continuation Passing

The spawn_and_wait_for_all method is a convenient way to wait for child tasks, but it incurs some inefficiency if a thread becomes idle. The idle thread attempts to keep busy by stealing tasks from other threads. The scheduler limits possible victim tasks to those deeper than the waiting task. This limit modifies the policy that the shallowest task should be chosen. The limit restrains memory demands in worst-case scenarios.

A way around the constraint is for the parent not to wait, but simply to spawn both children and return. The children are allocated not as children of the parent, but as children of the parent's *continuation task*, which is a task that runs when both children complete. Example 9-7 shows the *continuation-passing* variant of FibTask, with the addition of FibContinuation c.

Example 9-7. Continuation-passing Fibonacci

```
struct FibContinuation: public task {
    long* const sum;
    long x, y;
    FibContinuation( long* sum_ ) : sum(sum_) {}
    task* execute() {
        *sum = x+y;
        return NULL;
    }
};

struct FibTask: public task {
    const long n;
    long* const sum;
    FibTask( long n_, long* sum_ ) :
        n(n_), sum(sum_)
    {}
    task* execute() {
        if( n<CutOff ) {
            *sum = SerialFib(n);
            return NULL;
        } else {
            FibContinuation& c =
                *new( allocate_continuation() ) FibContinuation(sum);
            FibTask& a = *new( c.allocate_child() ) FibTask(n-2,&c.x);
            FibTask& b = *new( c.allocate_child() ) FibTask(n-1,&c.y);
            // Set ref_count to "two children".
            c.set_ref_count(2);
            c.spawn( b );
            c.spawn( a );
            return NULL;
        }
    }
};
```

The rest of this section explains the important differences between the original version and the continuation version here.

The big difference is that in the original version, x and y are local variables in the method execute. In the continuation-passing version, they cannot be local variables because the parent returns before its children complete. Instead, they are fields of the continuation task FibContinuation.

In addition, the allocation logic is changed. The continuation is allocated with allocate_continuation. It is similar to allocate_child, except that the depth of the continuation is the same as the parent, not one deeper, as it would be for a child. Also, it forwards the parent of this to c and sets the parent attribute of this to NULL. Figure 9-5 summarizes the effects.

One property of the transformation is that it does not change the reference count of the parent, and thus avoids interfering with reference-counting logic.

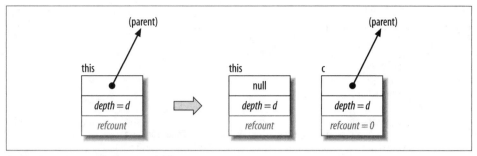

Figure 9-5. Action of allocate_child

The reference count is set to 2, the number of children. In the original version, it was set to 3 because spawn_and_wait_for_all required the augmented count. Furthermore, the code sets the reference count of the continuation instead of the parent because it is the execution of the continuation that waits for the children.

The pointer sum is passed to the continuation by the constructor because it is now FibContinuation that stores results into *sum. The children are still allocated with allocate_child, but notice that now they are allocated as children of the continuation c, not the parent. This is done so that c, and not this, becomes the *dependent* of the children; that is, c is automatically spawned when both children complete. If you accidentally used this.allocate_child( ), the parent task would run again after both children completed.

If you remember how the original top-level code, ParallelFib, was written, you might be worried now that continuation-passing style breaks the code—because now the root FibTask completes before the children are done and the top-level code uses spawn_root_and_wait to wait for the root FibTask. This is not a problem because spawn_root_and_wait is designed to work correctly with continuation-passing style. An invocation spawn_root_and_wait(x) does not actually wait for x to complete. Instead, it constructs a dummy dependent of x and waits for the dependent's reference count to be decremented. Because allocate_continuation forwards this dummy dependent to the continuation, the dummy dependent's reference count is not decremented until the continuation completes.

Scheduler bypass

Scheduler bypass is an optimization in which you directly specify the next task to run instead of letting the scheduler pick. Continuation-passing style often opens up an opportunity for scheduler bypass. For instance, in the continuation-passing example, it turns out that once FibTask::execute( ) returns, by the *getting* rules, task a is always the next task taken from the ready pool. Putting the task into the ready pool and then getting it back out incurs some overhead that can be avoided. To avoid the overhead, make sure that execute does not spawn the task but instead returns a pointer to it as the result. Example 9-8 shows the necessary changes.

Example 9-8. Scheduler bypass

```
struct FibTask: public task {
    ...
    task* execute( ) {
        if( n<CutOff ) {
            *sum = SerialFib(n);
            return NULL;
        } else {
            FibContinuation& c =
                *new( allocate_continuation( ) ) FibContinuation(sum);
            FibTask& a = *new( c.allocate_child( ) ) FibTask(n-2,&c.x);
            FibTask& b = *new( c.allocate_child( ) ) FibTask(n-1,&c.y);
            // Set ref_count to "two children".
            set_ref_count(2);
            c.spawn( b );
// was:       c.spawn( a );    // the return of &a will spawn a.
// was:       return NULL;
            return &a;
        }
    }
};
```

Recycling

Not only can you bypass the scheduler, you might be able to bypass task allocation and deallocation as well. This opportunity frequently arises for recursive tasks that do scheduler bypass because the child is initiated immediately upon return just as the parent completes. Example 9-9 shows the changes required to implement recycling in the scheduler bypass example.

Example 9-9. Scheduler bypass plus task alloc/dealloc bypass

```
struct FibTask: public task {
// was:      const long n;
    long n;
// was:      long* const sum;
    long* sum;
    ...
    task* execute( ) {
        if( n<CutOff ) {
            *sum = SerialFib(n);
            return NULL;
        } else {
            FibContinuation& c =
                *new( allocate_continuation( ) ) FibContinuation(sum);
            FibTask& a = *new( c.allocate_child( ) ) FibTask(n-2,&c.x);
            FibTask& b = *new( c.allocate_child( ) ) FibTask(n-1,&c.y);
            recycle_as_child_of(c);
            n -= 2;
            sum = &c.x;
            // Set ref_count to "two children".
            set_ref_count(2);
```

Example 9-9. Scheduler bypass plus task alloc/dealloc bypass (continued)

```
        c.spawn( b );
// was:  return &a;
        return this;
      }
   }
};
```

The child that was previously called a is now the recycled this. The call recycle_as_ child_of(c) has several effects:

- It marks this *not* to be automatically destroyed when execute returns.
- It sets the depth of this to be one more than the depth of c.
- It sets the dependent of this to be c. To prevent reference-counting problems, recycle_as_child_of has a prerequisite that this must have a NULL dependent. This is the case after allocate_continuation occurs.

When recycling, ensure that the original task's fields are not used after the task might start running. The example uses the scheduler bypass trick to ensure this. You can spawn the recycled task instead, as long as none of its fields is used after the spawning. This restriction applies even to const fields, because after the task is spawned, it might run and be destroyed before the parent progresses any further.

A similar method, task::recycle_as_continuation( ), recycles a task as a continuation instead of a child.

Empty tasks

You might need a task that does not do anything but wait for its children to complete. The header file *task.h* defines class empty_task for this purpose. Example 9-10 shows its definition.

Example 9-10. empty_task

```
// Task that does nothing. Useful for synchronization.
class empty_task: public task {
    /*override*/ task* execute( ) {
        return NULL;
    }
};
```

A good example of empty_task in action shown in Example 9-11. It invokes parallel_for in the method start_for::execute( ). The code there uses continuation-passing style. It creates two child tasks and uses an empty_task as the continuation when the child tasks complete. The top-level routine parallel_for waits on the root.

Example 9-11. empty_task usage from parallel_for

```
template<typename Range, typename Body>
task* start_for<Range,Body>::execute() {
  if( !my_range.is_divisible() ) {
   my_body( my_range );
   return NULL;
  } else {
   empty_task& c = *new(allocate_continuation()) empty_task;
   recycle_as_child_of(c);
   c.set_ref_count(2);
   start_for& b =
     *new(c.allocate_child()) start_for(Range(my_range,split()),my_body);
   c.spawn(b);
   return this;
  }
}
```

Lazy copying

It can be useful to copy a data structure only when another thread steals a task.
Example 9-12 uses the start_reduce::execute() method to implement parallel_
reduce. The code forks the loop body object you provide only when the thread runs a
stolen task. The forking permits the thief to run locally afterward until it is done and
joins its result to the original thread's result. Because the forks and joins incur some
overhead, they are worth doing only when stealing occurs.

Example 9-12. parallel_reduce start_reduce::execute() method

```
template<typename Range, typename Body>
  task* start_reduce<Range,Body>::execute() {
    Body* body = my_body;
    if( is_stolen_task() ) {
      finish_reduce<Body>* p = static_cast<finish_type*>(parent() );
      body = new(p->zombie_space.begin()) Body(*body,split());
      my_body = p->right_zombie = body;
    }
    task* next_task = NULL;
    if( !my_range.is_divisible() )
      (*my_body)( my_range );
    else {
      finish_reduce<Body>& c =
        *new(allocate_continuation()) finish_type(body);
      recycle_as_child_of(c);
      c.set_ref_count(2);
      start_reduce& b =
        *new(c.allocate_child()) start_reduce(Range(my_range,split()), body);
      c.spawn(b);
      next_task = this;
    }
    return next_task;
  }
}
```

The method task::is_stolen_task provides a way to detect stealing. It is called on a running task, typically by the task itself. Informally speaking, it returns true if the task is stolen. Formally, it returns true if the thread that owns the task is not the thread that owns the thread's dependent. For the usual fork-join task patterns, the informal and formal definitions have the same effect because usually when a task is created, it is created by the thread that owns its dependent. For example, the dependent is typically the parent or a continuation created by the parent. The exception to this rule can occur if the method allocate_additional_child_of(t) is used. A task can use this method to create a child of *another* task t, even if t already has running children.

Example 9-13 shows the method allocate_additional_child_of used by a running child task to create new siblings. In this case, task::is_stolen_task will return true unless the child is stolen by the thread that is running t. The name *task::might_be_running_on_different_thread_from_dependent()* would be more accurate but tedious.

Example 9-13. Creating new siblings with allocate_additional_child_of

```
block_type& t =
    *new(allocate_additional_child_of(my_barrier)) block_type(my_body);
```

Task Scheduler Interfaces

The scheduler employs task stealing. Each thread keeps a *ready pool* of tasks that are ready to run. The ready pool is structured as an array of lists of tasks, where the list for the *i*th element corresponds to tasks at level *i* in the tree. The lists are manipulated in last-in, first-out order. A task at level *i* spawns child tasks at level *i*+1. A thread pulls tasks from the deepest nonempty list in the array. If there are no nonempty lists, the thread randomly steals a task from the shallowest list of another thread. A thread also implicitly steals if it completes the last child, in which case it starts executing the task that was waiting on the children.

The task scheduler tends to strike a good balance between locality of reference, space efficiency, and parallelism. The scheduling technique is similar to that used by Cilk, a research project that implements efficient, unfair scheduling (*http://supertech.csail.mit.edu/cilk*).

---

task_scheduler_init Class

Class that represents thread's interest in task scheduling services.

```
#include "tbb/task_soinit;
```

Description

A task_scheduler_init is either *active* or *inactive*. Each thread that uses a task should have one active task_scheduler_init object that stays active over the duration that the thread uses task objects. A thread may have more than one active task_scheduler_init at any given moment.

The default constructor for a task_scheduler_init activates it, and the destructor deactivates it. To defer initialization, pass the value task_scheduler_init::deferred to the constructor. Such a task_scheduler_init may be initialized later by calling the initialize method. Destruction of an initialized task_scheduler_init implicitly deactivates it. To deactivate it earlier, call the terminate method.

An optional parameter to the constructor and initialize method allows you to specify the number of threads to be used for task execution. This parameter is useful for scaling studies during development, but should not be set for production use.

To minimize time overhead, it is best to have a thread create a single task_scheduler_init object whose activation spans all uses of the library's task scheduler. A task_scheduler_init is not assignable or copy-constructible.

 The template algorithms implicitly use the task class. Hence, creating a task_scheduler_init object is a prerequisite to using the template algorithms. The debug version of the library will report a failure to create the task_scheduler_init.

Example

```
#include "tbb/task_scheduler_init"

int main( ) {
    task_scheduler_init init;
     ... use task or template algorithms here...
    return 0;
}
Members
namespace tbb {

    class task_scheduler_init {
    public:
        static const int automatic = implementation-defined;
        static const int deferred = implementation-defined;
        task_scheduler_init( int number_of_threads=automatic );
        ~task_scheduler_init( );
        void initialize( int number_of_threads=automatic );
        void terminate( );
    };
} // namespace tbb
```

task_scheduler_init(int number_of_threads=automatic)

Requirements: number_of_threads object must be one of the values in Table 9-2.

Effects: if number_of_threads==task_scheduler_init::deferred, nothing happens, and the task_scheduler_init object remains inactive. Otherwise, the task_scheduler_init object is activated as follows. If the thread has no other active task_scheduler_init objects, the thread allocates internal thread-specific resources required for scheduling task objects. If there are no threads with active task_scheduler_init objects yet, internal worker threads are created as described in Table 9-2. These workers sleep until the task scheduler needs them.

Table 9-2. Value for number_of_threads

number_of_threads	Semantics
task_scheduler_init::automatic	Let library determine number_of_threads based on hardware configuration.
task_scheduler_init::deferred	Defer activation actions.
Positive integer	If no worker threads exist yet, create number_of_threads-1 worker threads. If worker threads exist, do not change the number of worker threads.

~task_scheduler_init( )

Effects: if the task_scheduler_init object is inactive, nothing happens. Otherwise, the task_scheduler_init object is deactivated as follows. If the thread has no other active task_scheduler_init objects, the thread deallocates the internal thread-specific resources required for scheduling task objects. If no existing thread has any active task_scheduler_init objects, the internal worker threads are terminated.

void initialize(int number_of_threads=automatic)

Requirements: the task_scheduler_init object must be inactive.

Effects: similar to the constructor.

void terminate( )

Requirements: the task_scheduler_init object must be active.

Effects: deactivates the task_scheduler_init object without destroying it. The description of the destructor specifies what deactivation entails.

task Class

Base class for tasks.

#include "tbb/task.h"

class task;

Description

This class is the base class for tasks. Programmers are expected to derive classes from it and override the virtual method task* task::execute( ).

Each instance of task has associated attributes, which are described in Table 9-3. Although they are not directly visible, they must be understood to fully grasp how task objects are used.

 Always allocate memory for task objects using the special overloaded new operators provided by the library. Otherwise, results are undefined. Destruction of a task is normally implicit.

Table 9-3. Task attributes

Attribute	Description
owner	The worker thread that is currently in charge of the task.
parent	Either NULL or the parent/continuation task that allocated this task.

Table 9-3. Task attributes (continued)

Attribute	Description
depth	The depth of the task in the task tree.
refcount	The number of tasks that have this as their parent. Increments and decrements of refcount must always be atomic.

 The copy constructor and assignment operators for task are not accessible. This prevents the accidental copying of a task, which would be ill-defined and would corrupt internal data structures.

Notation

Some member descriptions illustrate the effects of running the methods by diagrams such as Figure 9-6.

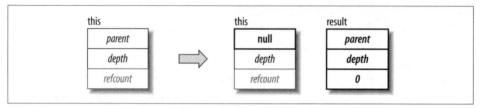

Figure 9-6. Example effect diagram

Conventions in the diagram, such as Figure 9-6, are as follows:

- Each task's state is shown as a box divided into parent, depth, and refcount subboxes.
- The arrow denotes the transition from the old state to the new state. Often, two objects take on a new state: the object that invokes the method (this), and the object returned by the method (the result).
- Gray denotes a state that is ignored. Sometimes an ignored state is simply left blank.
- Black denotes a state that is read.
- Bold black with a thick box outline denotes a state that is written.

Members

In the following description, the types proxy1...proxy4 are internal types. Methods returning such types should be used only in conjunction with the special overloaded new operators.

```
namespace tbb {
    class task {
    protected:
        task();

    public:
        virtual ~task() {}
```

```
virtual task* execute( ) = 0;

// task allocation and destruction
static proxy1 allocate_root( );
proxy2 allocate_continuation( );
proxy3 allocate_child( );
proxy4 allocate_additional_child_of( task& t );

// Explicit task destruction
void destroy( task& victim );

// Recycling
void recycle_as_continuation( );
void recycle_as_child_of( task& parent );
void recycle_to_reexecute( );

// task depth
typedef implementation-defined-signed-integral-type depth_type;
depth_type depth( ) const;
void set_depth( depth_type new_depth );
void add_to_depth( int delta );

// Synchronization
void set_ref_count( int count );
void wait_for_all( );
void spawn( task& child );
void spawn( task_list& list );
void spawn_and_wait_for_all( task& child );
void spawn_and_wait_for_all( task_list& list );
static void spawn_root_and_wait( task& root );
static void spawn_root_and_wait( task_list& root );

// task context
static task& self( );
task* parent( ) const;
bool is_stolen_task( ) const;

// task debugging
enum state_type {
    executing,
    reexecute,
    ready,
    allocated,
    freed
};
int ref_count( ) const;
state_type state( ) const;
    };
} // namespace tbb

void *operator new( size_t bytes, const proxy1& p );
void operator delete( void* task, const proxy1& p );
void *operator new( size_t bytes, const proxy2& p );
void operator delete( void* task, const proxy2& p );
```

```
void *operator new( size_t bytes, const proxy3& p );
void operator delete( void* task, const proxy3& p );
void *operator new( size_t bytes, proxy4& p );
void operator delete( void* task, proxy4& p );
```

Task derivation

task is an abstract base class. You *must* override the task::execute method. It should perform the necessary actions for running the task and then return the next task to execute, or return NULL if the scheduler should choose the next task to execute. Typically, if non-NULL, the returned task is one of the children of this. Unless one of the recycle/reschedule methods is called while the execute method is running, the this object will be implicitly destroyed after execute returns.

The derived class should override the virtual destructor if necessary to release resources allocated by the constructor.

Processing of execute( )

When the scheduler decides that a thread should begin executing a task, it performs the following steps:

1. It invokes execute( ) and waits for it to return.
2. If the task has not been marked for recycling by one of the recycle_* methods, it checks the task's parent. If the parent is non-NULL, it atomically decrements parent-> refcount, and if it becomes zero, it puts the parent into the ready pool.
3. It calls the task's destructor.
4. It frees the memory used by the task.
5. If the code has reached this point, the task has been marked for recycling. If it was marked by recycle_to_reexecute, the scheduler puts the task back into the ready pool. Otherwise, the task was marked by recycle_as_child or recycle_as_continuation. (See the section "Recycling tasks," later in this chapter.)

Task allocation

Always allocate memory for task objects using one of the special overloaded new operators. The allocation methods do not construct the task. Instead, they return a proxy object that can be used as an argument to an overloaded version of new provided by the library.

In general, the allocation methods must be called before any of the tasks allocated are spawned. The exception to this rule is allocate_additional_child_of(t), which can be called even if task t is already running. The proxy types are defined by the implementation. Because these methods are used idiomatically, the headings in the subsection show the idiom, not the declaration. The argument this is typically implicit, but it is shown explicitly in the headings to distinguish instance methods from static methods.

new(task::allocate_root( )) T

> Effects: allocates a task of type T with a depth that is one greater than the depth of the innermost task currently being executed by the current native thread. Figure 9-7 summarizes the state transition.
>
> Use the spawn_root_and_wait method to execute the task.

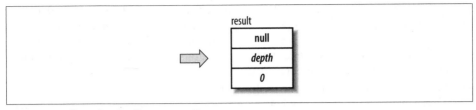

Figure 9-7. Effect of task::allocate_root()

```
new( this. allocate_continuation( ) ) T
```
Effects: allocates and constructs a task of type T at the same depth as this, and trans-
fers the parent from this to the new task. No reference counts change. Figure 9-8
summarizes the state transition.

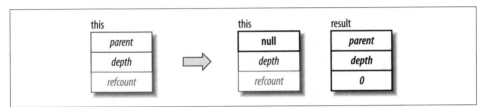

Figure 9-8. Effect of task::allocate_continuation()

```
new( this. allocate_child( ) ) T
```
Effects: allocates a task with a depth that is one greater than this, with this as its
parent. Figure 9-9 summarizes the state transition.

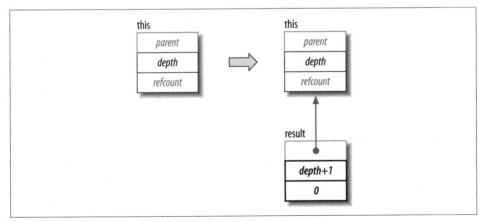

Figure 9-9. Effect of task::allocate_child()

If you are using explicit continuation passing, call the allocation method from the
continuation, not the parent, so that the parent member is set correctly. The task this
must be owned by the current thread.

If the number of tasks is not a small fixed number, consider building a task_list of the
children first and spawning them with a single call to task::spawn. If a task must

spawn some children before all are constructed, it should use task::allocate_
additional_child_of(*this) instead because that method atomically increments
refcount so that the additional child is properly counted. However, if using this proce-
dure, the task must protect against premature zeroing of refcount by using a blocking-
style task pattern (as was shown in Figure 9-2).

new(this.task::allocate_additional_child_of(parent))

Effects: allocates a task as a child of another task, parent. The result becomes a child of
parent, not this. The parent may be owned by another thread and may already be
running or have other children running. The task object this must be owned by the
current thread, and the result has the same owner as the current thread, not the
parent. Figure 9-10 summarizes the state transition.

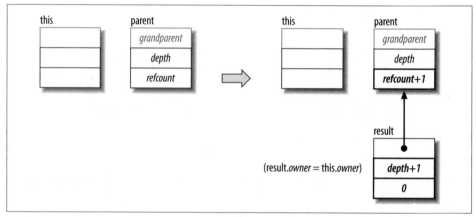

Figure 9-10. Effect of task::allocate_additional_child_of(parent)

Because parent may already have running children, the increment of parent.refcount is
thread-safe (unlike the other allocation methods, where the increment is not thread-safe).
When adding a child to a parent with other children running, it is up to the programmer to
ensure that the parent's refcount does not prematurely reach 0 and trigger execution of the
parent before the child is added.

Explicit task destruction

Usually, a task is automatically destroyed by the scheduler after its execute method returns.
But sometimes task objects are used idiomatically (e.g., for reference counting) without
ever running execute. Such tasks should be disposed of with the destroy method.

void destroy(task& victim)

Requirements: the reference count of victim should be 0. This requirement is checked
in the debug version of the library. The calling thread must own this.

Effects: calls the victim object's destructor and deallocates its memory. If this has a
non-NULL parent, the method atomically decrements parent->refcount. The parent is
not put into the ready pool if parent->refcount becomes 0. Figure 9-11 summarizes the
state transition.

The implicit argument this is used internally, but it is not visibly affected. A task is allowed to destroy itself, so this->destroy(*this) is permitted unless the task has been spawned but has not yet completed its execute method.

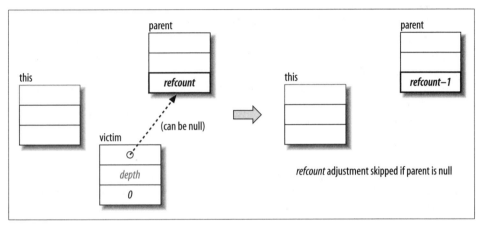

Figure 9-11. Effect of destroy(victim)

Recycling tasks

It is often more efficient to recycle a task object than it is to reallocate one from scratch. Often, the parent can be reused as the continuation of one of its children.

void recycle_as_continuation( )

>   Requirements: must be called while execute is running.

>   The refcount for the recycled task should be set to the number of current children of the continuation task.

>   The caller must guarantee that the task's refcount does not become 0 until after execute returns. If this is not possible, use the method recycle_as_safe_continuation( ) instead, and set refcount to one greater than the number of current children of the continuation task.

>   Effects: causes this not to be destroyed when its execute method returns.

void recycle_as_safe_continuation( )

>   Requirements: must be called while execute is running.

>   The refcount for the recycled task should be set to one greater than the number of children of the continuation task. The additional one represents the task to be recycled.

>   Effects: causes this not to be destroyed when its execute method returns.

>   This method avoids race conditions that can arise from using the method recycle_as_continuation. The race occurs when all of the following take place:

>   - The task's execute method recycles this as a continuation.
>   - The continuation creates children.
>   - All the children finish before the original task's execute method completes so that the continuation executes before the scheduler is done running this. The outcome is a corrupted scheduler.

The recycle_as_safe_continuation method avoids this race condition because the additional one in the refcount prevents the continuation from executing until the task completes.

void recycle_as_child_of(task& parent)

Requirements: must be called while execute is running.

Effects: causes this to become a child of parent and not be destroyed when execute returns.

void recycle _to_reexecute( )

Requirements: must be called while execute is running. execute must return a pointer to another task.

Effects: causes this to be automatically spawned after execute returns.

Task depth

For general fork-join parallelism, there is no need to explicitly set the depth of a task. However, in specialized task patterns that do not follow the fork-join pattern, it may be useful to explicitly set or adjust the depth of a task.

depth_type

The type task::depth_type is an implementation-defined, signed integral type.

depth_type depth( ) const

Returns: current depth attribute for the task.

void set_depth(depth_type new_depth)

Requirements: the value new_depth must be non-negative.

Effects: sets the depth attribute of the task to new_depth. Figure 9-12 shows the effects.

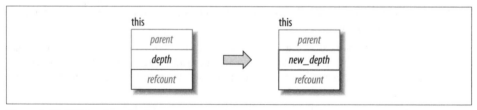

Figure 9-12. Effect of set_depth

void add_to_depth(int delta)

Requirements: the task must not be in the ready pool. The sum depth+delta must be non-negative.

Effects: sets the depth attribute of the task to depth+delta. Figure 9-13 illustrates the effect. The update is not atomic.

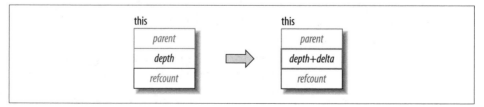

Figure 9-13. Effect of add_to-depth(delta)

Synchronization

Spawning a task either causes the calling thread to invoke task.execute( ), or causes task to be put into the ready pool. Any thread participating in task scheduling may then acquire the task and invoke task.execute( ). The calls that spawn tasks come in two forms:

- Calls that spawn a single task.
- Calls that spawn multiple task objects specified by a task_list and then clear task_list.

The calls distinguish between spawning root tasks and child tasks. A root task is one that is created using the allocate_root method.

 A task should not spawn any child until it has called set_ref_count to indicate both the number of children and whether it intends to use one of the wait_for_all methods.

void set_ref_count(int count)

> Requirements: count must be greater than 0. If the intent is to subsequently spawn *n* children and wait, count should be *n*+1. Otherwise, count should be *n*.

> Effects: sets the refcount attribute to count.

void wait_for_all( )

> Requirements: refcount=*n*+1, where *n* is the number of children still running.

> Effects: executes tasks in the ready pool until refcount is 1. Afterward, sets refcount to 0. Figure 9-14 summarizes the state transitions.

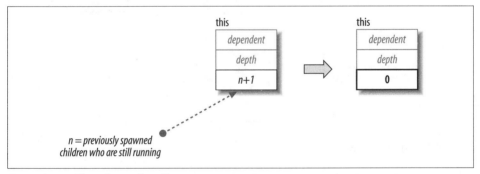

Figure 9-14. Effect of wait_for_all

void spawn(task& child)

> Requirements: child.refcount must be greater than 0. The calling thread must own this and child.

> Effects: puts the task into the ready pool and immediately returns. The this task that does the spawning must be owned by the caller thread. A task may spawn itself if it is owned by the caller thread. If no convenient task owned by the current thread is handy, use task::self( ).spawn(task) to spawn the child.

The parent must call set_ref_count before spawning any child tasks because once the child tasks are going, their completion will cause refcount to be decremented asynchronously. The debug version of the library detects when a required call to set_ref_count is not made, or is made too late.

void spawn (task_list& list)

Requirements: for each task in list, refcount must be greater than 0. The calling thread must own the task invoking the method and each task in list. Each task in list must have the same value for its depth attribute.

Effects: equivalent to executing spawn on each task in list and clearing list, but more efficient. If list is empty, there is no effect.

void spawn_and_wait_for_all(task& child)

Requirements: any other children of this must already be spawned. The task child must have a non-NULL parent attribute. There must be a chain of parent links from the child to the calling task. Typically, this chain contains a single link. That is, child is typically an immediate child of this.

Effects: similar to {spawn(task); wait_for_all();}, but often more efficient. Furthermore, it guarantees that task is executed by the current thread. This constraint can sometimes simplify synchronization. Figure 9-15 illustrates the state transitions.

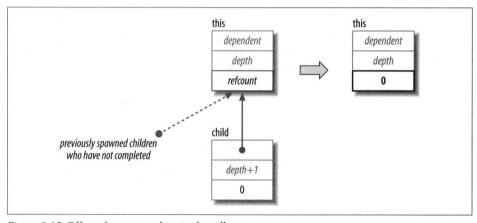

Figure 9-15. Effect of spawn_and_wait_for_all

void spawn_and_wait_for_all(task_list& list)

Effects: similar to {spawn(list); wait_for_all();}, but often more efficient.

static void spawn_root_and_wait(task& root)

Requirements: the memory for task root must have been allocated by task::allocate_root(). The calling thread must own root.

Effects: sets the parent attribute of root to an undefined value and executes root. Destroys root afterward unless it was recycled.

static void spawn_root_and_wait(task_list& root_list)

Requirements: each task object in root_list must meet the requirements for the parameter root of spawn_root_and_wait().

Effects: for each task object *t* in root_list, performs spawn_root_and_wait(*t*), possibly in parallel.

Task context

These methods expose relationships among task objects, and between task objects and the underlying physical threads:

`static task& self( )`
> Returns: reference to the innermost task that the calling thread is executing.

`task* parent( ) const`
> Returns: value of the parent attribute. The result is an undefined value if the task was allocated by `allocate_root` and is currently running under control of `spawn_root_and_wait`.

`bool is_stolen_task( ) const`
> Requirements: the attribute parent must be non-NULL and `this.execute( )` must be running. The calling task must not have been allocated with `allocate_root`.
>
> Returns: `true` if the attribute owner of this is unequal to the owner of parent.

Task debugging

Methods in this subsection are useful for debugging. They may change in future implementations.

`state_type state( ) const`
> Returns: current state of the task. Table 9-4 describes valid states. Any other value is the result of memory corruption, such as caused by using a task whose memory has been deallocated. Figure 9-16 summarizes possible state transitions for a task.

> This method is intended for debugging only. Its behavior or performance may change in future implementations. The definition of `task::state_type` may also change in future implementations. The information in this section is provided because it can be useful for diagnosing problems during debugging.

Table 9-4. Values returned by task::state()

Value	Description
allocated	The task is freshly allocated or recycled.
ready	The task is in the ready pool, or is in the process of being transferred to or from the pool.
executing	The task is running, and it will be destroyed after its `execute` method returns.
freed	The task is on the internal free list, or is in the process of being transferred to or from the list.
reexecute	The task is running, and will be respawned after its `execute` method returns.

`int ref_count( ) const`
> Returns: the value of the attribute refcount.

> This method is intended for debugging only. Its behavior or performance may change in future implementations.

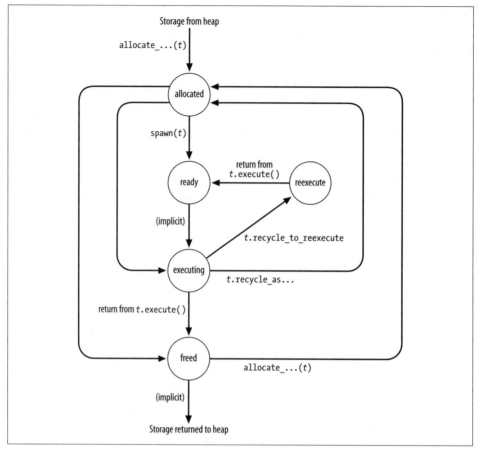

Figure 9-16. Typical task::state() transitions

empty_task Class

Subclass of task that represents doing nothing.

```
#include "tbb/task.h"
```

```
class empty_task;
```

Description

An empty_task is a task that does nothing. It is useful as a continuation of a parent task when the continuation should do nothing except wait for its children to complete.

Members

```
namespace tbb {
    class empty_task: public task {
        /*override*/ task* execute( ) {return NULL;}
    };
}
```

---

task_list Class

```
#include "tbb/task.h"
```

```
class task_list;
```

Description

A task_list is a list of references to task objects. The purpose of task_list is to allow a task to create a list of child tasks and spawn them all at once via the method task:: spawn(task_list&). A task can belong to, at most, one task_list at a time, and can be on that task_list once at most. A task that has been spawned but has not started running must not belong to a task_list. A task_list cannot be copy-constructed or assigned.

Members

```
namespace tbb {
    class task_list {
     public:
        task_list( );
        ~task_list( );
        bool empty( ) const;
        void push_back( task& task );
        task& pop_front( );
        void clear( );
    };
}
```

task_list( )
> Effects: constructs an empty list.

~task_list( )
> Effects: destroys the list. Does not destroy the task objects.

bool empty( ) const
> Returns: true if the list is empty; false otherwise.

push_back(task& task)
> Effects: inserts a reference to task at the back of the list.

task& task pop_front( )
> Effects: removes a task reference from the front of the list.
>
> Returns: the reference that was removed.

void clear( )
> Effects: removes all task references from the list. Does not destroy the task objects.

Task Scheduler Summary

The task scheduler works most efficiently for fork-join parallelism with lots of forks so that the task stealing can cause sufficient breadth-first behavior to occupy threads, which then conduct themselves in a depth-first manner until they need to steal more work.

The task scheduler is not the simplest-possible scheduler because it is designed for speed. If you need to use it directly, it may be best to hide it behind a higher-level interface, such as the templates `parallel_for`, `parallel_reduce`, and so on. Some of the details to remember are:

- Always use `new(allocation_method) T` to allocate a task, where `allocation_method` is one of the allocation methods of the class `task`. Do not create local or file-scope instances of a task.

- Allocate all siblings before any of them start to run, unless you are using `allocate_additional_child_of`.

- Exploit continuation passing, scheduler bypass, and task recycling to squeeze out maximum performance.

- If a task completes and was not marked for reexecution, it is automatically destroyed. Also, its dependent's reference count is decremented, and if it hits 0, the dependent is automatically spawned.

CHAPTER 10

Keys to Success

This chapter offers some advice and covers a number of issues that go beyond programming techniques for Intel Threading Building Blocks. These are important things you should know about: debugging, efficiency of the implementation, and compatibility with other thread packages.

Key Steps to Success

Our experience using Threading Building Blocks has helped us create a simple five-step program to success that has been working well for us at Intel:

1. Think Parallel. Understand where parallelism is and how you want to express it in terms of tasks.

2. Design using *relaxed sequential execution* (see the next section). Do not introduce anything in your code that will not allow single-thread execution.

3. When possible, use:

    a. The algorithm templates (Chapters 3 and 4) instead of raw tasks

    b. The algorithm templates instead of locking

    c. A scalable memory allocator (not malloc or the default new functions)

4. Debug:

    a. Debug the single-thread version first (enabled by step 1). Do this by giving tbb::task_scheduler_init a parameter value of 1.

    b. After that, try two threads, then four threads, and so on. It doesn't hurt to test with many more threads in case there are races lurking that might be hidden by unfair scheduling on a few processors.

    c. Use the Intel Thread Checker to check for race conditions, even if the program is working.

5. Look for tuning opportunities using the Intel Thread Profiler, which can give you insight into stalls induced by synchronization.

Relaxed Sequential Execution

Most parallel programs can run sequentially but will benefit from parallelism when it is present. However, it is very possible to design programs that *require* parallelism for correct behavior.

Consider a variable swap: A=B and B=A. If we start with A=14 and B=30, do we end with A=30 and B=14 or with A=30 and B=30? If the two assignments can be forced to run in parallel, we get the swap to occur. If that is what we expect, that code *must* be run in parallel.

This trivial example gives you a hint of what it means to require parallelism and strong synchronization. But such tight synchronization is not the only way to force parallelism. Nontrivial examples tend to be algorithms such as producer-consumer programs that *must* have two or more threads. For instance, consider a bounded container with a capacity for only two items and a program that has one thread doing PUT PUT PUT and another thread doing GET GET GET, each doing their actions only in triples. Such a program requires interleaving (concurrency).

A program that requires concurrency is more difficult to debug. That is why Threading Building Blocks (and many other concurrent systems, such as OpenMP) assume that a program has a valid sequential execution.

Threading Building Blocks implements a *relaxed sequential execution* model. The word *relaxed* refers to the notion that serial programs are actually overly constrained by implicit serial dependencies (such as the program counter) and that the concurrent library introduces as much parallelism as possible *without* removing the ability to run sequentially.

 You can think of this model as being as *relaxed* as possible and still being able to run correctly in a single thread. That is the goal.

Being able to run a program sequentially gives you a tremendous advantage when debugging your program. It lets you debug common programming errors before dealing with any concurrency issues that need to be debugged. Our advice is simple: start with debugging in a sequential mode, and then run the program in parallel to debug concurrency issues. Programs designed to require concurrency do not give you this option. Furthermore, programs designed to require concurrency will have performance pitfalls when the number of required threads exceeds the number of hardware threads because time-slicing artifacts can hit hard.

Design your programs *not* to require concurrency. You will be happier. Threading Building Blocks is designed to encourage you to use *relaxed sequential execution*.

Safe Concurrency for Methods and Libraries

It is recommended that you check the documentation for all the libraries you link with and use only thread-safe libraries in your Threading Building Blocks application. If you use libraries that are not thread-safe, you need to be very sure that they are not used improperly (without proper mutual exclusion) by multiple threads concurrently.

In particular, you should make sure you use the thread-safe runtime libraries in Windows (luckily, failure to do so will cause a compile-time error to help you remember this). Therefore, use the /MDd or /MD compiler option with the Intel or Microsoft compilers, for debug or release builds, respectively.

 Windows runtime libraries come in thread-safe and thread-unsafe forms. Using thread-unsafe versions with Intel Threading Building Blocks could cause undefined results.

In general, you should write your code so it does not need locks. Threading Building Blocks offers algorithms that promote implicit synchronization as an alternative to explicit synchronization with locks. But because that is not always possible, you need some guidance on locks.

The thread-safety rules for non-thread-safe libraries reduce to the following general principle: *do not invoke methods or functions concurrently on the same object*. Two tasks, or threads, can invoke a method or function concurrently on *different* objects, but not on the *same* object. A short way to say this is: you need to provide your own locking, and the kind of locking needed is the *intuitively obvious* locking.

Chapter 2 introduced mutual exclusion and locks, explained deadlock and race conditions, and pointed out what to look for in order to have thread-safe programs.

Chapter 7 discussed when your intuition might fail you when distinguishing reads from writes (i.e., when fancy data structures share and modify hidden state, or when state could be shared).

Descriptions of the classes in this book note any departures from the need for synchronization. For example, the concurrent containers are more liberal. By their nature, they permit concurrent operations on the same container object.

 Except where allowed, departure from these thread-safety rules will result in nondeterministic programs. A program may work today and then fail tomorrow. Care should be taken.

A later section of this chapter, "Mixing with Other Threading Packages," covers the use of Threading Building Blocks with other packages such as OpenMP.

Debug Versus Release

A few features should be used only when debugging. They won't cause production versions to fail, but they'll severely diminish the value of using Threading Building Blocks. Here is a list of things that should not be used in production code:

- Do not set the number of threads with task_scheduler_init. Let the setting be automatic (default) so that the program will run on a wide variety of hardware and make the best use of the processors.
- Leave TBB_DO_ASSERT undefined or set to zero.
- Leave TBB_DO_THREADING_TOOLS undefined or set to zero.

For Efficiency's Sake

There is no requirement to link in the scalable allocator just because you used a container, as it will default to dynamically loading the library or to using malloc. Performance will likely be better if you make sure the scalable allocator (Chapter 6) is indeed dynamically found and loaded.

Avoid using mutual exclusion if you can. Try to use implicit synchronization inherent in the algorithms covered in Chapters 3 and 4. If you cannot rewrite an algorithm to avoid sharing critical sections, avoid locks and protect shared memory usage using atomic operations if you can. Refer to Chapter 7 for more information.

Use the debug versions and assert macros only for debugging, as they introduce nontrivial overhead.

Enabling Debugging Features

The Threading Building Blocks headers define two macros that control certain debugging features. In general, it is useful to compile with these features turned on for development code, but to turn them off for production code.

The TBB_DO_ASSERT Macro

The macro TBB_DO_ASSERT controls whether error checking is enabled in the header files. Define TBB_DO_ASSERT as 1 to enable error checking.

If an error is detected, the library prints an error message on stderr and calls the standard C routine abort. To stop a program when internal error checking detects a failure, place a breakpoint on tbb::assertion_failure.

 On Windows systems, debug builds implicitly set TBB_DO_ASSERT to 1.

Do Not Ship Your Program Built with TBB_DO_ASSERT

TBB_DO_ASSERT not only adds assertion checking, it also turns off some inlining and enables extra hidden fields in some data structures. Therefore, it slows down performance. Furthermore, code compiled with TBB_DO_ASSERT is typically linked against the debug version of the library, which has some *significantly slow assertion checks*.

TBB_DO_ASSERT writes out failures to stderr; there is no way to request it to throw exceptions. The errors it detects are so egregious that they should be eliminated during debugging and are not the sort we expect anyone to plan to handle in production code.

On Windows, the debug version is linked against Microsoft's debug library, another reason it is unsuitable for production use. It is possible to use TBB_DO_ASSERT=1 and link against the release version of the Threading Building Blocks library, which gets you a few assertion checks. Still, we recommend setting TBB_DO_ASSERT=1 for development and debugging but having TBB_DO_ASSERT=0 for production code.

The TBB_DO_THREADING_TOOLS Macro

The macro TBB_DO_THREADING_TOOLS controls support for the following Intel threading analysis and debugging tools:

- Intel Thread Profiler
- Intel Thread Checker

More information is available at *http://intel.com/software/products*.

Define TBB_DO_THREADING_TOOLS as 1 to enable full support for these tools. The debug version of the library always has full support enabled.

Leave TBB_DO_THREADING_TOOLS undefined or 0 to enable top performance, at the expense of turning off some support for tools. In the current implementation, the only features affected are spin_mutex and spin_rw_mutex.

The Intel Thread Checker is a tool that helps you detect the potential for deadlock or race conditions in a program by observing it while it is running. The checker has special support for Threading Building Blocks, and by defining TBB_DO_THREADING_TOOLS for full support, you will get better diagnostics.

The checker works by recording when each thread *sends* or *receives* a synchronization message. For instance, when releasing a lock, a thread is effectively *sending* the message, "I'm done with the critical section," whereas acquiring a lock *receives* that message.

The checker recognizes standard Windows API calls, but it can have difficulty with Threading Building Blocks without a little help; hence, TBB_DO_THREADING_TOOLS. Some of the Threading Building Blocks calls may be inlined, which would generally make them escape detection without this help.

The checker lets you decorate calls with special *do-nothing subroutines* (used to flag the calls to the checker) that identify *send* and *receive* points. Unfortunately, a do-nothing subroutine has overhead that might be noticeable for very lightweight locks. There's also a spot in concurrent_hash_map that uses TBB_DO_THREADING_TOOLS to call an alternative out-of-line code sequence that hides a harmless race condition in the fast code sequence so that it is not reported.

Debug Versus Release Libraries

Threading Building Blocks includes dynamic shared libraries that come in debug and release versions, as described in Table 10-1.

Table 10-1. Dynamic shared libraries

Library	Description	When to use
tbb_debug tbbmalloc_debug	These versions have extensive internal checking for incorrect use of the library.	Use with code that is compiled with the TBB_DO_ASSERT macro set to 1.
tbb tbbmalloc	These versions deliver top performance.	Use with code compiled with TBB_DO_ASSERT undefined or set to 0.

All versions of the libraries support the Intel Thread Checker and Intel Thread Profiler. The debug versions always have full support enabled. The release version requires compiling code with the macro TBB_DO_THREADING_TOOLS set to 1 for full support.

The instrumentation support for the Intel Thread Checker becomes live after the first initialization of a task. If the library components are used before this initialization occurs, the Intel Thread Checker may falsely report race conditions that cannot actually occur.

Mixing with Other Threading Packages

Intel Threading Building Blocks can be mixed with other threading packages. No special effort is required to use the containers, synchronization primitives, or atomic operations with other threading packages. However, using the parallel algorithms or task scheduler requires extra effort because each thread that uses one of those features must construct its own task_scheduler_init object that is live while the feature is in use.

Mixing OpenMP (which was introduced in Chapter 1) with Threading Building Blocks is supported. Performance may be inferior to a pure OpenMP or pure Threading Building Blocks solution if the two forms of parallelism are nested.

An OpenMP parallel region that plans to use the task scheduler should create a task_scheduler_init inside the parallel region, because the parallel region may create new threads unknown to Threading Building Blocks. Each of these new OpenMP threads, like native threads, must create a task_scheduler_init object before using Threading Building Blocks algorithms.

Example 10-1 parallelizes an outer loop with OpenMP and an inner loop with Intel Threading Building Blocks.

Example 10-1. OpenMP and parallel_for used together

```
int M, N;

struct InnerBody {
    ...
};

void TBB_NestedInOpenMP( ) {
#pragma omp parallel
    {
        task_scheduler_init init;
#pragma omp for
        for( int i=0; i<M; ++j ) {
            parallel_for( blocked_range<int>(0,N,10), InnerBody(i) );
        }
    }
}
```

The details of InnerBody are omitted for brevity. What is important is the placement of the task_scheduler_init declaration. The #pragma omp parallel causes OpenMP to create a team of threads, and each thread executes the block statement associated with the pragma. Each thread must construct its own task_scheduler_init inside the block. The #pragma omp for statement indicates that the compiler should use the previously created thread team to execute the loop in parallel. Because this pragma does not create threads, it has no corresponding task_scheduler_init declaration.

Example 10-2 is the same as Example 10-1, but written using POSIX threads (pthreads). The initial function run by the pthread_create call that spawns each thread, OuterLoopIteration, simply defines a task_scheduler_init object.

Example 10-2. pthreads and parallel_for used together

```
int M, N;

struct InnerBody {
    ...
};

void* OuterLoopIteration( void* args ) {
    task_scheduler_init init;
    int i = (int)args;
    parallel_for( blocked_range<int>(0,N,10), InnerBody(i) );
}

void TBB_NestedInPThreads( ) {
    std::vector<pthread_t> id( M );
    // Create thread for each outer loop iteration
```

Example 10-2. pthreads and parallel_for used together (continued)

```
    for( int i=0; i<M; ++i )
        pthread_create( &id[i], NULL, OuterLoopIteration, NULL );
    // Wait for outer loop threads to finish
    for( int i=0; i<M; ++i )
        pthread_join( &id[i], NULL );
}
```

Using threading support from Intel for OpenMP and Intel Threading Building Blocks together will ensure a level of compatibility and cooperation in the threading packages that is not present with other combinations. There is some danger of oversubscription or lack of coordination between arbitrary threading packages. But in practice, there is generally no issue with correctness, although performance may not be optimal.

Naming Conventions

This section lists a few conventions and restrictions in the naming of variables and functions.

The tbb Namespace

The library puts all public classes and functions into the namespace tbb.

The tbb::internal Namespace

The library uses the namespace tbb::internal for internal identifiers. Client code should never directly reference the namespace tbb::internal or the identifiers inside it. Indirect reference via a public typedef provided by the header files is permitted.

An example of the distinction between direct and indirect use is type concurrent_vector<T>::iterator. This type is a typedef for an internal class internal::vector_iterator<Container,Value>. Source code should use the iterator typedef.

The _ _TBB Prefix

The library reserves the prefix _ _TBB for internal identifiers and macros that should never be directly referenced by your code.

CHAPTER 11

Examples

This chapter contains a rich collection of examples, together with explanations, to illustrate usage of Intel Threading Building Blocks. The early examples probably mimic the sorts of operations you will tackle first with Threading Building Blocks, and therefore are useful to get you started quickly. Then we include more complex examples that will help you understand Threading Building Blocks in more depth, and some later examples cover the domains of gaming and packet processing to show how you can develop specialized ways to utilize Threading Building Blocks tailored for your needs.

Starting with this chapter is a fine way to use this book. You can flip back to the earlier chapters for more in-depth discussions of particular features. Experimentation is recommended: pick an example, download and study it, and then modify and experiment with it.

 You can download the source code for all the examples in this chapter from *http://www.threadingbuildingblocks.org/book*. Look for errata and notes at this web site as well.

The Aha! Factor

a•ha /ä-ʹhä/ interjection, Middle English: Depending on manner of utterance, used to express surprise, pleasure, irony, derision, mockery, contempt, or triumph.

Studying these examples will hopefully have you saying Aha! a few times as the possibilities unfold. Here is a short list of some Aha! moments I have seen through the eyes of others, and on my own:

Splitting ranges can be complex operations
  Splitting a parallel range can be far more interesting than it first seems. You can play with the data in the region represented by the range. Oh, the possibilities! See Example 11-31.

Recursion maps to `parallel_for`

Recursive functions convert to parallelism using `parallel_for` easily. It is not obvious to use `parallel_for` for recursion—at least not until you have this Aha! moment. It makes sense because recursion is about splitting up work, and so is `parallel_for`. See the section "Quicksort: Visualizing Task Stealing," later in this chapter. Sometimes direct use of the task scheduler may seem better; see the section "A Better Matrix Multiply (Strassen)," later in this chapter.

Use implicit synchronization

Implicit synchronization is better than using locks. Develop a mindset to think about using implicit synchronization and avoiding locks. See the section "Advanced Task Programming," later in this chapter.

Memory is shared between tasks

It's all in the shared memory. When discussing pipelines and other algorithms, and being careful to partition access to data, it is possible to forget that all the data is in shared memory, which any task can access. This means you may need to use mutual exclusion (Chapter 7) if you did not split up your data completely, but it also means that pipelines do not really need to move data from input to output. See the section "Two Mouths: Feeding Two from the Same Task in a Pipeline," later in this chapter.

Dynamically adding tasks

Slipping in a task when you can identify work is easy and can be very powerful. See the section "Open Dynamics Engine," later in this chapter.

Empty tasks for synchronization

Tasks that do nothing are useful. They still synchronize actions. See the section "Advanced Task Programming."

Tasks that split help future-proof a program

Recursive splitting so that tasks fit available parallelism is very powerful. See Chapter 2 and Chapter 3. The number of processor cores will continue to grow in the future. Designing your program to have enough tasks to keep all processor cores busy will be increasingly important. But creating too many tasks is a problem due to additional overhead. Recursive splitting allows you to program in a manner that dynamically matches the needs of the system, and avoids having too many tasks or too few tasks. Recursive splitting lets the runtime break up as needed.

Code for parallelism need not disrupt program structure

Parallel and serial versions of code, through clever structured coding, can share drivers and low-level routines, leaving only a little code that is different. See the sections "The Game of Life," "A Better Matrix Multiply (Strassen)," and "ParallelPrime," later in this chapter.

What grainsize means

> grainsize is a parameter to some algorithms (Chapter 3) to guide recursive split-ting. It specifies the largest size range to *not* split. Because ranges that are larger than grainsize can be split, tasks could end up with ranges just above half the size of grainsize. This would be surprising if you were thinking of grainsize as a minimum size. It might also be surprising how much splitting is actually done. See Example 11-10.

I hope this chapter provides you with a few Aha! moments that help you learn Threading Building Blocks so that you can create your own masterpieces.

A Few Other Key Points

Although the items in this section are not quite Aha!-quality insights, you should consider them while exploring this chapter:

More examples

> More examples come with Threading Building Blocks—for instance, examples\ parallel_while\parallel_preorder, which uses parallel_while to do parallel preorder traversal of a sparse graph—I simply did not have the time or space to include them all in this chapter. The examples are set up as ready to build and try, although they currently include virtually no explanation about how they work internally. You just have to read the source code.

Even more examples

> Be sure to regularly visit the web sites for Threading Building Blocks, as we hope to add more and more examples, user forums, and so on.

Use a scalable memory allocator

> Have you ever analyzed the thread safety and scalability of your memory allocator? The results will send you looking for change. See the "Memory Alloca-tion" section in this chapter, and see Chapter 6.

Create only programs that can run serially (threads=1) for debugging purposes

> Always aim to be able to debug your code without concurrency as you write it. Experience will show that it is easier to debug common mistakes, which have nothing to do with parallelism, while running without concurrency. See Chapter 2 and Chapter 12.

The task scheduler is quite approachable

> Spawning tasks (Chapter 9) can be a better alternative to parallel_for when boundaries and computation granularity change between function calls. Take a look at how efficient it can be when you create and spawn tasks from the loop. See the example in the "Open Dynamics Engine" section (and other task examples in this chapter).

When in doubt, build a task graph that domain-decomposes your data structures from the top

And create about twice as many tasks as the number of cores you can imagine ever running upon. See "Game Threading Example," later in the chapter.

Controlling access to the shared data

This is made easy with the help of highly concurrent containers (Chapter 5): you can have multiple threads reading data containers without blocking each other, or you can modify a container with one writer exclusively. Moreover, if two writers modify different parts of the data containers, they will not block each other! See the example in the section "CountStrings: Using concurrent_hash_map," later in this chapter.

parallel_for Examples

The use of parallel_for is pretty straightforward. The first three examples in this section help you make sure you're comfortable with Threading Building Blocks basics. The last two examples, ParallelMerge and SubstringFinder, are a little more challenging and will help drill home how versatile parallel_for can be. The next section implements John Conway's Game of Life and is the only example to mix C++ and managed C++ in this chapter. Chapter 3 covers parallel_for in detail.

ParallelAverage

Example 11-1 defines a routine named ParallelAverage that sets output[i] to the average of input[i-1], input[i], and input[i+1], for $0 \leq i < n$.

Example 11-1. ParallelAverage

```
#include "tbb/parallel_for.h"
#include "tbb/blocked_range.h"

using namespace tbb;

class Average {
public:
    float* input;
    float* output;
    void operator()( const blocked_range<int>& range ) const {
        for( int i=range.begin(); i!=range.end(); ++i )
            output[i] = (input[i-1]+input[i]+input[i+1])*(1/3.0f);
    }
};

// Note: The input must be padded such that input[-1] and input[n]
// can be used to calculate the first and last output values.
void ParallelAverage( float* output, float* input, size_t n ) {
    Average avg;
```

Example 11-1. ParallelAverage (continued)

```
    avg.input = input;
    avg.output = output;
    parallel_for( blocked_range<int>( 0, n, 1000 ), avg );
}
```

Seismic

Here is a simple seismic wave simulation (wave propagation) based on `parallel_for` and `blocked_range`. The key parts of this example are shown here; the entire code is available for download.

The main program steps through the simulation of a seismic wave in a core loop that sets the impulse from the source of the disturbance, does the two tough computations of stress updates and velocities, and finally cleans up the edges of the simulation.

First we'll look at the stress algorithm, in Example 11-2 and Example 11-3. The first shows the serial version of the algorithm, and the second shows an equivalent parallel version.

Example 11-2. Seismic serial: Update stress

```
static void SerialUpdateStress() {
  drawing_area drawing(0, 0, UniverseWidth, UniverseHeight);
  for( int i=1; i<UniverseHeight-1; ++i ) {
    color_t* c = ColorMap[Material[i]];
    drawing.set_pos(1, i);
#pragma ivdep
    for( int j=1; j<UniverseWidth-1; ++j ) {
      S[i][j] += (V[i][j+1]-V[i][j]);
      T[i][j] += (V[i+1][j]-V[i][j]);
      int index = (int)(V[i][j]*(ColorMapSize/2)) + ColorMapSize/2;
      if( index<0 ) index = 0;
      if( index>=ColorMapSize ) index = ColorMapSize-1;
      drawing.put_pixel(c[index]);
    }
  }
}
```

Example 11-3. Seismic parallel: Update stress

```
struct UpdateStressBody {
  void operator()( const tbb::blocked_range<int>& range ) const {
    drawing_area drawing(0,
                         range.begin( ),
                         UniverseWidth,
                         range.end()-range.begin( ));
    int i_end = range.end( );
    for( int y = 0, i=range.begin( ); i!=i_end; ++i,y++ ) {
      color_t* c = ColorMap[Material[i]];
      drawing.set_pos(1, y);
```

Example 11-3. Seismic parallel: Update stress (continued)

```
#pragma ivdep
    for( int j=1; j<UniverseWidth-1; ++j ) {
      S[i][j] += (V[i][j+1]-V[i][j]);
      T[i][j] += (V[i+1][j]-V[i][j]);
      int index = (int)(V[i][j]*(ColorMapSize/2)) + ColorMapSize/2;
      if( index<0 ) index = 0;
      if( index>=ColorMapSize ) index = ColorMapSize-1;
      drawing.put_pixel(c[index]);
    }
   }
  }
};

static void ParallelUpdateStress( ) {
  tbb::parallel_for(
    tbb::blocked_range<int>( 1, UniverseHeight-1, GrainSize ),
                            UpdateStressBody( ) );
}
```

The parallel version, shown in Example 11-3, requires very little work to create from the serial version. The serial routine needs to be put into a function in a class. Note that struct UpdateStressBody { is equivalent to the class/public we use elsewhere in the book:

```
    class UpdateStressBody {
    public:
```

It seems worth letting you see it both ways. The function ParallelUpdateStress simply uses the parallel_for algorithm (Chapter 3), and specifies the range, the struct/class UpdateStressBody we created, and the grain size. The difference between the two versions of the code is minimal. If C++ were to support lambda functions (Chapter 12), the code would look almost identical. Similarly, compare the easy conversion of the serial version in Example 11-4 with the parallel version in Example 11-5.

Example 11-4. Seismic serial: Update velocity

```
static void SerialUpdateVelocity( ) {
  for( int i=1; i<UniverseHeight-1; ++i )
#pragma ivdep
    for( int j=1; j<UniverseWidth-1; ++j ) {
      V[i][j] += (S[i][j] - S[i][j-1] + T[i][j] - T[i-1][j])*M[i];
    }
}
```

Example 11-5. Seismic parallel: Update velocity

```
struct UpdateVelocityBody {
  void operator( )( const tbb::blocked_range<int>& range ) const {
    int i_end = range.end( );
    for( int i=range.begin( ); i!=i_end; ++i ) {
```

Example 11-5. Seismic parallel: Update velocity (continued)

```
#pragma ivdep
      for( int j=1; j<UniverseWidth-1; ++j ) {
        V[i][j] += (S[i][j] - S[i][j-1] + T[i][j] - T[i-1][j])*M[i];
      }
    }
  }
};

static void ParallelUpdateVelocity() {
  tbb::parallel_for(
    tbb::blocked_range<int>( 1, UniverseHeight-1, GrainSize ),
                             UpdateVelocityBody() );
}
```

Matrix Multiply

Example 11-6 shows a `SerialMatrixMultiply` that makes no use of Threading Building Blocks or any other parallelization, whereas Example 11-7 shows the corresponding `ParallelMatrixMultiply` that uses a `blocked_range2d` to specify a two-dimensional iteration space. The functions operate the same as far as the rest of the program is concerned. Obviously, we expect `ParallelMatrixMultiply` to run faster when on a machine with more than one processor core.

Example 11-6. Matrix multiply serial code

```
const size_t L = 150;
const size_t M = 225;
const size_t N = 300;

void SerialMatrixMultiply( float c[M][N], float a[M][L], float b[L][N] ) {
    for( size_t i=0; i<M; ++i ) {
        for( size_t j=0; j<N; ++j ) {
            float sum = 0;
            for( size_t k=0; k<L; ++k )
                sum += a[i][k]*b[k][j];
            c[i][j] = sum;
        }
    }
}
```

Example 11-7. Equivalent matrix multiply with blocked_range2d

```
#include "tbb/parallel_for.h"
#include "tbb/blocked_range2d.h"

using namespace tbb;

const size_t L = 150;
const size_t M = 225;
const size_t N = 300;
```

Example 11-7. Equivalent matrix multiply with blocked_range2d (continued)

```
class MatrixMultiplyBody2D {
    float (*my_a)[L];
    float (*my_b)[N];
    float (*my_c)[N];
public:
    void operator()( const blocked_range2d<size_t>& r ) const {
        float (*a)[L] = my_a; // a,b,c used in example to emphasize
        float (*b)[N] = my_b; // commonality with serial code
        float (*c)[N] = my_c;
        for( size_t i=r.rows().begin(); i!=r.rows().end(); ++i ){
            for( size_t j=r.cols().begin(); j!=r.cols().end(); ++j ) {
                float sum = 0;
                for( size_t k=0; k<L; ++k )
                    sum += a[i][k]*b[k][j];
                c[i][j] = sum;
            }
        }
    }
    MatrixMultiplyBody2D( float c[M][N], float a[M][L], float b[L][N] ) :
        my_a(a), my_b(b), my_c(c)
    {}
};

void ParallelMatrixMultiply(float c[M][N], float a[M][L], float b[L][N]){
    parallel_for( blocked_range2d<size_t>(0, M, 16, 0, N, 32),
                MatrixMultiplyBody2D(c,a,b) );
}
```

The blocked_range2d enables the two outermost loops of the serial version to become parallel loops. The parallel_for recursively splits the blocked_range2d until the pieces are no larger than 16×32. It invokes MatrixMultiplyBody2D::operator( ) on each piece.

ParallelMerge

The example in this section (Example 11-8) is more complex and requires a little familiarity with the Standard Template Library (STL) to fully understand. It shows the power of parallel_for beyond flat iteration spaces. The code performs a parallel merge of two sorted sequences. It works for any sequence with a random-access iterator. The algorithm operates recursively as follows:

1. If the sequences are too short for effective use of parallelism, it does a sequential merge. Otherwise, it performs steps 2–6.

2. It swaps the sequences if necessary so that the first sequence, [begin1,end1), is at least as long as the second sequence, [begin2,end2).

3. It sets m1 to the middle position in [begin1,end1). It calls the item at that location *key*.

4. It sets m2 to where *key* would fall in [begin2,end2).

5. It merges [begin1,m1) and [begin2,m2) to create the first part of the merged sequence.

6. It merges [m1,end1) and [m2,end2) to create the second part of the merged sequence.

The Intel Threading Building Blocks implementation of this algorithm uses the Range object to perform most of the steps. The predicate is_divisible performs the test in step 1, along with step 2. The splitting constructor performs steps 3–6. The body object does the sequential merges.

Example 11-8. Parallel merge

```
#include "tbb/parallel_for.h"
#include <algorithm>

using namespace tbb;

template<typename Iterator>
struct ParallelMergeRange {
    static size_t grainsize;
    Iterator begin1, end1;      // [begin1,end1) is 1st sequence to be merged
    Iterator begin2, end2;      // [begin2,end2) is 2nd sequence to be merged
    Iterator out;               // where to put merged sequence
    bool empty()    const {return (end1-begin1)+(end2-begin2)==0;}
    bool is_divisible() const {
      return std::min( end1-begin1, end2-begin2 ) > grainsize;
    }
    ParallelMergeRange( ParallelMergeRange& r, split ) {
      if( r.end1-r.begin1 < r.end2-r.begin2 ) {
          std::swap(r.begin1,r.begin2);
          std::swap(r.end1,r.end2);
      }
      Iterator m1 = r.begin1 + (r.end1-r.begin1)/2;
      Iterator m2 = std::lower_bound( r.begin2, r.end2, *m1 ) ;
      begin1 = m1;
      begin2 = m2;
      end1 = r.end1;
      end2 = r.end2;
      out = r.out + (m1-r.begin1) + (m2-r.begin2);
      r.end1 = m1;
      r.end2 = m2;
    }
    ParallelMergeRange( Iterator begin1_, Iterator end1_,
                Iterator begin2_, Iterator end2_,
                Iterator out_ ) :
      begin1(begin1_), end1(end1_),
      begin2(begin2_), end2(end2_), out(out_)
    {}
};
```

The `ParallelMergeRange` class has two constructors. The first contains the dummy variable, split, as explained in Chapter 3, to permit the library to split the range between two variables. The second is a conventional constructor. As before, the `ParallelMergeBody` class defines the operator( ) method that overloads ( ) to perform the desired operation, and the `ParallelMerge` class invokes the operation.

Because the algorithm moves many locations, it tends to be bandwidth-limited. Speedup varies, depending on the system.

SubstringFinder

`SubstringFinder` uses the `parallel_for` template in a substring matching program. For each position in a string, the program finds the length and location of the largest matching substring elsewhere in the string. For instance, take the string `OregonOrmereg`. Starting a scan at the first character (position 0), the largest substring with a match elsewhere in the string is `Or` at position 6. Starting at position 1, the largest match is `reg` at position 10. The position of such matches, and the length of the match, is recorded for every position in the string being searched.

Example 11-9 shows a serial version (lines 12–31) and a parallel version (lines 33–55). Note how lines 15–31 and 39–55 are nearly identical. The only difference is that the serial version does all the work directly on the input array, whereas the parallel version works on a range passed to it in the blocked_range r. For the sake of simplicity, both versions declare an array of static size to hold the output.

Example 11-9. Serial and parallel SubstringFinder

```
 1 #include <iostream>
 2 #include <string>
 3 #include <algorithm>
 4 #include "tbb/task_scheduler_init.h"
 5 #include "tbb/parallel_for.h"
 6 #include "tbb/blocked_range.h"
 7 #include "tbb/tick_count.h"
 8 using namespace tbb;
 9 using namespace std;
10 static const size_t N = 22;
11
12 void SerialSubStringFinder ( const string &str,
13                                 size_t *max_array,
14                                 size_t *pos_array) {
15   for ( size_t i = 0; i < str.size(); ++i ) {
16     size_t max_size = 0, max_pos = 0;
17     for (size_t j = 0; j < str.size(); ++j)
18       if (j != i) {
19         size_t limit = str.size()-( i > j ? i : j );
20         for (size_t k = 0; k < limit; ++k) {
21           if (str[i + k] != str[j + k]) break;
22           if (k > max_size) {
23             max_size = k;
24             max_pos = j;
```

Example 11-9. Serial and parallel SubstringFinder (continued)

```
25        }
26      }
27    }
28    max_array[i] = max_size;
29    pos_array[i] = max_pos;
30  }
31 }
32
33 class SubStringFinder {
34   const string str;
35   size_t *max_array;
36   size_t *pos_array;
37   public:
38   void operator( ) ( const blocked_range<size_t>& r ) const {
39     for ( size_t i = r.begin(); i != r.end(); ++i ) {
40       size_t max_size = 0, max_pos = 0;
41       for (size_t j = 0; j < str.size(); ++j)
42         if (j != i) {
43           size_t limit = str.size()-( i > j ? i : j );
44           for (size_t k = 0; k < limit; ++k) {
45             if (str[i + k] != str[j + k]) break;
46             if (k > max_size) {
47               max_size = k;
48               max_pos = j;
49             }
50           }
51         }
52       max_array[i] = max_size;
53       pos_array[i] = max_pos;
54     }
55   }
56
57   SubStringFinder(string &s, size_t *m, size_t *p) :
58     str(s), max_array(m), pos_array(p) { }
59 };
```

The main program (Example 11-11) sets up a string (with a Fibonacci string of "a" and "b" characters that is 17,711 characters long: "babbababbabbababbababbabbababbabbabb…").

The result of the SubstringFinder is an array of positions and an array of lengths of the matches found at the corresponding position. Two pairs of arrays are prepared: one filled in by the serial version and the other by the parallel version. The results are checked to be sure they are identical.

The parallel_for is used with a blocked_range with a grainsize of 100. The initial range is set to [0,17711).

When this example was run on a dual-core machine, the task scheduler made 254 calls to operator( ). At first, this may seem excessive. You might have assumed it would split the work into [0,8855) and [8856,17711) and let the two processor cores do equal work. But there are two reasons not to do this. The first is that operator( )

is assumed not to take the same amount of processing on every invocation. Because short substrings take less time to process than long ones, and other variations exist, the time will vary.

The second reason is that each thread is subject to differing demands on the processor core on which it is run. It is possible that one processor's core may be interrupted more often than the other. It is also possible in the future that processor cores will not all be the same.

For these reasons, in this simple example, the run split up the work into 254 tasks. Some of the ranges are shown in Example 11-10. You might also note that the grain size of 100 means that ranges can become as small as 50. (In this example, 69 was a favorite because 17711/2/2/2/2/2/2/2/2 = 69.1836). The split stopped at 69 because ranges larger than the grain size, which was set to 100, were considered splittable. You can also see how the ranges are kept far apart until the end in order to avoid cache contention. Interestingly enough, starting one thread in the middle and moving away from the other thread might perform slightly better by avoiding the slight potential for conflict at the end. There are always things to think about for future versions of the task scheduler.

 Aha! grainsize is the largest size not to split. Ranges half the size of grainsize are possible, or smaller depending on the logic of the splitter. All that is certain is that the splitter is supposed to reduce the range passed to it, so both subranges created will be smaller.

Example 11-10. Ranges passed to operator() on dual-core machine

```
 1  [0,69)
 2  [8924,8993)
 3  [69,138)
 4  [8993,9062)
 5  [138,207)
 6  [9062,9131)
 7  [207,276)
 8  [9131,9200)
 9  [276,345)
10  [9200,9269)
11  [345,414)
12  [9269,9338)
13  [9338,9408)
14  [414,483)
15  [9408,9477)
16  [483,553)
17  [553,622)
18  [9477,9546)
19  [622,691)
20  [9546,9615)
21  [691,760)
22  [9615,9685)
23  [760,829)
```

Example 11-10. Ranges passed to operator( ) on dual-core machine (continued)

```
24  [9685,9754)
25  [829,898)
26  [9754,9823)
27  [898,967)
28  [9823,9892)
29  [967,1036)
30  [9892,9962)
31  [1036,1106)
32  [9962,10031)
33  [1106,1175)
34  [10031,10100)
35  [10100,10169)
36  [1175,1244)
37  [10169,10238)
38  [1244,1313)
39  [10238,10307)
40  [1313,1382)
41  [10307,10376)
...
244 [8231,8301)
245 [17572,17641)
246 [8301,8370)
247 [17641,17711)
248 [8578,8647)
249 [8370,8439)
250 [8647,8716)
251 [8439,8508)
252 [8716,8785)
253 [8508,8578)
254 [8785,8855)
```

Example 11-11 runs the two substring finders, and the results are shown in Example 11-12, SubstringFinder. The speedup of 1.9 is near the ideal 2X (there were two processors used). The timer functions from Threading Building Blocks (described in Chapter 7) are used in this example to determine the times.

Example 11-11. Driver (main) for SubstringFinder

```
1   int main(size_t argc, char *argv[]) {
2     task_scheduler_init init;
3
4     string str[N] = { string("a"), string("b") };
5     for (size_t i = 2; i < N; ++i) str[i] = str[i-1]+str[i-2];
6     string &to_scan = str[N-1];
7
8     size_t *max = new size_t[to_scan.size()];
9     size_t *max2 = new size_t[to_scan.size()];
10    size_t *pos = new size_t[to_scan.size()];
11    size_t *pos2 = new size_t[to_scan.size()];
12    cout << " Done building string." << endl;
13
```

Example 11-11. Driver (main) for SubstringFinder (continued)

```
14   tick_count serial_t0 = tick_count::now( );
15   SerialSubStringFinder(to_scan, max2, pos2);
16   tick_count serial_t1 = tick_count::now( );
17   cout << " Done with serial version." << endl;
18
19   tick_count parallel_t0 = tick_count::now( );
20   parallel_for(blocked_range<size_t>(0, to_scan.size( ), 100),
21               SubStringFinder( to_scan, max, pos ) );
22   tick_count parallel_t1 = tick_count::now( );
23   cout << " Done with parallel version." << endl;
24
25   for (size_t i = 0; i < to_scan.size( ); ++i) {
26     if (max[i] != max2[i] || pos[i] != pos2[i]) {
27       cout << "ERROR: Serial and Parallel Results are Different!" << endl;
28     }
29   }
30   cout << " Done validating results." << endl;
31
32   cout << "Serial version ran in " <<
33         (serial_t1 - serial_t0).seconds( ) << " seconds" << endl
34     << "Parallel version ran in " <<
35         (parallel_t1 - parallel_t0).seconds( ) << " seconds" << endl
36     << "Resulting in a speedup of " <<
37         (serial_t1 - serial_t0).seconds( ) /
38         (parallel_t1 - parallel_t0).seconds( ) << endl;
39   return 0;
40 }
```

Example 11-12. SubstringFinder run on a dual-core machine

```
Done building string.
 Done with serial version.
 Done with parallel version.
 Done validating results.
Serial version ran in 19.476 seconds
Parallel version ran in 10.1276 seconds
Resulting in a speedup of 1.92305
```

The Game of Life

Here is a fun example written with a combination of C++ to use `parallel_for` from Threading Building Blocks and managed C++ code for the user interface code. This example implements the Game of Life invented by British mathematician, John Horton Conway. It was widely popularized when Martin Gardner described it in his "Mathematical Games" column in *Scientific American* in October 1970. It was popular from the start, but it also opened up a new field of mathematical research known as *cellular automata* and spurred work in the field of simulation games.

The Game of Life is played on a two-dimensional orthogonal grid of square *cells*, each of which is in one of two possible states: *live* or *dead*. Every cell interacts with its eight *neighbors*, which are the cells that touch the cell (horizontally, vertically, or diagonally). At every step in life, each cell lives, dies, stays empty, or is born because of a simple decision based on the surrounding population (number of neighbors).

Life persists in any cell where it is also present in two or three of the eight neighboring cells, and otherwise disappears (due to loneliness or overcrowding). Life is born in any empty cell for which there is life in exactly three of the eight neighboring cells. The decision-making is illustrated in Figure 11-1. A small grid containing five living cells is shown in Figure 11-2. As you can see, The Game of Life is beautifully parallel.

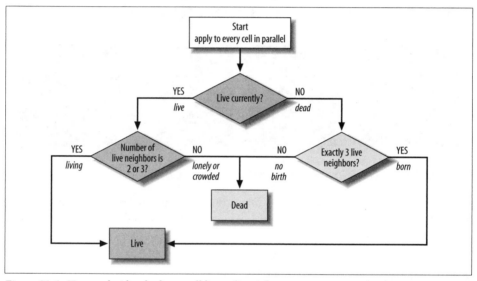

Figure 11-1. How to decide whether a cell lives, dies, is born, or stays empty for the next generation

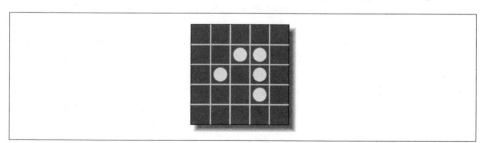

Figure 11-2. Grid with five living cells

Implementation

This program runs two simultaneous instances of this Game of Life. To show a side-by-side comparison, one of these instances is calculated using sequential programming and the other is calculated using parallel programming.

Each *generation* of a colony is calculated based on the position of the cells in the preceding generation. The decisions that determine what the next generation looks like are shown in Figure 11-1. Generation after generation, a colony grows, shrinks, and changes according to these very simple rules. Usually, it will eventually reach a state where every living cell stays alive, or where small figures oscillate between two or more repeating states. If we calculate the next four generations for the colony in Figure 11-2, we will see it progressing as shown in Figure 11-3.

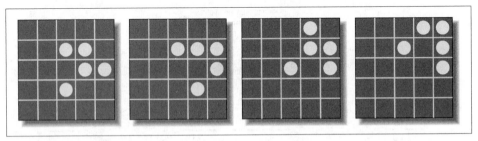

Figure 11-3. Game of Life: Four sample steps

The colony in this figure actually oscillates among four patterns, while at the same time moving diagonally across the grid. This pattern is known as the *glider* among Game of Life aficionados.

Automaton

We call our implementation *automaton* and, when run, it presents a pair of blank grids side by side. The lefthand grid displays cell colony generations with the calculations being done with sequential logic. The righthand grid displays cell colony generations with the calculations being done with parallel logic using Threading Building Blocks. Above each grid is the current generation number. Running on a single-processor core will work, but the results will vary based on the threads that get priority. Some will see the parallel side appear to be faster, even on a single-core processor, because it will have more resources competing fairly for the single-processor core than the sequential version (see the section "Fair Scheduling," in Chapter 9). Other machines show the opposite behavior because the sequential thread ends up with a priority. Neither result says anything about the efficiency of the parallel version. However, if you run this code on a quad-core (or better) processor, you will see a commensurate increase in speed for the parallel side due to true parallelism.

The Game of Life was originally assumed to take place on an infinite space. In this implementation, both of the grids wrap. The top edge is treated as though it is connected to the bottom edge, and the left edge is treated as though it is connected to the right edge. Therefore, a glider pattern moving off one edge will come into the grid from the opposite edge.

To seed both grids with the same starting cell pattern, you pull down the Game menu and select Seed. A random cell pattern is generated and placed into both grids. To begin the processing, pull down the Game menu again and select Run. Soon you will see a display similar to that shown in Figure 11-4.

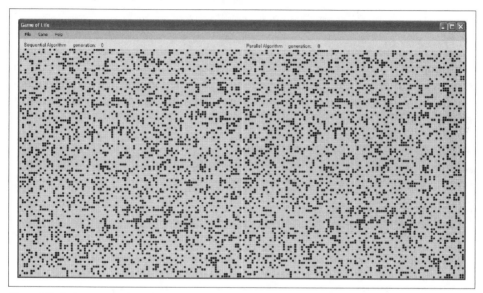

Figure 11-4. Automaton in action

Automata: Implementation

Automata are implemented as a mixture of managed and unmanaged C++. The user interface is entirely in managed code, with the calculation engine being a mixture of both.

The abstract class Evolution (Example 11-16) serves as a base class for the two implementations, SequentialEvolution (Example 11-17) and ParallelEvolution (Example 11-18). The actual generational calculations are performed by iterative calls to the Cell class, found in *Cell.h* and *Cell.cpp*.

The sequential calculation loop can be found in SequentialEvolution::Step( ), shown in Example 11-13.

Example 11-13. Automaton: SequentialEvolution step

```
// SequentialEvolution::Step() - override of step method
void SequentialEvolution::Step()
{
  Cell cell;

  for (int i=0; i<m_size; i++) {
    *(m_dest+i) = cell.CalculateState(
                        m_matrix->data,   // pointer to source data block
                        m_matrix->width,  // logical width of field
                        m_matrix->height, // logical height of field
                        i                 // number of cell position to examine
                        );
  }
}
```

This loop calls cell.CalculateState() for each cell in the source grid, and puts the resultant state in the same cell location in the destination grid. The corresponding parallel calculation can be found in ParallelEvolution::Step(), as shown in Example 11-14.

Example 11-14. Automaton: ParallelEvolution step

```
//
// ParallelEvolution::Step() - override of Step method
//
void ParallelEvolution::Step()
{
  size_t begin = 0;        // beginning cell position
  size_t end = m_size-1;   // ending cell position
  size_t grainSize = 4000; // grain (chunk) size for individual tasks

  // set matrix pointers
  tbb_parallel_task::set_values(m_matrix, m_dest);

  // do calculation loop
parallel_for (blocked_range<size_t> (begin, end, grainSize),
          tbb_parallel_task());
}
```

The routine sets up the parameters of the parallel_for (Chapter 3) by setting begin and end, and specifying the size of a parallel piece of work (grainsize = 4000) to be assigned to a thread by the underlying Threading Building Blocks logic. The actual loop code is implementead in the parallel class tbb_parallel_task as an override of the () operator. That operator override code is shown in Example 11-15 as part of the definition of tbb_parallel_task.

Example 11-15. Automaton tbb_parallel_task

```
//
// class tbb_parallel_task
//
```

Example 11-15. Automaton tbb_parallel_task (continued)

```
// TBB requires a class for parallel loop implementations. The actual
// loop "chunks" are performed using the () operator of the class. The
// blocked_range contains the range to calculate. Please see the TBB
// documentation for more information.
//
public class tbb_parallel_task
{
public:
  static void set_values(Matrix* source, char* dest)
  {
    void* x;
    m_source = source;
    m_dest = dest;
    x = m_source;
    x = m_dest;
    return;
  }

  void operator()( const blocked_range<size_t>& r ) const
  {
    int begin = (int)r.begin();// capture lower range number for this chunk
    int end = (int)r.end();    // capture upper range number for this chunk
    Cell cell;

    for (int i=begin; i<=end; i++)
    {
      *(m_dest+i) = cell.CalculateState(
                       m_source->data,  // pointer to source data block
                       m_source->width, // logical width of field
                       m_source->height,// logical height of field
                       i                // number of cell position to examine
                    );
    }
  }

  // constructor
  tbb_parallel_task () {}

private:
  // private data

  static Matrix* m_source;
  static char* m_dest;
};
```

Threading Building Blocks decides at runtime how many individual tasks to create. It schedules those tasks on threads as it sees fit, passing in the limits of the subloop to perform via the blocked_range parameter (Chapter 3). The more processing cores that are available, the more tasks it will create and the more threads it will utilize. Thus, it scales to fit the local hardware configuration.

Example 11-16. Automaton abstract class evolution

```
//
// Evolution constructor
//
Evolution::Evolution(
      Matrix *m,           // beginning matrix including initial pattern
      Board^ board,        // the board to update
      HWND messageWindow // window to which WM_DISPLAY_MATRIX message
                           // will be sent
      ) : m_matrix(m), m_board(board), m_hWnd(messageWindow), m_dest(NULL),
          m_size(m_matrix->height * m_matrix->width)
{
  // allocate memory for second matrix data block
  m_dest = new char[m_size];
  m_done = false;
}


//
// Evolution destructor
//
Evolution::~Evolution( )
{
  // release allocated memory
  delete m_dest;
}


//
// Evolution::PrepareForCalculation( )
// moves the previous destination data to the
// source data block and zeros out destination.
//
void Evolution::PrepareForCalculation( )
{
  for (int i=0; i<m_size; i++) {
    *(m_matrix->data+i) = *(m_dest+i);
    *(m_dest+i) = 0;
  }
}
```

Example 11-17. Automaton SequentialEvolution

```
//
// SequentialEvolution constructor
//
SequentialEvolution::SequentialEvolution(Matrix *m, Board^ board,
                                         HWND messageWindow)
                   : Evolution(m, board, messageWindow)
{
}


//
// SequentialEvolution::Run - begins looped evolution
//
```

Example 11-17. Automaton SequentialEvolution (continued)

```
void SequentialEvolution::Run( )
{
  // copy source matrix to destination matrix to set up data for call to
  // PrepareForCalculation( ).
  for (int i=0; i<m_size; i++) {
    *(m_dest+i) = *(m_matrix->data+i);
  }

  while (!m_done)
  {
    PrepareForCalculation( );
    Step( );
    m_board->draw( );
  }
}

//
// SequentialEvolution::Step( ) - override of step method
//
void SequentialEvolution::Step( )
{
  Cell cell;

  for (int i=0; i<m_size; i++) {
    *(m_dest+i) = cell.CalculateState(
                      m_matrix->data,     // pointer to source data block
                      m_matrix->width,   // logical width of field
                      m_matrix->height,  // logical height of field
                      i          // number of cell position to examine
                      );
  }
}
```

Example 11-18. Automaton ParallelEvolution

```
//
// ParallelEvolution constructor
//
ParallelEvolution::ParallelEvolution(Matrix *m, Board^ board,
                                      HWND messageWindow)
                 : Evolution(m, board, messageWindow)
{
  // instantiate a task_scheduler_init object and save a pointer to it
  m_pInit = NULL;
}

//
// ParallelEvolution destructor
//
ParallelEvolution::~ParallelEvolution( )
{
```

Example 11-18. Automaton ParallelEvolution (continued)

```
  // delete task_scheduler_init object
  if (m_pInit != NULL)
    delete m_pInit;
}

//
// ParallelEvolution::Run - begins looped evolution
//
void ParallelEvolution::Run( )
{
  // start task scheduler as necessary
  if (m_pInit == NULL)
    m_pInit = new task_scheduler_init( );

  // copy source matrix to destination matrix to set up data for call to
  // PrepareForCalculation( ).
  for (int i=0; i<m_size; i++)
  {
    *(m_dest+i) = *(m_matrix->data+i);
  }

  while (!m_done)
  {
    PrepareForCalculation( );
    Step( );
    m_board->draw( );
  }
}
```

Extending the Application

This application is ready for demonstrating the basic Game of Life, but you could extend it to offer more interesting features. Here are some of the ways you might extend the application:

- Experiment with grain size or the auto partitioner (see Chapter 3).
- Allow the user to specify the size of the cell grids.
- The program could measure actual performance differences between the sequential and parallel implementations and display the running results next to the generation numbers.
- Allow the user to optionally seed the grids with patterns entered via mouse clicks.
- Offer interesting starting cell configurations, such as the glider, as starting seeds.
- Make two side-by-side grids fit the screen or be otherwise adjustable.

Futher Reading

- Gardner, M. (1970). "Mathematical Games: The fantastic combinations of John Conway's new solitaire game 'life.'" *Scientific American*, 223, 120–123.
- John Conway's Game of Life, *http://www.bitstorm.org/gameoflife*.
- "Mathematical Games," *http://ddi.cs.uni-potsdam.de/HyFISCH/Produzieren/lis_projekt/proj_gamelife/ConwayScientificAmerican.htm*.
- "Patterns, Programs, and Links for Conway's Game of Life," *http://www.radicaleye.com/lifepage*.

Parallel_reduce Examples

Parallel_reduce is an extension of the parallel ranges used in earlier examples, but it adds the complexity of combining results and eventually reducing them back to a single answer. Studying the examples in this section should make you very comfortable with parallel_reduce (Chapter 3).

ParallelSum

Example 11-19 sums the values in an array.

Example 11-19. ParallelSum

```
#include "tbb/parallel_reduce.h"
#include "tbb/blocked_range.h"

using namespace tbb;

struct Sum {
    float value;
    Sum() : value(0) {}
    Sum( Sum& s, split ) {value = 0;}
    void operator()( const blocked_range<float*>& range ) {
        float temp = value;
        for( float* a=range.begin(); a!=range.end(); ++a ) {
            temp += *a;
        }
        value = temp;
    }
    void join( Sum& rhs ) {value += rhs.value;}
};

float ParallelSum( float array[], size_t n ) {
    Sum total;
    parallel_reduce( blocked_range<float*>( array, array+n, 1000 ),
                     total );
    return total.value;
}
```

This example is easily converted to do a reduction for any associative operation op as follows:

1. Replace occurrences of 0 with the identity element for op.
2. Replace occurrences of += with op= or its logical equivalent.
3. Change the name Sum to something more appropriate for op.

The operation is allowed to be noncommutative. For example, op could be matrix multiplication.

ParallelSum without Having to Specify a Grain Size

Example 11-20 does away with the need to supply a grain size by converting the prior example to use an auto_partitioner. Note how the block_range loses the grainsize parameter, and the parallel_reduce has a parameter added specifying our desire to use the auto_partitioner.

Example 11-20. ParallelSum with auto_partitioner

```
#include "tbb/parallel_reduce.h"
#include "tbb/blocked_range.h"

using namespace tbb;

struct Sum {
    float value;
    Sum( ) : value(0) {}
    Sum( Sum& s, split ) {value = 0;}
    void operator( )( const blocked_range<float*>& range ) {
        float temp = value;
        for( float* a=range.begin(); a!=range.end( ); ++a ) {
            temp += *a;
        }
        value = temp;
    }
    void join( Sum& rhs ) {value += rhs.value;}
};

float ParallelSum( float array[], size_t n ) {
    Sum total;
    parallel_reduce( blocked_range<float*>( array, array+n ),
                     total, auto_partitioner( ) );
    return total.value;
}
```

ParallelPrime

This example is a parallel version of the *Sieve of Eratosthenes*, which finds prime numbers, written using parallel_reduce. This program computes prime numbers up to *n*. The algorithm here is a fairly efficient version of the Sieve of Eratosthenes, even though the Sieve is not the most efficient way to find primes. Figure 11-5 shows how the Sieve of Eratosthenes finds primes through an elimination process.

The parallel version demonstrates how to use `parallel_reduce`, and in particular, how to exploit lazy splitting.

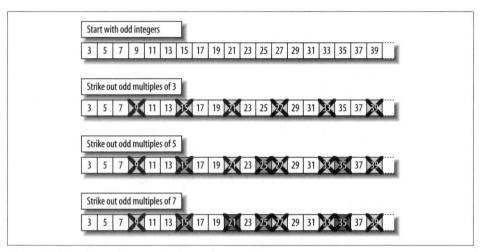

Figure 11-5. Finding primes via the Sieve of Eratosthenes

For comparison purposes, let's look at a serial version of the Sieve in Example 11-21.

 Aha! Parallel and serial versions of code differ in the middle, and clever coding can have a shared driver and can share low-level routines, leaving only a little code different.

Example 11-21. Serial version of count primes

```
//! Count number of primes between 0 and n
/** This is the serial version. */
Number SerialCountPrimes( Number n ) {
    // Two is special case
    Number count = n>=2;
    if( n>=3 ) {
        Multiples multiples(n);
        count += multiples.n_factor;
        if( PrintPrimes )
            printf("---\n");
        Number window_size = multiples.m;
        for( Number j=multiples.m; j<=n; j+=window_size ) {
            if( j+window_size>n+1 )
                window_size = n+1-j;
            count += multiples.find_primes_in_window( j, window_size );
        }
    }
    return count;
}
```

The equivalent code to do this in parallel is in Example 11-22. The code for the Multiples class, including find_primes_in_window, is in Example 11-23. The Multiples class is used by the parallel and serial versions. Both the serial and parallel versions have subroutines working to find primes in the window.

Example 11-22. Parallel version of count primes

```
//! Count number of primes between 0 and n
/** This is the parallel version. */
Number ParallelCountPrimes( Number n ) {
    // Two is special case
    Number count = n>=2;
    if( n>=3 ) {
        Sieve s(n);
        count += s.multiples.n_factor;
        if( PrintPrimes )
            printf("---\n");
        parallel_reduce( SieveRange( s.multiples.m, n,
                                     s.multiples.m, GrainSize ),
                         s );
        count += s.count;
    }
    return count;
}
```

Example 11-23. The Multiples class used by the serial and parallel sieves

```
#include <cassert>
#include <cstdio>
#include <cstring>
#include <math.h>
#include <cstdlib>
#include <cctype>
#include "tbb/parallel_reduce.h"
#include "tbb/task_scheduler_init.h"
#include "tbb/tick_count.h"

using namespace std;
using namespace tbb;

typedef unsigned long Number;

//! If true, then print primes on stdout.
static bool PrintPrimes = false;

//! Grainsize parameter // someday we should
                        // convert program to use auto_partitioner
static Number GrainSize = 1000;

class Multiples {
    inline Number strike( Number start,
                          Number limit,
                          Number stride ) {
```

Example 11-23. The Multiples class used by the serial and parallel sieves (continued)

```
        // Hoist "my_is_composite" into register for sake of speed.
        bool* is_composite = my_is_composite;
        assert( stride>=2 );
        for( ;start<limit; start+=stride )
            is_composite[start] = true;
        return start;
    }
    //! Window into conceptual sieve
    bool* my_is_composite;

    //! Indexes into window
    /** my_striker[k] is an index into
        my_composite corresponding to
        an odd multiple of my_factor[k]. */
    Number* my_striker;

    //! Prime numbers less than m.
    Number* my_factor;
public:
    //! Number of factors in my_factor.
    Number n_factor;
    Number m;
    Multiples( Number n ) :
        is_forked_copy(false)
    {
        m = Number(sqrt(double(n)));
        // Round up to even
        m += m&1;
        my_is_composite = new bool[m/2];
        my_striker = new Number[m/2];
        my_factor = new Number[m/2];
        n_factor = 0;
        memset( my_is_composite, 0, m/2 );
        for( Number i=3; i<m; i+=2 ) {
            if( !my_is_composite[i/2] ) {
                if( PrintPrimes )
                    printf("%d\n",(int)i);
                my_striker[n_factor] = strike( i/2, m/2, i );
                my_factor[n_factor++] = i;
            }
        }
    }

    //! Find primes in range [start,window_size),
    //   advancing my_striker as we go.
    /** Returns number of primes found. */
    Number find_primes_in_window( Number start,
                                  Number window_size ) {
        bool* is_composite = my_is_composite;
        memset( is_composite, 0, window_size/2 );
        for( size_t k=0; k<n_factor; ++k )
            my_striker[k] = strike( my_striker[k]-m/2,
```

Example 11-23. The Multiples class used by the serial and parallel sieves (continued)

```
                                window_size/2,
                                my_factor[k] );
        Number count = 0;
        for( Number k=0; k<window_size/2; ++k ) {
            if( !is_composite[k] ) {
                if( PrintPrimes )
                    printf("%ld\n",long(start+2*k+1));
                ++count;
            }
        }
        return count;
    }

    ~Multiples( ) {
        if( !is_forked_copy )
            delete[] my_factor;
        delete[] my_striker;
        delete[] my_is_composite;
    }

    //---------------------------------------------------
    // Begin extra members required by parallel version

    //! True if this instance was forked from another instance.
    const bool is_forked_copy;

    Multiples( const Multiples& f, split ) :
        n_factor(f.n_factor),
        m(f.m),
        my_is_composite(NULL),
        my_striker(NULL),
        my_factor(f.my_factor),
        is_forked_copy(true)
    {}

    bool is_initialized( ) const {
        return my_is_composite!=NULL;
    }

    void initialize( Number start ) {
        assert( start>=1 );
        my_is_composite = new bool[m/2];
        my_striker = new Number[m/2];
        for( size_t k=0; k<n_factor; ++k ) {
            Number f = my_factor[k];
            Number p = (start-1)/f*f % m;
            my_striker[k] = (p&1 ? p+2*f : p+f)/2;
            assert( m/2<=my_striker[k] );
        }
    }
    // End extra methods required by parallel version
    //---------------------------------------------------
};
```

For the parallel version, a parallel range is required, as shown in Example 11-24. The class Sieve—which effectively is the body for parallel_reduce—is shown in Example 11-25.

Example 11-24. Parallel range designed for the sieve

```cpp
//! Range of a sieve window.
//
// Actually very simple creation of a
// range specialized for the Sieve
//
class SieveRange {
    //! Width of full-size window into sieve.
    const Number my_stride;

    //! Always multiple of my_stride
    Number my_begin;

    //! One past last number in window.
    Number my_end;

    //! Width above which it is worth forking.
    const Number my_grainsize;

    bool assert_okay() const {
        assert( my_begin%my_stride==0 );
        assert( my_begin<=my_end );
        assert( my_stride<=my_grainsize );
        return true;
    }
public:
    //----------------------------------------------
    // Begin signatures required by parallel_reduce

    // should we split? (is it worth the overhead?)
    bool is_divisible() const {
        return my_end-my_begin>my_grainsize;
    }

    // is the range empty?
    bool empty() const {return my_end<=my_begin;}

    // called to split the range
    SieveRange( SieveRange& r, split ) :
        my_stride(r.my_stride),
        my_grainsize(r.my_grainsize),
        my_end(r.my_end)
    {
        assert( r.is_divisible() );
        assert( r.assert_okay() );
        Number middle = r.my_begin +
                        (r.my_end-r.my_begin+r.my_stride-1)/2;
```

Example 11-24. Parallel range designed for the sieve (continued)

```
        middle = middle/my_stride*my_stride;
        my_begin = middle;
        r.my_end = middle;
        assert( assert_okay() );
        assert( r.assert_okay() );
    }
    // End of signatures required by parallel_reduce
    //------------------------------------------------------------

    Number begin() const {return my_begin;}
    Number end() const {return my_end;}
    SieveRange( Number begin,
                Number end,
                Number stride,
                Number grainsize ) :
        my_begin(begin),
        my_end(end),
        my_stride(stride),
        my_grainsize(grainsize<stride?stride:grainsize)
    {
        assert( assert_okay() );
    }
};
```

Example 11-25. Sieve class used in the parallel sieve

```
//! Loop body for parallel_reduce.
/** parallel_reduce splits the sieve into subsieves.
    Each subsieve handles a subrange of [0..n]. */
class Sieve {
public:
    //! Prime multiples to consider, and
    //  working storage for this subsieve.
    Multiples multiples;

    //! Number of primes found so far by this subsieve.
    Number count;

    //! Construct Sieve for counting primes in [0..n].
    Sieve( Number n ) :
        multiples(n),
        count(0)
    {}

    //------------------------------------------------------------
    // Begin signatures required by parallel_reduce

    void operator()( const SieveRange& r ) {
        Number m = multiples.m;
        if( multiples.is_initialized() ) {
            // Simply reuse "multiples" structure
            //  from previous window
```

Example 11-25. Sieve class used in the parallel sieve (continued)

```
            // This works because parallel_reduce always applies
            // *this from left to right.
        } else {
            // Need to initialize "multiples" because
            // *this is a forked copy
            // that needs to be set up to start at r.begin().
            multiples.initialize( r.begin() );
        }
        Number window_size = m;
        for( Number j=r.begin(); j<r.end(); j+=window_size ) {
            assert( j%multiples.m==0 );
            if( j+window_size>r.end() )
                window_size = r.end()-j;
            count += multiples.find_primes_in_window( j, window_size );
        }
    }

    void join( Sieve& other ) {
        count += other.count;
    }

    Sieve( Sieve& other, split ) :
        multiples(other.multiples,split()),
        count(0)
    {}
    // End of signatures required by parallel_reduce
    //----------------------------------------------------
};
```

Lazy splitting is supported through the reuse of Multiples. This avoids an explosion of memory allocation and usage, which would occur if all Multiples were created at once. This can be quite important. Note the extra is_initialized flag that is designed to help reduce the runtime on reused Multiples. See Example 11-26 for code that calls SerialCountPrimes and ParallelCountPrimes.

Example 11-26. Code that calls SerialCountPrimes and ParallelCountPrimes

```
//! A closed range of Number.
struct NumberRange {
    Number low;
    Number high;
    void set_from_string( const char* s );
    NumberRange( Number low_, Number high_ ) : low(low_), high(high_) {}
};

void NumberRange::set_from_string( const char* s ) {
    char* end;
    high = low = strtol(s,&end,0);
    switch( *end ) {
    case ':':
        high = strtol(end+1,0,0);
        break;
```

Example 11-26. Code that calls SerialCountPrimes and ParallelCountPrimes (continued)

```
        case '\0':
            break;
        default:
            printf("unexpected character = %c\n",*end);
        }

}

//! Number of threads to use.
static NumberRange NThread(0,4);

//! If true, then at end wait for user to hit return
static bool PauseFlag = false;

//! Parse the command line.
static Number ParseCommandLine( int argc, char* argv[] ) {
    Number n = 100000000;
    int i = 1;
    if( i<argc && strcmp( argv[i], "pause" )==0 ) {
        PauseFlag = true;
        ++i;
    }
    if( i<argc && !isdigit(argv[i][0]) ) {
        // Command line is garbled.
        fprintf(stderr,
                "Usage: %s [['pause'] n [nthread [grainsize]]]\n",
                argv[0]);
        fprintf(stderr,"where n is a positive integer [%lu]\n",n);
        fprintf(stderr,
                "%s the form low:high [%ld:%lu]\n",
                "\tnthread is a non-negative integer, or range of",
                NThread.low,NThread.high);
        fprintf(stderr,
                "\tgrainsize is an optional positive integer [%lu]\n",
                GrainSize);
        exit(1);
    }
    if( i<argc )
        n = strtol(argv[i++],0,0);
    if( i<argc )
        NThread.set_from_string(argv[i++]);
    if( i<argc )
        GrainSize = strtol(argv[i++],0,0);
    return n;
}

static void WaitForUser() {
    char c;
    printf("Press return to continue\n");
    do {
        c = getchar();
    } while( c!='\n' );
}
```

Example 11-26. Code that calls SerialCountPrimes and ParallelCountPrimes (continued)

```
int main( int argc, char* argv[] ) {
    Number n = ParseCommandLine(argc,argv);

    // Try different numbers of threads
    for( Number p=NThread.low; p<=NThread.high; ++p ) {
        task_scheduler_init init(task_scheduler_init::deferred);
        // If p!=0, we are doing a parallel run
        if( p )
            init.initialize(p);

        Number count;
        tick_count t0 = tick_count::now( );
        if( p==0 ) {
            count = SerialCountPrimes(n);
        } else {
            count = ParallelCountPrimes(n);
        }
        tick_count t1 = tick_count::now( );

        printf("#primes from [2..%lu] = %lu (%.2f sec with ",
                (unsigned long)n,
                (unsigned long)count,
                (t1-t0).seconds( ));
        if( p )
            printf("%lu-way parallelism)\n", p );
        else
            printf("serial code)\n");
    }
    if( PauseFlag ) {
        WaitForUser( );
    }
    return 0;
}
```

CountStrings: Using concurrent_hash_map

The container concurrent_hash_map (Chapter 5) is similar to the associative containers of STL, but it permits concurrent accesses to its elements. The hash table provides a way to use *associative arrays* that allows you to store data indexed by keys of any type you desire. For this example, we will start with a program that uses a standard STL map (hash map) to count the occurrences of distinct strings in an array and uses the parallel_for template to run in parallel. Because the STL map is *not* thread-safe (STL containers are not thread-safe in general), synchronization is required to avoid corruption of the map when more than one thread tries to access it concurrently.

Example 11-27 shows our initial hybrid implementation. Step by step, we'll examine how to replace the uses of the STL map with a Threading Building Blocks concurrent_hash_map. Because concurrent_hash_map is thread-safe, this will allow us to remove the coarse-grained synchronization using a native lock, which STL required.

Example 11-27. CountStrings using STL map with a coarse-grained lock

```
 1  #include "my_native_lock_wrappers.h"
 2  #include <map>
 3  #include "tbb/blocked_range.h"
 4  #include "tbb/parallel_for.h"
 5  #include "tbb/tick_count.h"
 6  #include "tbb/task_scheduler_init.h"
 7  #include <string>
 8  #include <cctype>
 9
10  using namespace tbb;
11  using namespace std;
12
13  LOCK_TYPE my_lock;
14
15  //! maps strings to ints.
16  typedef map<string,int> StringTable;
17
18  //! Function object for counting occurrences of strings.
19  struct Tally {
20      StringTable& table;
21      Tally( StringTable& table_ ) : table(table_) {}
22      void operator()( const blocked_range<string*> range ) const {
23          for( string* p=range.begin(); p!=range.end( ); ++p ) {
24              LOCK_WRAPPER(&my_lock);
25              table[*p] += 1;
26              UNLOCK_WRAPPER(&my_lock);
27          }
28      }
29  };
30
31  const size_t N = 1000000;
32
33  static string Data[N];
34
35  static void CountOccurrences( ) {
36      StringTable table;
37      LOCK_INIT_WRAPPER(&my_lock);
38      tick_count t0 = tick_count::now( );
39      parallel_for( blocked_range<string*>( Data, Data+N, 1000 ),
40                    Tally(table) );
41      tick_count t1 = tick_count::now( );
42
43      int n = 0;
44      for( StringTable::iterator i=table.begin(); i!=table.end( ); ++i ) {
45          n+=i->second;
46      }
47      printf("total=%d time = %g\n",n,(t1-t0).seconds( ));
48      LOCK_DESTROY_WRAPPER(&my_lock);
49  }
50
51  static const string Adjective[] =
52      { "sour", "sweet", "bitter", "salty", "big", "small" };
53
```

Example 11-27. CountStrings using STL map with a coarse-grained lock (continued)

```
54  static const string Noun[] =
55      { "apple", "banana", "cherry", "date", "eggplant",
56        "fig", "grape", "honeydew", "icao", "jujube" };
57
58  static void CreateData( ) {
59      size_t n_adjective = sizeof(Adjective)/sizeof(Adjective[0]);
60      size_t n_noun = sizeof(Noun)/sizeof(Noun[0]);
61      for( int i=0; i<N; ++i ) {
62          Data[i] = Adjective[rand( )%n_adjective];
63          Data[i] += " ";
64          Data[i] += Noun[rand( )%n_noun];
65      }
66  }
67
68  int main( int argc, char* argv[] ) {
69      srand(2);
70      task_scheduler_init init;
71      CreateData( );
72      CountOccurrences( );
73  }
```

The example code uses an STL map protected by a coarse-grained native lock because the STL map is not safe for concurrent use. This coarse-grained lock is necessary to ensure that the STL map is not corrupted, but limits concurrency.

On line 39, the CountOccurrences method uses a parallel_for template with a Tally object as the body and a blocked_range<string *> object to describe the range, including a grain size of 1000.

The operator( ) in Tally, lines 22–28, performs the actual calculation in which each thread iterates through its assigned portion of data and increments the corresponding element in the STL map table. The single lock that controls access to the entire map is acquired at line 24 and then released at line 26.

Line 47 prints the total time used to tally the occurrences as well as the total number of strings that were inspected (this total should always equal the data set size of N).

Switching from an STL map

Now we'll change the definition of the table from an STL map to a Threading Building Blocks concurrent_hash_map. First, we include the Intel Threading Building Blocks concurrent_hash_map class at line 1 (Example 11-28) instead of the STL map class that was at line 2 in the original listing (Example 11-27). Next, we define a *traits class* for the map, which shows how the map will perform its two central functions: deriving the hash value and determining whether two values being compared are equal. MyHashCompare, defined at line 4, provides the hash function to use in mapping, as well as a function that evaluates the equality of two keys.

The typedef on line 19 of the new example replaces the typedef on line 16 in the original listing for the StringTable type.

Example 11-28. Converting to use concurrent_hash_map

```
 1 #include <tbb/concurrent_hash_map.h>
 2
 3 //! Structure that defines hashing and comparison operations for user's type.
 4 struct MyHashCompare {
 5
 6     static size_t hash( const string& x ) {
 7         size_t h = 0;
 8         for( const char* s = x.c_str(); *s; s++ )
 9             h = (h*17)^*s;
10         return h;
11     }
12     //! True if strings are equal
13         static bool equal( const string& x, const string& y ) {
14             return x==y;
15         }
16     };
17
18 //! maps strings to ints.
19 typedef concurrent_hash_map<string,int,MyHashCompare> StringTable;
```

In the next version (Example 11-29), we remove the coarse-grained lock code from Tally::operator() and use an accessor instead to gain exclusive access to the concurrent_hash_map element.

A concurrent_hash_map acts as a container of elements of type std::pair<const Key,T>. Typically, when accessing a container element, you either want to update it or read it. The concurrent_hash_map template class supports these two purposes with the accessor and const_accessor classes, respectively. These act as smart pointers and enable atomic access to elements.

An accessor represents *update (write)* access. As long as it points to an element, all other attempts to look up that key in the table will block until the accessor is done (destroyed).

The lock and unlock at lines 24 and 26 of Example 11-27 are removed here. Instead, at line 7, an accessor object is created. The element associated with key=*p is exclusively acquired at line 8. If an element already exists for this key, the insert method returns that element; otherwise, it creates a new one. The value associated with the key is updated at line 9. The accessor releases the element when it is destroyed at the end of the operator() method's scope, at line 10.

The lock declaration, initialization, and destruction are no longer needed (lines 13, 37, and 48 in Example 11-27).

Example 11-29. Switching away from the coarse-grained locks that STL map required

```
1  //! Function object for counting occurrences of strings.
2  struct Tally {
3      StringTable& table;
4      Tally( StringTable& table_ ) : table(table_) {}
5      void operator()( const blocked_range<string*> range ) const {
6          for( string* p=range.begin(); p!=range.end(); ++p ) {
7              StringTable::accessor a;
8              table.insert( a, *p );
9              a->second += 1;
10         }
11     }
12 };
```

We have measured the performance of the different `CountStrings` examples and found the following:

- An STL map using a Win32 mutex for locks achieved less than one-tenth the performance of the original sequential version for two, three, or four threads.

- An STL map using Win32 `CRITICAL_SECTION` for locks achieved about 75 percent of the performance of the original sequential version for two, three, or four threads.

- concurrent_hash_map achieved about 125 percent of the performance of the original sequential version for two threads and about 150 percent for three or four threads.

A Win32 mutex is a kernel object that is visible across processes. Although guarding each access to the STL map with a single mutex object ensures thread safety, doing so also incurs a very high overhead. On the other hand, a Win32 `CRITICAL_SECTION` is a lightweight, user-space, intra-process mutex object, and therefore is the option more likely to be selected by an experienced developer.

Even though the coarse-grained lock covers only a small increment of a key in the map, the concurrency provided by the Threading Building Blocks concurrent container enables speedup over the original sequential program, whereas the coarse-grained locking of an STL container can not. Example 11-30 shows the final program.

Example 11-30. CountStrings using concurrent_hash_map instead of STL map

```
#include "tbb/concurrent_hash_map.h"
#include "tbb/blocked_range.h"
#include "tbb/parallel_for.h"
#include "tbb/tick_count.h"
#include "tbb/task_scheduler_init.h"
#include <string>
#include <cctype>

using namespace tbb;
using namespace std;
```

Example 11-30. CountStrings using concurrent_hash_map instead of STL map (continued)

```
//! Set to true to counts.
static bool Verbose = false;
//! Working threads count
static int NThread = 1;
//! Problem size
const size_t N = 1000000;

//! Structure that defines hashing and comparison operations for user's type.
struct MyHashCompare {
    static size_t hash( const string& x ) {
        size_t h = 0;
        for( const char* s = x.c_str(); *s; s++ )
            h = (h*17)^*s;
        return h;
    }
    //! True if strings are equal
    static bool equal( const string& x, const string& y ) {
        return x==y;
    }
};

//! A concurrent hash table that maps strings to ints.
typedef concurrent_hash_map<string,int,MyHashCompare> StringTable;

//! Function object for counting occurrences of strings.
struct Tally {
    StringTable& table;
    Tally( StringTable& table_ ) : table(table_) {}
    void operator()( const blocked_range<string*> range ) const {
        for( string* p=range.begin(); p!=range.end(); ++p ) {
            StringTable::accessor a;
            table.insert( a, *p );
            a->second += 1;
        }
    }
};

static string Data[N];

static void CountOccurrences() {
    StringTable table;

    tick_count t0 = tick_count::now();
    parallel_for( blocked_range<string*>( Data, Data+N, 1000 ), Tally(table) );
    tick_count t1 = tick_count::now();

    int n = 0;
    for( StringTable::iterator i=table.begin(); i!=table.end(); ++i ) {
        if( Verbose )
            printf("%s %d\n",i->first.c_str(),i->second);
        n+=i->second;
    }
```

```
    }
    printf("threads = %d   total = %d   time = %g\n", NThread, n, (t1-t0).seconds( ));
}

static const string Adjective[] =
    { "sour", "sweet", "bitter", "salty", "big", "small" };

static const string Noun[] = {
    { "apple", "banana", "cherry", "date", "eggplant",
      "fig", "grape", "honeydew", "icao", "jujube" };

static void CreateData( ) {
    size_t n_adjective = sizeof(Adjective)/sizeof(Adjective[0]);
    size_t n_noun = sizeof(Noun)/sizeof(Noun[0]);
    for( int i=0; i<N; ++i ) {
        Data[i] = Adjective[rand( )%n_adjective];
        Data[i] += " ";
        Data[i] += Noun[rand( )%n_noun];
    }
}

static void ParseCommandLine( int argc, char* argv[] ) {
    int i = 1;
    if( i<argc && strcmp( argv[i], "verbose" )==0 ) {
        Verbose = true;
        ++i;
    }
    if( i<argc && !isdigit(argv[i][0]) ) {
        fprintf(stderr,"Usage: %s [verbose] number-of-threads\n",argv[0]);
        exit(1);
    }
    if( i<argc ) NThread = strtol(argv[i++],0,0);
}

int main( int argc, char* argv[] ) {
    srand(2);
    ParseCommandLine( argc, argv );
    task_scheduler_init init(NThread);
    CreateData( );
    CountOccurrences( );
}
```

Quicksort: Visualizing Task Stealing

Although Quicksort is a recursive algorithm, no explicit recursion is needed in
Threading Building Blocks. Aside from studying the code for Quicksort, look to this
example as an illustration of task stealing and range splitting. Let's go through how it
would work using Threading Building Blocks.

Part of the magic is realizing that when you are splitting a parallel range, you are free to adjust the data in that range before considering it split and handing it off. It is safe to do this because when a range is being split, there is no concurrent use on that particular range.

The Quicksort range shown in Example 11-31 is where the partitioning step is done (using std::swap). Partitioning involves making sure that all the numbers on one side of a pivot are smaller than or equal to the pivot, and the numbers on the other side are larger than or equal to it. Without this step, you would end up with a bunch of sort sections in the array. They appear sorted overall only because of this partitioning. See Example 11-32 for the Quicksort functions.

 Aha! Recursive splitting so that tasks fit available parallelism is very powerful.

Example 11-31. Quicksort range

```
template<typename RandomAccessIterator, typename Compare>
struct quick_sort_range {
   static const size_t grainsize = 500;
   const Compare &comp;
   RandomAccessIterator begin;
   size_t size;

   quick_sort_range( RandomAccessIterator begin_,
                     size_t size_,
                     const Compare &comp_ ) :
      comp(comp_), begin(begin_), size(size_) {}

   bool empty() const {return size==0;}
   bool is_divisible() const {return size>=grainsize;}

   quick_sort_range( quick_sort_range& range, split ) : comp(range.comp) {
      RandomAccessIterator array = range.begin;
      RandomAccessIterator key0 = range.begin;
      size_t m = range.size/2u;
      std::swap ( array[0], array[m] );

      size_t i=0;
      size_t j=range.size;
      // Partition interval [i+1,j-1] with key *key0.
      for(;;) {
        __TBB_ASSERT( i<j, NULL );
        // Loop must terminate since array[l]==*key0.
        do {
           --j;
           __TBB_ASSERT( i<=j, "bad ordering relation?" );
        } while( comp( *key0, array[j] ));
```

Example 11-31. Quicksort range (continued)

```
        do {
            __TBB_ASSERT( i<=j, NULL );
            if( i==j ) goto partition;
            ++i;
        } while( comp( array[i],*key0 ));
        if( i==j ) goto partition;
        std::swap( array[i], array[j] );
        }
partition:
    // Put the partition key where it belongs
    std::swap( array[j], *key0 );
    // array[l..j) is less or equal to key.
    // array(j..r) is greater than or equal to key.
    // array[j] is equal to key
    i=j+1;
    begin = array+i;
    size = range.size-i;
    range.size = j;
    }
};
```

 Aha! Splitting a parallel range can be interesting code. It can be a very active routine. You can play with the data in the region represented by the range! Oh, the possibilities! See Example 11-31.

Example 11-32. Quicksort functions

```
template<typename RandomAccessIterator, typename Compare>
struct quick_sort_body {
    void operator()( const quick_sort_range<RandomAccessIterator,
                     Compare>& range ) const {
    //SerialQuickSort( range.begin, range.size, range.comp );
        std::sort( range.begin, range.begin + range.size, range.comp );
    }
};

template<typename RandomAccessIterator, typename Compare>
void parallel_quick_sort( RandomAccessIterator begin,
                          RandomAccessIterator end,
                          const Compare& comp ) {
    parallel_for( quick_sort_range<RandomAccessIterator,Compare>
                  (begin, end-begin, comp ),
                  quick_sort_body<RandomAccessIterator,Compare>() );
}

template<typename RandomAccessIterator, typename Compare>
void parallel_sort( RandomAccessIterator begin,
                    RandomAccessIterator end, const Compare& comp) {
    const int min_parallel_size = 500;
    if( end > begin ) {
        if (end - begin < min_parallel_size) {
```

Example 11-32. Quicksort functions (continued)

```
        std::sort(begin, end, comp);
    } else {
      parallel_quick_sort(begin, end, comp);
    }
  }
}

template<typename RandomAccessIterator>
inline void parallel_sort( RandomAccessIterator begin,
                           RandomAccessIterator end ) {
   parallel_sort( begin, end, std::less< typename std::iterator_
traits<RandomAccessIterator>::value_type >() );
}

template<typename T>
inline void parallel_sort( T * begin, T * end ) {
   parallel_sort( begin, end, std::less< T >() );
}
```

Figure 11-6 through Figure 11-15 show how recursion and task stealing might progress for a simple instantiation of tbb::parallel_sort(color,color+64). Four threads are shown, which is what Threading Building Blocks would create on a quad-core, processor-based machine. If you ran this on a dual-core machine, you would get only two threads. The shading in the figures shows which of the four threads handles each data set. As you read through the figures, look at the bottom of each one to see what's changed—that is, to see how data sets split and are taken by different threads.

The ten steps have been sequenced to help illustrate the key steps. Because splitting and sorting run in parallel, and the only synchronization occurs when task stealing takes place, the timeline for progress is more rapid than these figures might lead you to believe.

The task scheduler built into Threading Building Blocks has each thread do a very simple job: pick up work from the local task pool, and split it if it is deemed splittable; otherwise, it sorts it. If the local task queue is empty, the thread looks to steal from another queue. It is that simple.

 Aha! Recursive functions convert to parallelism easily using parallel_ for. It is not obvious to use parallel_for for recursion, such as Quicksort, at least not until you have this Aha! moment. It makes sense because recursion is about splitting up work, and so is parallel_for.

The task stealing is biased toward stealing from the cold end of the task pool in order to leave behind the work that is most likely to have data in the cache of the other thread. The task pool is used as last-in first-out locally, but it is stolen from as first-in

---

first-out. This helps avoid cache thrash and tends to give priority to moving larger chunks of work at a time. Avoiding cache thrash is not going to show up in this small example, but it turns out to be reasonably important in real-life applications.

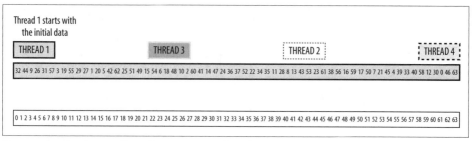

Figure 11-6. Quicksort: all work starts assigned to Thread 1

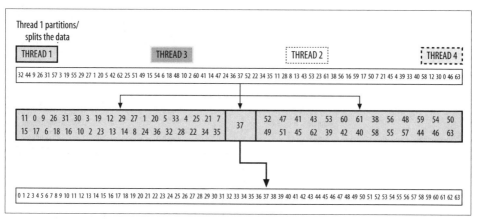

Figure 11-7. Quicksort: Thread 1 splits the workload

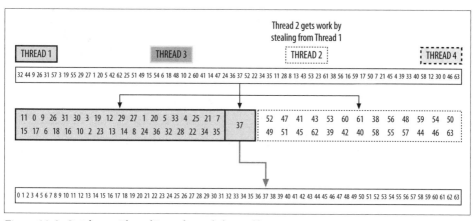

Figure 11-8. Quicksort: Thread 2 steals work for itself

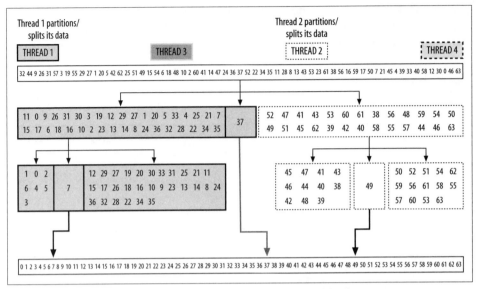

Figure 11-9. Quicksort: both Thread 1 and Thread 2 split their workloads

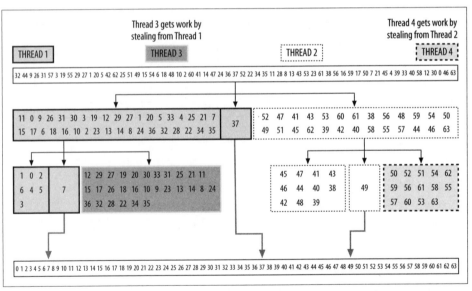

Figure 11-10. Quicksort: Threads 3 and 4 steal work

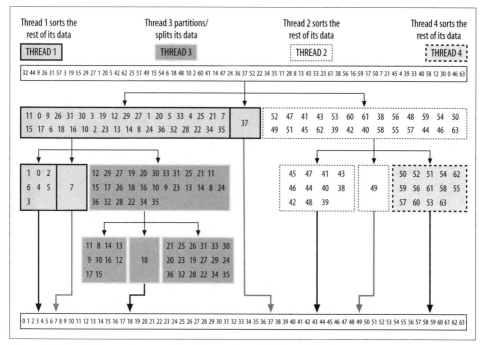

Figure 11-11. *Quicksort: some workloads are split while others finish*

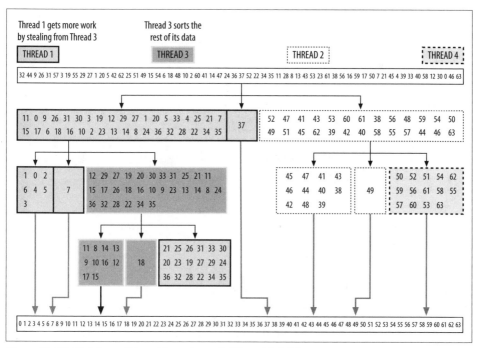

Figure 11-12. *Quicksort: Thread 1 steals work, Thread 3 finishes*

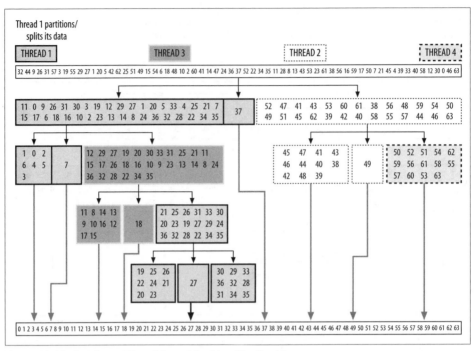

Figure 11-13. Quicksort: Thread 1 workload is still splittable

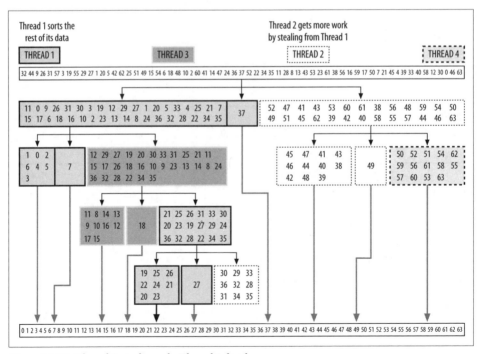

Figure 11-14. Thread 2 steals work, Thread 1 finishes

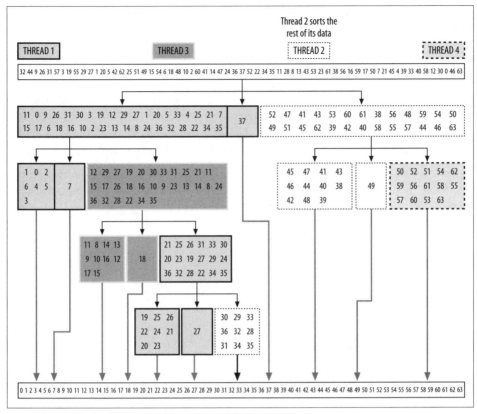

Figure 11-15. When Thread 2 finishes, all work is done

A Better Matrix Multiply (Strassen)

This implementation uses the task scheduler to run a seven-task version of the Strassen algorithm. It is an excellent and simple introduction to using the task scheduler (Chapter 9).

The Strassen algorithm is faster than the standard matrix multiply process for large matrixes. Volker Strassen published his algorithm in 1969 and was the first to point out that the standard method of *Gaussian elimination* is not optimal. His paper touched off a search for even faster algorithms.

The parallel implementation is found in the StrassenMultiply class. Instead of a recursive function call, we create a new task of type StrassenMultiply that will operate with the submatrixes (see Example 11-35). Seven new tasks are created to compute $p_1...p_7$. Those new tasks are put into the tbb::task_list (Chapter 9) and then they are all spawned by the spawn_and_wait_for_all (list) function. After all of the children are finished, it calculates the resulting submatrixes. The recursion ends when the matrix size becomes less than the cutoff parameter, and it uses a serial algorithm to multiply these smaller matrixes.

The serial version uses two temporary arrays (a_cum and b_cum) to store things such as (a11+a22) and (b21+b22) (operands for the recursive call to compute p_j). Those arrays are being reused to compute $p_1 \ldots p_7$. For Threading Building Blocks, this would not work and the memory will be spoiled by the part that prepares arguments for the following p_j. So, we have to allocate new arrays for each child task. All memory allocation is performed by the alloca function that allocates memory on the function stack, so it gets cleaned up when the function returns. It should work faster than malloc.

There are three versions of matrix multiplication: matrix_mult (serial simple algorithm, not shown), strassen_mult (Strassen serial, not shown), and strassen_mult_par (Strassen parallel, shown in Example 11-33).

Example 11-33. strassen_mult_par (Strassen parallel)

```
void strassen_mult_par (
  // dimensions of A, B, and C submatrices
  int n,
  // (ax,ay) = origin of A submatrix for multiplicand
  double *A, int ax, int ay, int as,
  // (bx,by) = origin of B submatrix for multiplicand
  double *B, int bx, int by, int bs,
  // (cx,cy) = origin of C submatrix for result
  double *C, int cx, int cy, int cs,
  // current depth of Strassen's recursion
  int d,
  // Strassen's recursion limit for array dimensions
  int s
)
{
  StrassenMultiply& t = *new (tbb::task::allocate_root ())
    StrassenMultiply (n, A, ax, ay, as,
                      B, bx, by, bs,
                      C, cx, cy, cs, d, s);
  tbb::task::spawn_root_and_wait (t);
}
```

Example 11-34 shows timing results from a quad-core system with 1024×1024 matrixes. It shows a 2.43X speedup for Strassen due to parallelism through an implementation without any tuning work or special compiler switches, so there may be more opportunity to tune after this first step of making it run in parallel. Example 11-35 shows the StrassenMultiply task, and Example 11-36 shows the main program to call the various matrix multiply routines.

 Aha! Parallel and serial versions of code differ in the middle, and clever coding can have a shared driver and shared low-level routines, leaving only a little code different.

Example 11-34. Strassen timing results

```
Simple serial: 12.6384 seconds
Srassen serial: 1.39001 seconds
Strassen parallel: 0.571969 seconds
```

Example 11-35. The StrassenMultiply task

```
/*
 * Perform A x B => C  for square submatrices of
 * A, B, and C assuming the submatrix
 * dimension is divisible by two.
 *
 * First, decompose matrices as follows:
 *      n_2 = n/2 = order of partitioned matrices
 *
 *
 *          ------------- -------------      -------------
 *      n/2 ! a11 ! a12 ! ! b11 ! b12 !      ! c11 ! c12 ! n/2
 *          !-----!-----!*!-----!-----! =    !-----!-----!
 *      n/2 ! a21 ! a22 ! ! b21 ! b22 !      ! c21 ! c22 ! n/2
 *          ------------- -------------      -------------
 *          n/2   n/2     n/2   n/2          n/2   n/2
 *
 *      algorithm:
 * Then, compute temp. Matrices as follows:
 *      p1 = (a11+a22)*(b11+b22)
 *      p2 = (a21+a22)*b11
 *      p3 = a11*(b12-b22)
 *      p4 = a22*(b21-b11)
 *      p5 = (a11+a12)*b22
 *      p6 = (a21-a11)*(b11+b12)
 *      p7 = (a12-a22)*(b21+b22)
 *
 * In the end, when all temp. matrices are ready,
 * compute the result matrix C:
 *      c11 = p1+p4-p5+p7
 *      c12 = p3+p5
 *      c21 = p2+p4
 *      c22 = p1+p3-p2+p6
 *
 * Each matrix multiplication is implemented as a
 * recursive call to strassen_mult.
 */
class StrassenMultiply : public tbb::task {
  int n, ax, ay, as, bx, by, bs, cx, cy, cs, d, s;
  double *A, *B, *C;
public:
  // dimensions of A, B, and C submatrices
  StrassenMultiply ( int _n,
  // (ax,ay) = origin of A submatrix for multiplicand
    double *_A, int _ax, int _ay, int _as,
  // (bx,by) = origin of B submatrix for multiplicand
    double *_B, int _bx, int _by, int _bs,
  // (cx,cy) = origin of C submatrix for result
    double *_C, int _cx, int _cy, int _cs,
```

Example 11-35. The StrassenMultiply task (continued)

```
// current depth of Strassen's recursion
int _d,
// Strassen's recursion limit for array dimensions
int _s
): n(_n), A(_A), B(_B), C(_C),
   ax(_ax), ay(_ay), as(_as), bx(_bx), by(_by), bs(_bs),
     cx(_cx), cy(_cy), cs(_cs), d(_d), s(_s) {}

 tbb::task* execute () {
   if (n < s) {
      // just do the simple algorithm for small matrices
      matrix_mult(n, n, n, A, ax, ay, as,
                    B, bx, by, bs, C, cx, cy, cs, d);
   } else {

      // we are going to create a list of seven tasks -
      // those tasks may create seven more each
      tbb::task_list list;
      int count = 1;

      int n_2 = n >> 1;
      double *work;
      double *p1, *p2, *p3, *p4, *p5, *p6, *p7;

      work = (double *) alloca (sizeof(double) * n_2 * n_2 * 9);
      p1  =  work;
      p2  = p1 + n_2 * n_2;
      p3  = p2 + n_2 * n_2;
      p4  = p3 + n_2 * n_2;
      p5  = p4 + n_2 * n_2;
      p6  = p5 + n_2 * n_2;
      p7  = p6 + n_2 * n_2;

      // p1 = (a11 + a22) x (b11 + b22)
      double* a_cum1 =
              (double *) alloca (sizeof(double) * n_2 * n_2);
      double* b_cum1 =
              (double *) alloca (sizeof(double) * n_2 * n_2);
      matrix_add(n_2, n_2, A, ax, ay, as,
                 A, ax+n_2, ay+n_2, as, a_cum1, 0, 0, n_2);
      matrix_add(n_2, n_2, B, bx, by, bs,
                 B, bx+n_2, by+n_2, bs, b_cum1, 0, 0, n_2);
      ++count;
      list.push_back (*new (allocate_child ())
        StrassenMultiply (n_2, a_cum1, 0, 0, n_2,
                           b_cum1, 0, 0, n_2, p1, 0, 0, n_2, d+1, s));

      // p2 = (a21 + a22) x b11
      double* a_cum2 = (double *) alloca (sizeof(double) * n_2 * n_2);
      matrix_add(n_2, n_2, A, ax+n_2,
                 ay, as, A, ax+n_2, ay+n_2, as, a_cum2, 0, 0, n_2);
```

Example 11-35. The StrassenMultiply task (continued)

```
++count;
list.push_back (*new (allocate_child ())
  StrassenMultiply (n_2, a_cum2, 0, 0, n_2,
                    B, bx, by, bs, p2, 0, 0, n_2, d+1, s));

// p3 = a11 x (b12 - b22)
double* b_cum3 = (double *) alloca (sizeof(double) * n_2 * n_2);
matrix_sub(n_2, n_2, B, bx,
           by+n_2, bs, B, bx+n_2, by+n_2, bs, b_cum3, 0, 0, n_2);
++count;
list.push_back (*new (allocate_child ())
  StrassenMultiply (n_2, A, ax, ay, as,
                    b_cum3, 0, 0, n_2, p3, 0, 0, n_2, d+1, s));

// p4 = a22 x (b21 - b11)
double* b_cum4 = (double *) alloca (sizeof(double) * n_2 * n_2);
matrix_sub(n_2, n_2, B, bx+n_2,
           by, bs, B, bx, by, bs, b_cum4, 0, 0, n_2);
++count;
list.push_back (*new (allocate_child ())
  StrassenMultiply (n_2, A, ax+n_2, ay+n_2, as,
                    b_cum4, 0, 0, n_2, p4, 0, 0, n_2, d+1, s));

// p5 = (a11 + a12) x b22
double* a_cum5 = (double *) alloca (sizeof(double) * n_2 * n_2);
matrix_add(n_2, n_2, A, ax,
           ay, as, A, ax, ay+n_2, as, a_cum5, 0, 0, n_2);
++count;
list.push_back (*new (allocate_child ())
  StrassenMultiply (n_2, a_cum5, 0, 0, n_2,
                    B, bx+n_2, by+n_2, bs, p5, 0, 0, n_2, d+1, s));

// p6 = (a21 - a11) x (b11 + b12)
double* a_cum6 = (double *) alloca (sizeof(double) * n_2 * n_2);
double* b_cum6 = (double *) alloca (sizeof(double) * n_2 * n_2);
matrix_sub(n_2, n_2, A, ax+n_2,
           ay, as, A, ax, ay, as, a_cum6, 0, 0, n_2);
matrix_add(n_2, n_2, B, bx,
           by, bs, B, bx, by+n_2, bs, b_cum6, 0, 0, n_2);
++count;
list.push_back (*new (allocate_child ())
  StrassenMultiply (n_2, a_cum6, 0, 0, n_2,
                    b_cum6, 0, 0, n_2, p6, 0, 0, n_2, d+1, s));

// p7 = (a12 - a22) x (b21 + b22)
double* a_cum7 = (double *) alloca (sizeof(double) * n_2 * n_2);
double* b_cum7 = (double *) alloca (sizeof(double) * n_2 * n_2);
matrix_sub(n_2, n_2, A, ax,
           ay+n_2, as, A, ax+n_2, ay+n_2, as, a_cum7, 0, 0, n_2);
matrix_add(n_2, n_2, B, bx+n_2,
           by, bs, B, bx+n_2, by+n_2, bs, b_cum7, 0, 0, n_2);
```

Example 11-35. The StrassenMultiply task (continued)

```
        ++count;
        list.push_back (*new (allocate_child ())
          StrassenMultiply (n_2, a_cum7, 0, 0, n_2,
                            b_cum7, 0, 0, n_2, p7, 0, 0, n_2, d+1, s));

        set_ref_count (count);
        spawn_and_wait_for_all (list);

        // c11 = p1 + p4 - p5 + p7
        matrix_add(n_2, n_2, p1, 0,
                   0, n_2, p4, 0, 0, n_2, C, cx, cy, cs);
        matrix_sub(n_2, n_2, C, cx,
                   cy, cs, p5, 0, 0, n_2, C, cx, cy, cs);
        matrix_add(n_2, n_2, C, cx,
                   cy, cs, p7, 0, 0, n_2, C, cx, cy, cs);

        // c12 = p3 + p5
        matrix_add(n_2, n_2, p3, 0,
                   0, n_2, p5, 0, 0, n_2, C, cx, cy+n_2, cs);

        // c21 = p2 + p4
        matrix_add(n_2, n_2, p2, 0,
                   0, n_2, p4, 0, 0, n_2, C, cx+n_2, cy, cs);

        // c22 = p1 + p3 - p2 + p6
        matrix_add(n_2, n_2, p1, 0,
                   0, n_2, p3, 0, 0, n_2, C, cx+n_2, cy+n_2, cs);
        matrix_sub(n_2, n_2, C, cx+n_2,
                   cy+n_2, cs, p2, 0, 0, n_2, C, cx+n_2, cy+n_2, cs);
        matrix_add(n_2, n_2, C, cx+n_2,
                   cy+n_2, cs, p6, 0, 0, n_2, C, cx+n_2, cy+n_2, cs);
    }
    return NULL;
  }
};
```

Example 11-36. The main program to call the various matrix multiply routines

```
void init (size_t size, double* A, double* B) {
  srand((unsigned int)time(NULL));
  for (size_t i = 0; i < size; i++) {
      for (size_t j = 0; j < size; j++) {
          A[i*size + j] = ((float) rand()) / ((float) RAND_MAX);
          B[i*size + j] = ((float) rand()) / ((float) RAND_MAX);
      }
  }
}

int main(int argc, char *argv[])
{
  double *A, *B, *C, *D, *E;
```

```cpp
// Allocate array storage
A = new double [size * size];
B = new double [size * size];
C = new double [size * size];
D = new double [size * size];
E = new double [size * size];

// Set up input matrices with random values
init (size, A, B);

std::cerr << "Parameters:" << std::endl <<
   "  array size: " << size << "x" << size << std::endl <<
   "  threads: " << threadreq << std::endl <<
   "  strassen minimum: " << strass << std::endl <<
   "  matmul blocksize: " << block << std::endl;

// Blocked serial matrices multiplication
tbb::tick_count simple1 = tbb::tick_count::now ();
matrix_mult (size, size, size,
             A, 0, 0, size,
             B, 0, 0, size,
             D, 0, 0, size, 0);
tbb::tick_count simple2 = tbb::tick_count::now ();
std::cerr << "Simple serial algorithm: " <<
   (simple2-simple1).seconds () << " seconds" << std::endl;

// Strassen algorithm [Serial]
tbb::tick_count serial1 = tbb::tick_count::now ();
strassen_mult (size, A, 0, 0, size,
                     B, 0, 0, size,
                     C, 0, 0, size, 1, strass);
tbb::tick_count serial2 = tbb::tick_count::now ();
std::cerr << "Strassen algorithm serial: " <<
   (serial2-serial1).seconds () << " seconds" << std::endl;

// Strassen algorithm [Parallel]
tbb::task_scheduler_init init (threadreq);
tbb::tick_count parallel1 = tbb::tick_count::now ();
strassen_mult_par (size, A, 0, 0, size,
                         B, 0, 0, size,
                         E, 0, 0, size, 1, strass);
tbb::tick_count parallel2 = tbb::tick_count::now ();
std::cerr << "Strassen algorithm parallel: " <<
   (parallel2-parallel1).seconds () << " seconds" << std::endl;

delete[] A;
delete[] B;
delete[] C;
delete[] D;
delete[] E;

return 0;
}
```

Advanced Task Programming

This section could be called "Dummy Tasks to the Rescue" because, although the design of Threading Building Blocks is very simple at the core, there are times when you want a little more help.

This section has two examples that use a dummy task to create relationships among tasks that at first seem impossible because they have non-treelike dependence graphs. In the first example, we give a sibling task to the main program that is usually the base of the tree. In the second example, we set up a pipeline with a fork in it. It is a classic example of avoiding locks through implicit synchronization. We'll name the two examples as follows:

- Start a Large Task in Parallel with the Main Program
- Two Mouths: Feeding Two from the Same Task in a Pipeline

Start a Large Task in Parallel with the Main Program

Instead of having all threads execute portions of a problem, it is possible to start a task in parallel with the main application. We've seen a number of requests for how to do this. The trick is to use a nonexecuting dummy task as the parent on which to synchronize, as shown in Example 11-37. Something very close to this trick is already used in *tbb/parallel_while.h* and *tbb/parallel_scan.h*, shown earlier.

One of the beautiful things about this approach is that each half of the program is free to invoke as much parallelism as it desires. The task-based approach of Threading Building Blocks does the load balancing and manages the assignment of tasks to threads without causing oversubscription.

Example 11-37. Using a dummy task for synchronization

```
 1  // The technique is similar to one used in tbb/parallel_while.h
 2
 3  #include "tbb/task.h"
 4  #include "tbb/task_scheduler_init.h"
 5  #include <stdio.h>
 6  #include <stdlib.h>
 7
 8  //! Some busywork
 9  void TwiddleThumbs( const char * message, int n ) {
10      for( int i=0; i<n; ++i ) {
11          printf(" %s: i=%d\n",message,i);
12          static volatile int x;
13          for( int j=0; j<20000000; ++j )
14              ++x;
15      }
16  }
17
```

Example 11-37. Using a dummy task for synchronization (continued)

```
18  //! SideShow task
19  class SideShow: public tbb::task {
20      tbb::task* execute( ) {
21          TwiddleThumbs("Sideshow task",4);
22          return NULL;
23      }
24  };
25
26  //! Start up a SideShow task.
27  //! Return pointer to dummy task that acts as parent of the SideShow.
28  tbb::empty_task* StartSideShow( ) {
29      tbb::empty_task* parent = new( tbb::task::allocate_root( ) ) tbb::empty_task;
30      // 2 = 1 for SideShow and C
31      parent->set_ref_count(2);
32      SideShow* s = new( parent->allocate_child( ) ) SideShow;
33      parent->spawn(*s);
34      return parent;
35  }
36
37  //! Wait for SideShow task.  Argument is dummy parent of the SideShow.
38  void WaitForSideShow( tbb::empty_task* parent ) {
39      parent->wait_for_all( );
40      // parent not actually run, so we need to destroy it explicitly.
41      // (If you forget this line, the debug version of tbb reports a task leak.)
42      parent->destroy(*parent);
43  }
44
45  //! Optional command-line argument is number of threads to use.  Default is 2.
46  int main( int argc, char* argv[] ) {
47      tbb::task_scheduler_init init( argc>1 ? strtol(argv[1],0,0) : 2 );
48      // Loop over n tests various cases where SideShow/Main finish twiddling first.
49      for( int n=3; n<=5; ++n ) {
50          printf("\ntest with n=%d\n",n);
51
52          // Start up a Sideshow task
53          tbb::empty_task* e = StartSideShow( );
54
55          // Do some useful work
56          TwiddleThumbs("master",n);
57
58          // Wait for Sideshow task to complete
59          WaitForSideShow(e);
60      }
61      return 0;
62  }
```

In the example, the main program starts up an additional task called SideShow as the child of a dummy parent task. The parent task is never started and is therefore well suited to use in synchronization to determine whether and when the SideShow has completed. The example in the following section builds on this one to solve a common problem in parallel programs.

The main and SideShow tasks are free to create more tasks by using parallel algorithms from Threading Building Blocks or the task scheduler. There is no danger of oversubscription, so there is no need for the SideShow developer and the developer of the main program to coordinate their decisions on parallelism unless they share some data. If SideShow and the main program share, the developers need only talk about safe concurrent access to data. There is still no need to discuss load balancing because it is automatic when using Threading Building Blocks to manage your parallelism.

The program is instrumented with some simple printf calls to show the various cases where the main program completes before and after the SideShow task. Table 11-1 shows the output from a dual-core system running Windows Vista and using Intel Threading Building Blocks 1.1 for Windows. The program was run with input arguments of one, two, and four threads, to set the number of threads for the purposes of illustration. With only one thread you can see there is no parallelism.

Table 11-1. Output from TwiddleThumbs in the example

Only one thread run (run on a two-core system)	Run with two threads (run on a two-core system)	Run with four threads (run on a two-core system)

test with n=3
  master: i=0
  master: i=1
  master: i=2
  Sideshow task: i=0
  Sideshow task: i=1
  Sideshow task: i=2
  Sideshow task: i=3
	test with n=3
	  master: i=0
	  Sideshow task: i=0
	  master: i=1
	  Sideshow task: i=1
	  master: i=2
	  Sideshow task: i=2
	  Sideshow task: i=3
		test with n=3
		  master: i=0
		  Sideshow task: i=0
		  Sideshow task: i=1
		  master: i=1
		  Sideshow task: i=2
		  master: i=2
		  Sideshow task: i=3

test with n=4
  master: i=0
  master: i=1
  master: i=2
  master: i=3
  Sideshow task: i=0
  Sideshow task: i=1
  Sideshow task: i=2
  Sideshow task: i=3
	test with n=4
	  master: i=0
	  Sideshow task: i=0
	  Sideshow task: i=1
	  master: i=1
	  master: i=2
	  Sideshow task: i=2
	  master: i=3
	  Sideshow task: i=3
		test with n=4
		  master: i=0
		  Sideshow task: i=0
		  master: i=1
		  Sideshow task: i=1
		  master: i=2
		  Sideshow task: i=2
		  master: i=3
		  Sideshow task: i=3

test with n=5
  master: i=0
  master: i=1
  master: i=2
  master: i=3
  master: i=4
  Sideshow task: i=0
  Sideshow task: i=1
  Sideshow task: i=2
  Sideshow task: I=3
	test with n=5
	  master: i=0
	  Sideshow task: i=0
	  master: i=1
	  Sideshow task: i=1
	  master: i=2
	  master: i=3
	  Sideshow task: i=2
	  master: i=4
	  Sideshow task: i=3
		test with n=5
		  master: i=0
		  Sideshow task: i=0
		  Sideshow task: i=1
		  Sideshow task: i=2
		  master: i=1
		  master: i=2
		  Sideshow task: i=3
		  master: i=3
		  master: i=4

Two Mouths: Feeding Two from the Same Task in a Pipeline

Imagine you have a couple of pipelines and you want to merge results from different pipelines in a task.

Additionally, suppose the output of at least one task feeds more than a single task. Normally, a task can feed only one other task in a pipeline. The solution is to use a dummy task inside a task to link in the data for the task that feeds two dependents.

Figure 11-16 shows a diagram for a desired pipeline that contains a split such that the output of one stage is used by two other stages. This is a pretty typical-looking set of parallel pipelines such as you might find in any variety of signal-processing or multimedia applications. The temptation is to give up after the third step and do the merges back into the main program, but that would give up the parallelism available during the merges. Likewise, we do not want to execute the middle pipeline (ending with FILTER B) twice.

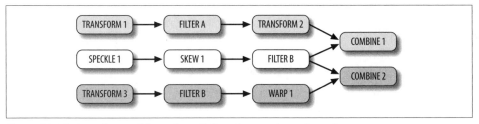

Figure 11-16. A pipeline with lots of parallelism, but a twist at the end

To focus on the problem we're solving, we need only look at the last two phases, as shown in Figure 11-17. The actual solution is to create a DUMMY task solely for the sake of synchronization, as shown in Figure 11-18. Example 11-38 shows the code of the worker tasks and dummy task, and Example 11-39 shows the main program that spawns the three worker tasks. Keep in mind that because all data is in memory and is accessible by any thread, there is no real data movement. The dummy task does not need to move data, nor does it impose any real overhead.

 Aha! It's all in the shared memory. When discussing pipelines and other algorithms, and being careful to partition access to data, it is possible to forget that all the data is in shared memory, which any task can access.

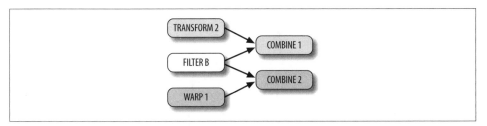

Figure 11-17. The example will focus on the final part of the pipeline

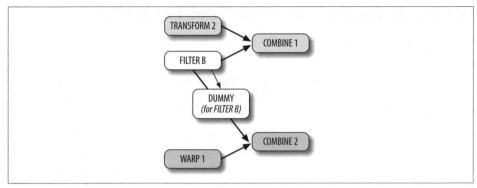

Figure 11-18. This is how the example actually implements the pipeline

Example 11-38. Pipelined tasks with a dummy task to help in a TwoMouths pattern

```
1  #include "tbb/task.h"
2  #include "tbb/task_scheduler_init.h"
3  #include <stdio.h>
4  #include <stdlib.h>
5
6  //! Some busywork
7  void TwiddleThumbs( const char * message, int n ) {
8      for( int i=0; i<n; ++i ) {
9          printf(" %s: i=%d\n",message,i);
10         static volatile int x;
11         for( int j=0; j<20000000; ++j )
12             ++x;
13     }
14 }
15
16 // Time delays
17 int m1, m2, t1, t2;
18
19 class Combine1: public tbb::task {
20 public:
21     tbb::task* execute( ) {
22         TwiddleThumbs("Combine1",m1);
23         return NULL;
24     }
25 };
26
27 class Combine2: public tbb::task {
28 public:
29     tbb::task* execute( ) {
30         TwiddleThumbs("Combine2",m2);
31         return NULL;
32     }
33 };
34
```

Example 11-38. Pipelined tasks with a dummy task to help in a TwoMouths pattern (continued)

```
35  class Filterb: public tbb::task {
36  public:
37      tbb::empty_task* dummy;
38      tbb::task* execute( ) {
39          TwiddleThumbs("Filterb",4);
40          // When all the work is done -
41          //  start dummy, which does nothing and signals the
42          //  second parent to continue.
43          dummy->spawn(*dummy);
44          return NULL;
45      }
46  };
47
48  class Transform2: public tbb::task {
49  public:
50      tbb::task* execute( ) {
51          TwiddleThumbs("Transform2",t1);
52          return NULL;
53      }
54  };
55
56  class Warp1: public tbb::task {
57  public:
58      tbb::task* execute( ) {
59          TwiddleThumbs("Warp1",t2);
60          return NULL;
61      }
62  };
```

Example 11-39. The main program that sets up the pipeline for TwoMouths

```
1   //! Optional command-line argument is number of threads to use.  Default is 3.
2   int main( int argc, char* argv[] ) {
3       tbb::task_scheduler_init init( argc>1 ? strtol(argv[1],0,0) : 3 );
4       // Test various time delays
5       for( m1=3; m1<=5; ++m1 ) {
6           for( m2=3; m2<=5; ++m2 ) {
7               for( t1=3; t1<=5; ++t1 ) {
8                   for( t2=3; t2<=5; ++t2 ) {
9                       printf("\nm1=%d m2=%d t1=%d t2=%d\n",m1,m2,t1,t2);
10                      tbb::empty_task* root =
11                          new( tbb::task::allocate_root() ) tbb::empty_task;
12                      root->set_ref_count(3);
13                      Combine1* combine1 = new( root->allocate_child() ) Combine1;
14                      combine1->set_ref_count(2);
15                      Combine2* combine2 = new( root->allocate_child() ) Combine2;
16                      combine2->set_ref_count(2);
17                      Filterb* filterb = new( combine1->allocate_child() ) Filterb;
18                      filterb->dummy =
19                          new( combine2->allocate_child() ) tbb::empty_task;
20                      filterb->spawn( *filterb );
```

```
21                        Transform2* transform2 =
22                            new( combine1->allocate_child( ) ) Transform2;
23                        combine1->spawn( *transform2 );
24                        Warp1* warp1 =
25                            new( combine2->allocate_child( ) ) Warp1;
26                        combine2->spawn( *warp1 );
27                        root->wait_for_all( );
28                        root->destroy(*root);
29                    }
30                }
31            }
32        }
33 }
```

The main program loops with a variety of timing delays that exist only to demonstrate a variety of timings among the pipeline stages (tasks). The main program has the job of creating the tasks shown in Figure 11-18. Therefore, main creates the tasks TRANSFORM 2, FILTER B, WARP 1, COMBINE 1, and COMBINE 2. The FILTER B task is informed about DUMMY inside it so that it can use that task to signal COMBINE 2. The tasks TRANSFORM 2, FILTER B, and WARP 1 are spawned (started) at this point.

If we had implemented the original design as shown in Figure 11-16, we would have created six more tasks (TRANSFORM 1, FILTER A, SPECKLE 1, SKEW 1, TRANSFORM 3, and FILTER B), and we would have started the leftmost three tasks (TRANSFORM 1, SPECKLE 1, and TRANSFORM 3) instead of TRANSFORM 2, FILTER B, and WARP 1. FILTER B gets started by the task to the left (SKEW 1), and it has to do the same trick of using DUMMY to signal COMBINE 2.

The trick is that Filterb::execute does the spawning of DUMMY just before it exits, so logically, the graph behaves *as though* FILTER B has both COMBINE 1 and COMBINE 2 waiting on it.

This is a classic example of choosing to utilize implicit synchronization instead of using explicit synchronization such as a lock. This is a fundamental mindset to cultivate. If we had used native threads, COMBINE 1 and COMBINE 2 would have to block on some synchronization event (lock) that FILTER B has to signal when it is done. With Threading Building Blocks, the DUMMY task eliminates the need to use a lock to synchronize.

Aha! Implicit synchronization is better than using locks. You want to develop a mindset to think about using implicit synchronization and avoiding locks.

The output is very long. Table 11-2 shows some of it. The program was run on a dual-core system running Windows Vista and using Intel Threading Building Blocks 1.1 for Windows. The program was run with input arguments of 1 and 2 to set the number of threads for the purposes of illustration. With only one thread, you can see there is no parallelism.

Table 11-2. Some of the output from the TwoMouths pattern example

Only one thread run (run on a two-core system)	Run with two threads (run on a two-core system)
. . .	. . .

```
m1=3 m2=3 t1=4 t2=5          m1=3 m2=3 t1=4 t2=5
  Warp1: i=0                   Filterb: i=0
  Warp1: i=1                   Warp1: i=0
  Warp1: i=2                   Filterb: i=1
  Warp1: i=3                   Warp1: i=1
  Warp1: i=4                   Filterb: i=2
  Transform2: i=0              Warp1: i=2
  Transform2: i=1              Filterb: i=3
  Transform2: i=2              Warp1: i=3
  Transform2: i=3              Transform2: i=0
  Filterb: i=0                 Warp1: i=4
  Filterb: i=1                 Combine2: i=0
  Filterb: i=2                 Transform2: i=1
  Filterb: i=3                 Combine2: i=1
  Combine2: i=0                Transform2: i=2
  Combine2: i=1                Combine2: i=2
  Combine2: i=2                Transform2: i=3
  Combine1: i=0                Combine1: i=0
  Combine1: i=1                Combine1: i=1
  Combine1: i=2                Combine1: i=2

m1=3 m2=3 t1=5 t2=3          m1=3 m2=3 t1=5 t2=3
  Warp1: i=0                   Warp1: i=0
  Warp1: i=1                   Transform2: i=0
  Warp1: i=2                   Transform2: i=1
  Transform2: i=0             Warp1: i=1
  Transform2: i=1             Transform2: i=2
  Transform2: i=2             Warp1: i=2
  Transform2: i=3             Transform2: i=3
  Transform2: i=4            Filterb: i=0
  Filterb: i=0                Transform2: i=4
  Filterb: i=1                Filterb: i=1
  Filterb: i=2                Filterb: i=2
  Filterb: i=3                Filterb: i=3
  Combine2: i=0               Combine1: i=0
  Combine2: i=1               Combine2: i=0
  Combine2: i=2               Combine2: i=1
  Combine1: i=0               Combine1: i=1
  Combine1: i=1               Combine2: i=2
  Combine1: i=2               Combine1: i=2
```

. . .   . . .

Packet Processing Pipeline

This example illustrates how you can use pipelines (Chapter 4) and a concurrent hash map (Chapter 5) to implement packet processing such as you might find in a router.

Packet processing is an ideal application for Threading Building Blocks. Packet processing is often done on special devices as well as on computer systems, so this is a good example of how Threading Building Blocks can help embedded designs that take advantage of multi-core processors.

Devices on the Internet communicate using packets of information. Each packet is like a postcard; it has an address to *send to* and a *return address* plus a *message*. On the way from the sender to the receiver, it passes through switches and routers that direct traffic and do other processing on the packets. Packet processing is not unlike mail processing; the router must receive a packet on a connection and send it out to the appropriate connections. It also provides a service called network address translation (NAT), which allows the outside world to communicate with a collection of computers and devices through one address without even knowing it is not a single computer at that one address. This is not unlike the postcard that arrives addressed to an apartment building without the number that indicates the apartment to which to deliver it. The postal delivery person will use other clues, such as the name on the postcard, to determine where it should be delivered.

Parallel Programming for an Internet Device

Devices that connect the worldwide network of unique addressed devices to local networks are known as *devices at the edge* of the network. More generally, you can create subnetworks yourself that have devices on their edges to hook to other subnetworks. Devices at the edge of the network perform sophisticated processing in order to handle the packets coming in over the different subnetworks they aggregate. Examples of edge devices are appliances at the frontend of a data center that perform functions such as XML acceleration, load balancing, or other content processing, as well as devices at the entry point of an enterprise that perform security-related functions such as firewalls, intrusion detection, and virus checking. Designing network-edge software is very complex today and consumes nontrivial processing power. With the advent of multiple-core processors, we can address the processing needed with a hybrid model of both parallel packet processing and pipelined packet processing. We illustrate the latter with a Threading Building Blocks example. For the sake of the example, we will assume a small network (Figure 11-19) such as you might find in a home or small business, and we will have only special processing for file transfer protocol (FTP) packets. This simplified example will allow us to discuss all the key points of how to use Threading Building Blocks, and you can extend it to process many more types of packets.

The packet processing applications on network-edge devices exhibit some common characteristics. They usually fit into a regular flow of data pattern (Figure 2-16). They typically access a lot of memory, including state information that exhibits temporal locality (fits in caches well). These applications exhibit numerous forms of parallelism including packet-level, connection-level, and service-level parallelism. Maximizing the performance of such applications requires programmable parallel hardware. The trend toward processors with multiple cores aligns well with these needs.

Worldwide and Local IP Addresses

At one time, the rapid growth of Internet addressable devices was of grave concern because we were on pace to run out of the unique addresses required for every computer in the world to be connected to each other. Addresses were allocated in blocks and you would, as an individual, usually pay to receive a single number from your Internet service provider. Organizations such as businesses obtained blocks of addresses, but with rapid growth, even they faced running out of numbers. Businesses also worried about the security of giving every computer or device within their company a unique address that outsiders could learn.

Most Internet addressing is done with a 4-byte Internet Protocol (IP) address that is written as a set of four 8-bit numbers separated by dots. An example address is 198.175.96.33. In order to allow organizations and individuals to run local networks with addresses that are never assigned unique numbers, three blocks of addresses have been reserved for local area network (LAN) usage only. One block, 10.x.x.x, has only 8 bits as a prefix; the other 24 bits are available for use internally in the local network, thereby allowing a local network using this range to have more than 16 million devices. Another block, 172.16.x.x through 172.31.x.x, has 12 bits of prefix. And the third block, 192.168.x.x, is known as the 16-bit prefix block and can handle networks of more than 65,000 unique addresses for the local network. Addresses such as 10.10.20.20, 172.19.3.2, and 192.168.0.1 are examples of numbers that can be used only locally and never as a unique worldwide address. Large organizations are free to create local networks hooked to local networks, so there is really no limit on how many devices can be given addresses.

Local networks require a method to talk with the worldwide network, which is achieved using network address translation (NAT). NAT is a simple concept: hook many local devices to the world using a single address owned by a special routing device (*router*). Outgoing requests are rewritten with instructions to respond to the one single address. Responses coming to the router from outside the local network are routed to the appropriate device inside the local network. The example will show specific cases of NAT.

Threading Building Blocks supports functional simulation because network-edge devices have strict performance requirements. For efficient packet processing, some primary goals are as follows:

- Nearly all the time, task switching should be fast. A packet processor cannot afford to fall behind.

- You should be able to guarantee that no tasks are starved. A packet must never get stalled indefinitely.

Threading Building Blocks should be able to handle programming most packet processing applications. Linear pipelines, such as the Threading Building Blocks pipeline class, are most common, yet packet processing can occasionally have branches, multicasts, and loopbacks.

Here are some of the topics we will cover in our discussion of the local network router:

Local network router example
What are some common functions and how is it structured? Up front, it must be said that this example is the simplest one possible to demonstrate the concept of using the Threading Building Blocks pipeline class.

Simple stages of a local network router
Including NAT, Application Layer Gateway (ALG), and packet forwarding.

Implementation
Points out how the functions described have been implemented in Threading Building Blocks.

Example filter code
The key parts of the example are included here. You can download the complete example from the web site for this book.

Local Network Router Example

In looking for an example that is simple enough to cover in a few pages, is realistic in functionality, and can be completed with a Threading Building Blocks pipeline, a local network router came to mind. Figure 11-19 shows how a local network router used for a home is structured. (The home could be a business as well.) Here are the key points:

- IP addresses within the local network, inside the home, are private. Packets leaving the local network *must* be modified as they go through the router.

- The local network for the home has one IP address known outside the home. Packets coming back from the Internet are sent to this address. The real destination must be determined by the router and the packet must be forwarded to the appropriate home device.

- Some application protocols pass address or port information inside the packet, called the *payload*, on top of the Transmission Control Protocol/Internet Protocol (TCP/IP). This information is used by the application to connect to the right address or port. Hence, for correct operation a router that transparently modifies the TCP/IP port or address information must also modify such information in the payload. In this example, we will only write code that can work with FTP payloads.

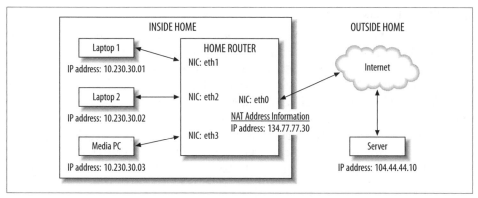

Figure 11-19. Local network (at home) router structural diagram

Pipelined Components for the Local Network Router

Protocol processing is very frequently organized into a pipeline. The main reason is that it simplifies packet processing by layer and by function. It also allows a functional dataflow parallel programming style. Although these layers and functions must be performed serially on a single packet, when executed with a pipeline we find that different packets may be processed in parallel. The pipeline in the example functionally simulates three stages. Let's describe each.

Network address translation (NAT)

Network address translation is a technique wherein IP addresses are mapped from one address realm to another. A typical use of NATs is at the edge of a local network where the addresses within the network are private, unregistered addresses. This flexibility makes networking easier. NAT allows devices on the local network to communicate with end systems on the Internet by transparently routing the packets so that they appear to come from one IP address. A more global benefit of NAT is that it helps stem depletion of IP addresses. Because the addresses inside the home are not advertised, multiple networks could use the same set of addresses without causing any problems. A simple NAT operation would be to map, usually via a table, a private network IP plus port number to a router port number so that outbound packets appear to be sourced from the router's IP with a port that the router has selected. In this way, the router can map reply packets to that port back to the private-side IP and port.

NATs have evolved to support various flavors such as *Bidirectional*, *Twice NAT*, and *Realm Specific IP* that a real NAT implementation would have to support. These are beyond the scope of this example.

Application Layer Gateway (ALG)

ALGs are frequently used with NATs to handle cases where peer addresses or ports are embedded in application-layer payloads. Packets with such payloads require special treatment. The ALG modifies the content of the packet and may adjust the header information to reflect address translations required in a router. In the example, we offer just one well-known special case—namely, the processing of an FTP PORT command. For an active FTP connection, the FTP PORT command from a client on the home network requests the server to send FTP data back to the port specified in the payload of the client's PORT command. Therefore, the ALG needs to correct the IP and port mapping of this basic network address port translation (NAPT).

An ALG should treat several other application considerations—for example, DNA and SIP, where packets carry the addresses for sessions to be established, IPv4/IPv6 translation, or security considerations where end-to-end encryption may encrypt IP addresses or the router may be required to filter for exposed IP addresses.

Packet forwarding

The third stage in this example simply touches on the most basic responsibility of a router: to move packets from one network interface controller (NIC) in the router to another. The example considers the connections from a remote device's IP to NIC to be fixed. When a packet wants to go to a destination IP, a static table is used to determine what the next hop NIC is.

Our example

We make numerous simplifying assumptions in this example implementation for the sake of brevity. Specifically, we do not actually send or receive packets over the network.

We simulate this with a packet trace. That is, we read from an input file representing a simplified packet record containing only the relevant fields of a packet. The fields include values from the IP header, TCP header, and certain application payload information. This allows us to focus on the parts of the application that we want to pipeline. Furthermore, for the application stages themselves, we implement only sufficient functionality to provide insight into the benefits of pipelining.

In terms of NAT, we implement only a simplified version of NAPT. We do not delete mapping entries in the table once a connection has been closed, which a real implementation would do in order to reuse port numbers.

In terms of ALG, we consider only an FTP ALG in this example. Specifically, we look at the PORT command in an active FTP connection wherein the client sends its IP address and port information in the packet payload. We do not update the checksum and other header information that a real implementation would have to modify when the packet payload is modified.

Nevertheless, this example demonstrates how a pipeline class would be used and how it would benefit a programmer creating a real packet processing application.

Figure 11-20 through Figure 11-23 show how this router will need to process packets through with its three stages. The first figure shows the router sending out a packet and remembering the port it has assigned so that when responses come back, as shown in Figure 11-21, it can route them to the appropriate computer on the local network. Figure 11-22 shows the router doing similar processing but also tampering with the payload to complete the address translation.

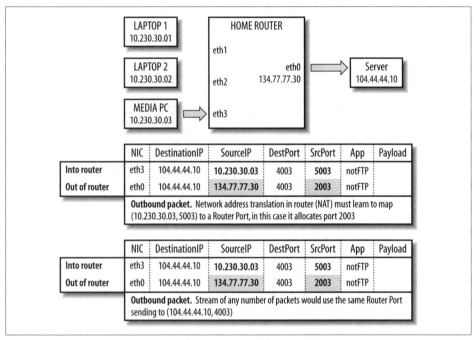

Figure 11-20. Packets from inside the home get NAT and are sent to the server

Implementation

Let's walk through the implementation, including use of a Threading Building Blocks pipeline (Chapter 4), to understand it. We'll start with pipeline creation and execution. Then we will review the synchronized structures for transforming the packets in the trace and storing port and NIC mappings. Finally, we'll discuss the filters.

The Threading Building Blocks pipeline

The three stages described earlier are implemented in a Threading Building Blocks pipeline with five filters. An input filter to simulate packets coming into the pipeline comes first. An output filter has been added at the end to simulate packets going

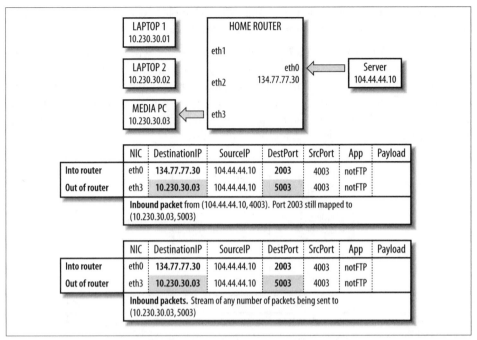

Figure 11-21. The Response requires a NAT lookup to finish delivery

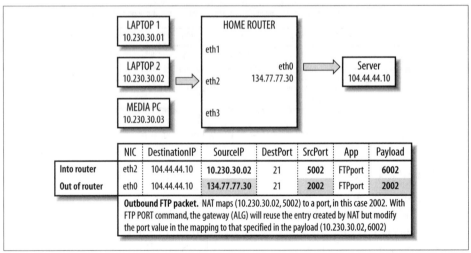

Figure 11-22. FTP port mapping from inside the home to the server

back out through the device. The three packet processing stages between the input and output filters are the network_address_translator filter, application_level_gateway filter, and packet_forwarding filter.

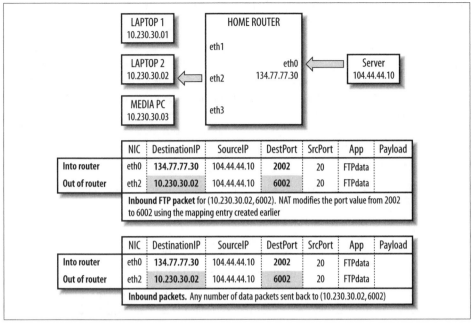

Figure 11-23. Inbound FTP data returned to the proper laptop inside the home

In the main routine, the five pipeline filters are plugged together in a straightforward way:

```
tbb::pipeline pipeline;
// Stage 0: Input Packet
get_next_packet receive_packet (in_file);
pipeline.add_filter (receive_packet);

// Stage 1: Network Address Translator
translator network_address_translator (router_ip, router_nic,
                                        mapped_ports);
pipeline.add_filter (network_address_translator);

// Stage 2: Application Level Gateway
gateway application_level_gateway (router_ip, router_nic,
                                   mapped_ports);
pipeline.add_filter (application_level_gateway);

// Stage 3: Packet Forwarding Stage
forwarding packet_forwarding (router_ip, router_nic,
                              network_config);
pipeline.add_filter (packet_forwarding);

// Stage 4: Output Packet
output_packet send_packet (out_file);
pipeline.add_filter (send_packet);
```

And the pipeline is started on the packet trace:

```
pipeline.run (number_of_live_items);
pipeline.clear ( );
```

For compute-intensive pipelines, the speedup of a pipeline is limited to the number of stages, subject to the proportion of time in the slowest stage. Packet processing pipelines may have I/O stalls waiting for packet transmission delays. Allowing the number of packets in the pipeline, number_of_live_items, to grow above five would allow for frequent interruptions in the input and output stages. In the example, that number is set to 10, but you can experiment with several values. Note that any thread may be processing several packets in the same or different filters.

If you want to experiment with scaling, you should increase the size of the packet trace file (download), which is pretty small right now. You can easily expand the back-and-forth traffic mentioned in Figure 11-21, Figure 11-22, and Figure 11-23 as "Any number of data packets...."

Synchronization with the pipeline item and concurrent hash maps

You synchronize packet information between stages using the Threading Building Blocks pipeline template. Each filter returns a packet_trace instance that is passed to the next stage.

The pipeline template is given a packet trace structure that consists of:

```
typedef struct {
    nic_t packetNic;       // the NIC packet into and out of router
    ip_t packetDestIp;     // destination IP into and out of router
    ip_t packetSrcIp;      // source IP into and out of router
    port_t packetDestPort; // destinationPort paired w/destination IP
    port_t packetSrcPort;  // source Port paired w/source IP
    protocol_t packetProtocol;// packet protocol type
    port_t packetPayloadApp;  // any of the packet worth simulating
} packet_trace;
```

A packet will be transformed, filter by filter, from what would come into the router into what would go out of the router. For example, for an outbound packet, the NAT would change the packetSrcIp to be the IP of the router outgoing_ip. That is how every device in the Ethernet will see the local network. And it will change the packetSrcPort to the router port mapped in its mapped_ports_table.

The other synchronized structures are the data tables in the local network router. The network_table is used to map the IP to the NIC in packet forwarding. It is implemented using a concurrent hash map (Chapter 5).

```
typedef tbb::concurrent_hash_map<ip_t, nic_t, ip_addr_comparator>
                                            network_table;
```

The key data structure for mapping a router port is the mapped_ports_table. The NAPT function for outbound packets is mapping the outbound (Local Device IP, Local Device Port) to a router port, and then reversing that mapping, from a router port to a (Local Device IP, Local Device Port), for inbound packets. Therefore, a good hash key into a concurrent hash map would be a port moving in either direction, represented by a port_t type. The map would return a pointer to an accessor address class we created, which can access an IP address with get_ip_address, or a port number with get_port_number.

```
typedef tbb::concurrent_hash_map<port_t, address*, port_comparator> mapped_ports_
table;
class address {
public:
    virtual bool get_ip_address (mapped_ports_table& /*in*/,
                                 ip_t& /*out*/) = 0;
    virtual bool get_port_number (port_t& /*out*/) = 0;
};
```

A concurrent hash map is used because multiple packets will be flowing through the pipeline simultaneously. They may have to add a new port mapping if the local device wants to use another port associated with its IP. Port mappings can change in both the NAT and ALG stages.

Filter Classes

The source code for the setup, hash table, and filters is presented here for you to study. You can download the complete source code (about 400 lines) from *http://www.threadingbuildingblocks.org/book*. Look for errata and notes at this web site as well.

The *includes* and *constants* sections (Example 11-40) are pretty straightforward. Some constant values are also read from the packet trace file.

Example 11-40. Filter classes setup

```
#include <iostream>
#include <sstream>
#include <fstream>
#include <string>
#include "tbb\task_scheduler_init.h"
#include "tbb\pipeline.h"
#include "tbb\concurrent_hash_map.h"
#include "tbb\atomic.h"
#include "tbb\pipeline.h"

using namespace std;
// All packet attributes stored as std::strings (for simplicity)
typedef string nic_t, ip_t, port_t, app_t, protocol_t;

// Constants
static const string empty = "";
static const port_t FTPcmdPort  = "21";
static const port_t FTPdataPort = "20";
```

Example 11-40. Filter classes setup (continued)

```
// Request contains FTP command
static const protocol_t IPwithFTP = "IPwithFTP";

// Default filenames
static const char* in_file_name   = "input.txt";
static const char* out_file_name  = "output.txt";

// Marker for packets stream
static const string end_of_map    = "PacketTrace";
```

Example 11-41 shows the concurrent hash map definitions we need. Hash maps are used for storing both router port to (Local Device IP, Local Device Port) mapping, mapped_ports_table, and Local Device IP to Router NIC mapping, network_table. string_comparator is the hash compare type in both cases. The network_table is an easy-to-understand example of how to use a hash map. For the port mapping, outbound the lookup has to return a router port and inbound it has to return a (Local Device IP, Local Device Port). Hence, it is a bit complex to follow.

Example 11-41. Concurrent hash map for port mapping

```
// Hash compare type for tbb::concurrent_hash_map
class string_comparator {
public:
    static size_t hash( const string& x ) {
        size_t h = 0;
        for( const char* s = x.c_str(); *s; s++ )
            h = (h*17)^*s;
        return h;
    }
    static bool equal( const string& x, const string& y ) {
        return x==y;
    }
};

class address;
typedef string_comparator port_comparator, ip_addr_comparator;
// Hash map key is a port_t. This can be either router assigned port number or local
device port number
// If key is a router port number, then the value is the local device assigned port;
// If key is an local device port number, then the value is a pair = (IP, router port
number).
// The router port numbers are duplicated to avoid linear search at the NAT stage
typedef tbb::concurrent_hash_map<port_t, address*, port_comparator> mapped_ports_table;
// Network configuration table: IP->NIC
typedef tbb::concurrent_hash_map<ip_t, nic_t, ip_addr_comparator> network_table;

// This is an interface class for value type of mapped_ports_table: PORT->ADDRESS*
// where ADDRESS points to either port_number (local device port number) or
// to ip_address (associated with the local device port number)
```

Example 11-41. Concurrent hash map for port mapping (continued)

```
class address {
public:
    virtual bool get_ip_address (mapped_ports_table& /*in*/, ip_t& /*out*/) = 0;
    virtual bool get_port_number (port_t& /*out*/) = 0;
};

// If mapped_ports_table is port_number, then router mapped port number is known
// (stored in the object), IP address can be found in the table via local device port
class port_number : public address {
public:
    port_t port;
    port_number (port_t& _port) : port(_port) {}
    bool get_ip_address (mapped_ports_table& mapped_ports, ip_t& addr) {
        mapped_ports_table::const_accessor a;
        if (mapped_ports.find (a, port)) {
            return a->second->get_ip_address (mapped_ports, addr);
        }
        return false;
    }
    bool get_port_number (port_t& p) { p = port; return true; }
};

// if mapped_ports_table is ip_address,
// then the router mapped port and associated IP
// address are known (stored in the object)
class ip_address : public address {
public:
    ip_t ip;
    port_t router_port;
    ip_address (ip_t& _ip, port_t& _router_port) : ip(_ip), router_port(_router_port) {}
    bool get_ip_address (mapped_ports_table& mapped_ports /*in*/, ip_t& addr /*out*/) {
        addr = ip;
        return true;
    }
    bool get_port_number (port_t& p) { p = router_port; return true; }
};
```

Each packet trace record read from the input file and written to the output file is a packet_trace instance. Packet trace streaming operations define this in Example 11-42.

Example 11-42. Packet attributes and I/O

```
// Packet attributes
typedef struct {
    nic_t packetNic;
    ip_t packetDestIp;
    ip_t packetSrcIp;
    port_t packetDestPort;
    port_t packetSrcPort;
    protocol_t packetProtocol;
    port_t packetPayloadApp;
} packet_trace;
```

Example 11-42. Packet attributes and I/O (continued)

```
//Input packet
istream& operator>> (istream &s, packet_trace& a)
{
    // No input data verification for simplicity
    s >> a.packetNic >> a.packetDestIp >> a.packetSrcIp >>
    a.packetDestPort >> a.packetSrcPort >> a.packetProtocol;
    if (a.packetProtocol == IPwithFTP)
        s >> a.packetPayloadApp;
    else
        a.packetPayloadApp = empty;
    return s;
}

// Output packet
ostream& operator<< (ostream &s, packet_trace& a) {
    return s << a.packetNic << " " << a.packetDestIp << " " <<
    a.packetSrcIp << " " << a.packetDestPort << " " <<
    a.packetSrcPort << " " << a.packetProtocol << " " <<
    a.packetPayloadApp << endl;
}
```

Initialization is shown in Example 11-43. The main program arguments are the names of the input and output files. Initialization mostly loads the network_table.

Example 11-43. Initialization for the packet processing example

```
void get_args (int argc, char* argv[]) {
    // Parse command line
    switch (argc) {
        case 3:  out_file_name = argv[2];
        case 2:  in_file_name = argv[1]; break;
        case 1:  break;
        default: cerr << "Usage:\trouter input-file output-file"
                        << endl;
    };
    cerr << "Router: input file - " << in_file_name
        << ", output file - " << out_file_name << endl;
}

bool init_home_router (ip_t& outgoing_ip,
                       nic_t& outgoing_nic,
                       network_table& network_config,
                       ifstream& in_file)
{
    // Router outgoing IP and NIC: first line of input file
    if (!in_file.eof()) in_file >> outgoing_nic >> outgoing_ip;
    else return false;

    // Initialize network configuration map: IP => NIC
    string nic, ip;
    network_table::accessor a;
    while (!in_file.eof()) {
        in_file >> nic;
```

Example 11-43. Initialization for the packet processing example (continued)

```
        if (nic == end_of_map) break;
        in_file >> ip;
        network_config.insert (a, ip);
        a->second = nic;
    }
    return true;
}
```

Class get_next_packet : public tbb::filter

The filter class get_next_packet (Example 11-44) reads each packet from a packet trace in the input file.

Example 11-44. Filter to get the next packet

```
class get_next_packet : public tbb::filter {
    istream& in_file;
public:
    get_next_packet (ifstream& file) : in_file (file),
                    filter (true) {}
    void* operator( ) (void*) {
        packet_trace* packet = new packet_trace ( );
        in_file >> *packet;
        if (packet->packetNic == empty) {
            delete packet;
            return NULL;
        }
        return packet;
    }
};
```

Class output_packet : public tbb::filter

The filter class output_packet (Example 11-45) writes each packet from a packet structure to the output file.

Example 11-45. Filter to output a packet

```
class output_packet : public tbb::filter {
    ostream& out_file;
public:
    output_packet (ofstream& file) : out_file (file), filter (true) {}
    void* operator( ) (void* item) {
        packet_trace* packet = static_cast<packet_trace*> (item);
        out_file << *packet;
        delete packet;
        return NULL;
    }
};
```

Class translator : public tbb::filter

The filter class translator (Example 11-46) performs the NAT function. In this simple example, it separates inbound packets from outbound packets. For outbound
packets, it maps the local device (IP,Port) to the router port by hashing into the
mapped_ports_table, creating a mapping if one is needed. It also inserts the router's
IP into the packet source IP slot in case the destination will send a packet back. For
inbound packets, it does the reverse by looking up the router port to local device
(IP,Port).

Example 11-46. Filter that does the actual NAT

```
class translator : public tbb::filter {
    const ip_t outgoing_ip;
    const nic_t outgoing_nic;
    // port => address, where port={router mapped port | home device port}
    // and address = {home device port | pair(IP, router mapped port)}
    mapped_ports_table& mapped_ports;
    static tbb::atomic<int> spare_port; // Previous spare port number

public:
    translator (ip_t& _outgoing_ip, nic_t& _outgoing_nic,
                mapped_ports_table& _mapped_ports) :
                outgoing_ip(_outgoing_ip), outgoing_nic(_outgoing_nic),
                mapped_ports(_mapped_ports), filter (true /* is_serial*/) { spare_port =
2002; }
    void* operator() (void* item) {
        packet_trace* packet = static_cast<packet_trace*> (item);
        if (packet->packetNic == outgoing_nic) {
            // this is an external incoming packet
            ip_t app_ip;
            port_t app_port;
            if (get_port_mapping (packet->packetDestPort,
                                  app_ip, app_port)) {
                packet->packetDestIp   = app_ip;
                packet->packetDestPort = app_port;
            }
            else
                cerr << "Packet destination unknown" << endl;
        }
        else {
            // this is an internal outgoing packet
            port_t mappedPort;
            if (! get_router_port (mappedPort, packet->packetSrcIp,
                                   packet->packetSrcPort)) {
                mappedPort = add_new_mapping (packet->packetSrcIp,
                                              packet->packetSrcPort,
                                              get_new_port());
            }
            packet->packetSrcPort = mappedPort;
        }

        return packet;
    }
```

Example 11-46. Filter that does the actual NAT (continued)

```
    // IP, home device port <= router mapped port
    bool get_port_mapping (port_t& router_port /*in*/,
                           ip_t& ip  /*out*/, port_t& app_port /*out*/)
    {
        mapped_ports_table::/*const_*/accessor a;
        if (mapped_ports.find (a, router_port))
        {
            address* addr = a->second;
            if (! addr->get_port_number (app_port)) return false;
            a.release();

            return addr->get_ip_address (mapped_ports, ip);
        }
        return false;
    }
    // Router mapped port <= home device assigned port, IP
    bool get_router_port (port_t& router_port /*out*/,
                          ip_t& ip  /*in*/, port_t& app_port /*in*/)
    {
        mapped_ports_table::/*const_*/accessor a;
        if (mapped_ports.find (a, app_port))
        {
            address* addr = a->second;
            return addr->get_port_number (router_port);
        }
        return false;
    }

    // Allocates next spare port
    port_t get_new_port () {
        int port = ++spare_port; // this is an atomic operation
        stringstream s;
        s << port;
        return s.str ();
    }

    port_t& add_new_mapping (ip_t& ip, port_t& port, port_t& new_port) {
        mapped_ports_table::accessor a; // acquires writer lock
        if (mapped_ports.insert (a, new_port)) {
            port_number* mapped_port = new port_number (port);
            a->second = mapped_port;
            if (mapped_ports.insert (a, port)) {
                ip_address*  addr = new ip_address (ip, new_port);
                a->second = addr;
            }
        }
        return new_port;
    }
};

tbb::atomic<int> translator::spare_port;
```

Class gateway : public tbb::filter

The filter class gateway (Example 11-47), in this simple example, only checks for FTP applications. If it is an FTP command, it looks at the application payload that would contain a command port somewhere. (In this packet trace input, all the rest of the packet has been thrown away.) The ALG modifies the mapped_ports_table to anticipate receiving FTP packets for this command port.

Example 11-47. Filter to check for specific (FTP) applications

```
class gateway : public tbb::filter {
    const ip_t outgoing_ip;
    const nic_t outgoing_nic;
    // port => address,
    // where port={router mapped port | home device port}
    // and
    // address = {home device port | pair(IP, router mapped port)}
    mapped_ports_table& mapped_ports;
public:
    gateway    (ip_t& _outgoing_ip, nic_t& _outgoing_nic,
            mapped_ports_table& _mapped_ports) :
            outgoing_ip(_outgoing_ip), outgoing_nic(_outgoing_nic),
            mapped_ports(_mapped_ports),
                        filter (true /* is_serial*/) {  }

    void* operator() (void* item) {
        packet_trace* packet = static_cast<packet_trace*> (item);
        if (packet->packetDestPort == FTPcmdPort) {
            // outbound packet sends FTP command
            // packetPayloadApp contains data port -
            // save it in ports table
            add_new_mapping (packet->packetSrcIp,
                            packet->packetPayloadApp,
                            packet->packetSrcPort);
            packet->packetSrcIp = outgoing_ip;
            packet->packetPayloadApp = packet->packetSrcPort;
        }
        return packet;
    }
    port_t& add_new_mapping (ip_t& ip, port_t& port,
                            port_t& new_port) {
        port_number* mapped_port = new port_number (port);
        ip_address*  addr = new ip_address (ip, new_port);
        mapped_ports_table::accessor a; // acquires writer lock
        if (! mapped_ports.find (a, new_port))
            mapped_ports.insert (a, new_port);
        else
            delete a->second;
        // The port has already been mapped at the NAT stage
        // Re-map the port to the one specified by packet->PayloadApp
        a->second = mapped_port;
        mapped_ports.insert (a, port);
```

Example 11-47. Filter to check for specific (FTP) applications (continued)

```
        a->second = addr;
        return new_port;
    }
};
```

Class forwarding : public tbb::filter

The filter class forwarding (Example 11-48) performs a very simple packet forwarding operation. If the packet is inbound, it uses the network_table to select a NIC.
Outbound packets can go to only one place, which is the NIC connected to the outbound Ethernet link. (In the NIC IP bindings in the input file, we made the simplifying assumption that the first pair was the outward link.) See Example 11-49 for the
packet processing main program.

Example 11-48. Forwarding filter

```
class forwarding : public tbb::filter {
    const ip_t outgoing_ip;
    const nic_t outgoing_nic;
    network_table& network_config;
public:
    forwarding (ip_t& _outgoing_ip, nic_t& _outgoing_nic,
                network_table& _network_config) :
            outgoing_ip(_outgoing_ip), outgoing_nic(_outgoing_nic),
            network_config(_network_config),
                            filter (false /* is_serial*/) {  }

    void* operator() (void* item) {
        packet_trace* packet = static_cast<packet_trace*> (item);
        if (packet->packetNic == outgoing_nic) {
            // packet is inbound, so translate it to the target Mac
            nic_t nextNic;
            if (find_next_hop (packet->packetDestIp, nextNic))
                packet->packetNic = nextNic;
            else
                cerr << "No next hop found" << endl;
        }
        else {
            // packet is outbound, only one place it can go
            packet->packetSrcIp = outgoing_ip;
            packet->packetNic = outgoing_nic;
        }
        return packet;
    }

    bool find_next_hop (ip_t& ip, nic_t& nic) {
        network_table::const_accessor a; // acquires reader lock
        if (network_config.find (a, ip)) {
            nic = a->second;
            return true;
```

Example 11-48. Forwarding filter (continued)

```
        }
        return false;
    }
};
```

Example 11-49. Packet processing main program

```
int main (int argc, char** argv)
{
    mapped_ports_table mapped_ports; // Router assigned ports
    network_table network_config; // Network configuration: IP => NIC

    ip_t router_ip;        // Router outgoing IP
    nic_t router_nic;      // Router outgoing NIC
    const size_t number_of_live_items = 10; // Pipeline's throughput

    // Parse command-line arguments
    get_args (argc, argv);

    // Open file streams
    ifstream in_file (in_file_name);
    if (!in_file) {
        cerr << "Cannot open input file " << in_file_name << endl;
        exit (1);
    }
    ofstream out_file (out_file_name);
    if (!out_file) {
        cerr << "Cannot open output file " << out_file_name << endl;
        exit (1);
    }

    // Initialize home router: build network configuration table
    // and read outgoing IP and NIC from input file
    if (! init_home_router (router_ip, router_nic,
                            network_config, in_file)) exit (1);

    // Create home router instance
    //home_router router (port_map (port_table),
    //                    network_map (net_map),
    //                    router_nic, router_ip);

    // Initialize Threading Building Blocks
    tbb::task_scheduler_init tbb_init;

    // Create Threading Building Blocks pipeline
    tbb::pipeline pipeline;

    // Stage 0: Input Packet
    get_next_packet receive_packet (in_file);
    pipeline.add_filter (receive_packet);
```

Example 11-49. Packet processing main program (continued)

```
    // Stage 1: Network Address Translator
    translator network_address_translator (router_ip, router_nic,
                                            mapped_ports);
    pipeline.add_filter (network_address_translator);

    // Stage 2: Application Level Gateway
    gateway application_level_gateway (router_ip, router_nic,
                                       mapped_ports);
    pipeline.add_filter (application_level_gateway);

    // Stage 3: Packet Forwarding Stage
    forwarding packet_forwarding (router_ip, router_nic,
                                  network_config);
    pipeline.add_filter (packet_forwarding);

    // Stage 4: Output Packet
    output_packet send_packet (out_file);
    pipeline.add_filter (send_packet);

    cerr << "Starting packets processing..." << endl;
    pipeline.run (number_of_live_items);
    pipeline.clear ();
    cerr << "All packets are processed. Exiting..." << endl;

    return 0;
}
```

Additional reading

- Srisuresh, P., and M. Holdrege (1999). IP Network Address Translator (NAT) Terminology and Considerations, *http://www.ietf.org/rfc/rfc2663.txt?number=2663*.

Memory Allocation

There are two examples for memory allocation. The first is for replacing new and delete. The second is one for C programmers with notes about replacing malloc, calloc, realloc, and free.

Replacing new and delete

Example 11-50 shows a method to replace new and delete. As described in Chapter 6, all versions of new and delete must be replaced at once, which amounts to four versions of new and four versions of delete. It is necessary to link with the scalable memory library (see Chapter 6).

Please note that you do not have to initialize the task scheduler to be able to use the memory allocator. We do initialize it in this example because it uses parallel_for in order to demonstrate the use of memory allocation and deallocation in multiple tasks. Similarly, the only header file that is required for the memory allocator is *tbb/scalable_allocator.h*.

There are four basic signatures for new and delete: a set for individual objects, and a set for arrays of objects. If memory cannot be allocated, new calls the new handler function if set, or it throws the std::bad_alloc( ) exception. This example chooses to ignore any new handler because there are thread-safety issues (see the sidebar "Thread-Safety Issues in Implementing new"), and it always throws std::bad_alloc( ). The variation of the basic signature includes the additional parameter const std:: nothrow_t& that means that this operator will not throw an exception but will return NULL if the allocation fails. These four non-throwing exception operators can be used for C runtime libraries. See Example 11-51 for a driver program that also demonstrates the replacement of new and delete.

Example 11-50. Replacement of new and delete functions, demonstration

```
#include "tbb\task_scheduler_init.h"
#include "tbb\blocked_range.h"
#include "tbb\parallel_for.h"
#include "tbb\scalable_allocator.h"

// No retry loop because we assume that scalable_malloc does
// all it takes to allocate the memory, so calling it repeatedly
// will not improve the situation at all
//
// No use of std::new_handler because it cannot be done in portable
// and thread-safe way (see sidebar)
//
// We throw std::bad_alloc( ) when scalable_malloc returns NULL
//(we return NULL if it is a no-throw implementation)

void* operator new (size_t size) throw (std::bad_alloc)
{
    if (size == 0) size = 1;
    if (void* ptr = scalable_malloc (size))
        return ptr;
    throw std::bad_alloc ( );
}

void* operator new[] (size_t size) throw (std::bad_alloc)
{
    return operator new (size);
}

void* operator new (size_t size, const std::nothrow_t&) throw ( )
{
    if (size == 0) size = 1;
    if (void* ptr = scalable_malloc (size))
        return ptr;
    return NULL;
}
```

Example 11-50. Replacement of new and delete functions, demonstration (continued)

```
void* operator new[] (size_t size, const std::nothrow_t&) throw ()
{
    return operator new (size, std::nothrow);
}

void operator delete (void* ptr) throw ()
{
    if (ptr != 0) scalable_free (ptr);
}

void operator delete[] (void* ptr) throw ()
{
    operator delete (ptr);
}

void operator delete (void* ptr, const std::nothrow_t&) throw ()
{
    if (ptr != 0) scalable_free (ptr);
}

void operator delete[] (void* ptr, const std::nothrow_t&) throw ()
{
    operator delete (ptr, std::nothrow);
}
```

Example 11-51. Driver program to demonstrate replacement of new and delete

```
class do_for {
    const size_t chunk;
public:
    do_for (size_t _chunk): chunk (_chunk) {}
    void operator() (tbb::blocked_range<int> &r) const {
        for (int i = r.begin(); i != r.end(); ++i) {
            // scalable_malloc will be called to allocate the memory
            // for this array of int's
            int *p = new int [chunk];
            // scalable_free will be called to deallocate the memory
            // for this array of int's
            delete[] p;
        }

    }
};

int main (int argc, char** argv)
{
    const size_t size = 1000;
    const size_t chunk = 10;
    const size_t grain_size = 200;
    // Initialize TBB
    tbb::task_scheduler_init tbb_init;
```

Example 11-51. Driver program to demonstrate replacement of new and delete (continued)

```
    // scalable_malloc will be called to allocate the memory
    //  for this array of int's
    int *p = new int[size];

    tbb::parallel_for (tbb::blocked_range<int> (0, size, grain_size),
                       do_for (chunk));

    return 0;
}
```

Replacing malloc, calloc, realloc, and free

Four simple interfaces that provide equivalent functionality to malloc, free, realloc, and calloc exist:

```
#include "tbb/scalable_allocator.h"
void * scalable_malloc (size_t size);
void   scalable_free (void* ptr);
void * scalable_realloc (void* ptr, size_t size);
void * scalable_calloc (size_t nobj, size_t size);
```

These can be used to replace the C language malloc, free, realloc, and calloc memory functions by calling them instead. In general, that is the safest and easiest choice.

> You do not want to make malloc a call to scalable_allocator because scalable_malloc(n) returns a pointer with sufficient alignment for any type, whereas scalable_allocator<char>( ).allocate(n) is guaranteed only to return a pointer with sufficient alignment for type char.

Be sure that memory from scalable_malloc is freed using scalable_free, and that memory from malloc is freed using free. Mixing these up can have results which are difficult to debug. Therefore, Threading Building Blocks does not attempt to replace malloc, free, realloc, and calloc for you. If you are diligent and make sure you are not mixing malloc with free and scalable_malloc with scalable_free (including if you use a module compiled to use the standard malloc to obtain objects you later free), you can also replace the definitions using extern statements and macros. The code to do this is in Example 11-52.

Example 11-52. Replacing malloc, calloc, realloc, and free

```
extern "C" void * scalable_malloc(size_t size);
extern "C" void   scalable_free(void* object);
extern "C" void * scalable_realloc(void* ptr, size_t size);
extern "C" void * scalable_calloc(size_t nobj, size_t size);
#define calloc  scalable_calloc
#define malloc  scalable_malloc
#define realloc scalable_realloc
#define free    scalable_free
```

In some cases, scalable_malloc and scalable_free make calls to malloc and free, so replacing them by linking in routines with these names that in turn call the scalable allocator would cause a big problem. This may change in a future implementation, but for now you should not redefine malloc or free in a way which would have malloc or free call the scalable allocator.

Thread-Safety Issues in Implementing new

The implementation for the new operator described in the C++ standard does not guarantee thread safety. A simple implementation could look like Example 11-53.

Lines 12 and 13 are troubling because the only way to get the address of the current handler is via line 12, which also sets it to zero, and that can affect other threads. Line 13 has the potential to be setting a new handler to an address that was obtained—with poor timing—based on another thread executing line 10 at the wrong time.

We could try to force lines 12 and 13 to be indivisible by using a lock. The use of a lock around lines 12 and 13 would help keep this function from clobbering another one, but it would do nothing to protect it from other calls to these routines that don't have locks around them.

There seems to be no portable solution here. We choose just to throw bad_alloc in Example 11-50 and avoid the problem, but potentially this will not create the behavior your program expects. You should feel free to address this shortcoming as you see fit.

Example 11-53. Example of new which is not thread-safe

```
1  // described in the sidebar
2  void* operator new (size_t size) throw (std::bad_alloc)
3  {
4    if (size == 0) size = 1;
5    // operator tries to allocate memory multiple times
6    //   if the first time fails
7    while (true) {
8      if (void* ptr = scalable_malloc (size))
9        return ptr;  // memory was allocated
10                     //   successfully, return a ponter
11     // if allocation fails then the standard behavior is
12     //to try to call new_handler function
13     std::new_handler cur_new_handler = std::set_new_handler (0);
14     std::set_new_handler (cur_new_handler);
15     // if new_handler function was set (!= 0) then we call it
16     if (cur_new_handler)
17       (*cur_new_handler) ();
18     //(it may be able to resolve the memory issue
19     // so we can repeat the attempt)
20     else
```

Example 11-53. Example of new which is not thread-safe

```
21          throw std::bad_alloc (); // otherwise, we throw exception and
22                                   // leave the loop
23     }
24 }
```

Game Threading Example

This example clearly illustrates how rethinking parallelism can result in a decomposition that is better suited to scaling. This example also emphasizes building your own structures with Threading Building Blocks tailored to your particular specialty. You'll find more information and downloads on the Web for the particular gaming framework used here. For the purposes of this book, we'll focus on the key design decisions and show the code that uses the task scheduler directly.

Games, like many programs, have been threaded for the sake of convenience rather than performance. Specifically, games have often been threaded along function lines and nothing more. In order to fully utilize many cores, this example shows how to thread a game using a functional pipeline with domain decomposition. This example demonstrates several ways to reach the next level of scalability in game architecture. Most threading of games has traditionally focused on functional parallelism and data parallelism. The former is pretty straightforward: one thread for rendering, one thread for physics, and so forth. Data parallelism generally comes in waves with serial interludes, as shown in Figure 11-24.

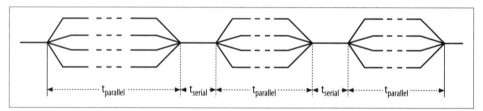

Figure 11-24. Data parallelism with serial section between

In this example, we concern ourselves with rendering stars after determining positions based on physics. We go beyond data parallelism to discuss domain decomposition, which has the structure shown in Figure 11-25.

The principle performance advantage of this structure is that a *group of stars each form a domain task that is treated as a large single task with several data parallel sections,* instead of scheduling each region and then each star separately. The computations take advantage of knowing that several nearby stars are in the same domain to avoid most of the threading synchronization overhead. It has been shown in many supercomputer applications that this *simple* domain decomposition principle helps scalable performance considerably. This is especially true in games where some significant sections are serial and the need to produce many frames-per-second synchronization penalties are paid many times over.

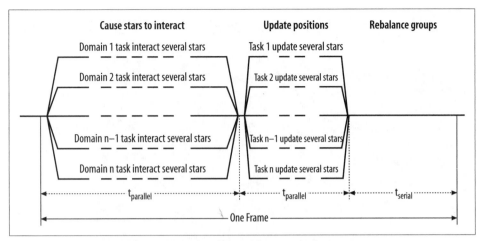

Figure 11-25. Domain decomposition of each frame from example

By developing a simple example game architecture, you can keep the threading architecture design issues simple and clear enough to experiment with, and thus demonstrate the best threading methods for real games.

When you run the example, a window will appear that shows marble-like stars moving around in space under the force of gravity between each of the other stars and a black hole. Figure 11-26 shows a view of the game in progress. By setting the Count of object stars and the simulated computational Load in the fill-ins on the right, you can model the complexity of a simulated k-d tree data structure. At the top of the window, you can see various performance data, such as the frames per second (FPS), the operations performed in Serial mode, and the number of stars in each of the eight object domains: 15 15 09 12 11 11 14 13.

Threading Architecture: Physics + Rendering

This threading architecture splits the data structures of the game, such as the scene graph, into domains, and has threads that walk around the domains in the scene graph.

This version implements compound functional and domain decomposed threading of a game. At the functional level, two things are occurring, each of which represents a greatly simplified game component:

Physics interactions
> Star objects move toward each other and toward a black hole under the force of gravity. They do a gravity interaction and an update-positions phase in each frame. The set of stars is decomposed with the data structures and with Threading Building Blocks tasks into domains.

Rendering
> The scene graph goes into a display list and is displayed.

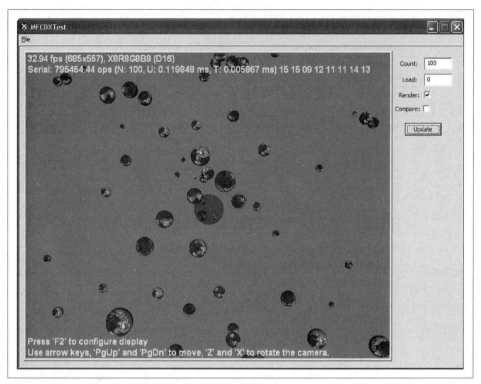

Figure 11-26. Screen capture from example

On two-processor cores, physics and rendering are each given a core resulting in a pipeline on two threads. On four-processor cores, physics has multiple Threading Building Blocks threads that execute different domains.

Overview of Keys to Scalability

The first thing that really matters in achieving scalability is having abundant parallelism in an application. Games do have abundant parallelism. At least 60 times per second, everything could change and need to be recomputed. And with relatively few dependencies, it could all be computed in parallel. So, we describe the general places to look to avoid losing performance. Recalling Amdahl's Law (Chapter 2), the speedup can decrease rapidly with small performance losses.

One thing to be cautious of in highly parallel applications is that to get computations to run in parallel, you may need to add some *extra computations*. You have to measure performance carefully to make sure that any added computation is not slowing down the serial computation, giving extra credit for making the game faster. We will identify added computation shortly.

The second thing that really matters is that the overhead of threading on a multi-core processor stays low. Three dimensions must be reviewed:

- Task setup and scheduling
- Synchronization
- Cache and shared memory efficiency

These three are largely orthogonal issues. You can attack each one. Conversely, improving the program structure strategically, you can improve more than one at a time. For these three areas a qualitative four-point rating of importance is given. To give you an idea, there will be comments on overhead, characterized from *not-good* (1 out of 4 on the overhead scale), to *bad* (2), to *terrible* (3), to *worst* (4). The names may exaggerate a bit to make a point: avoid overhead. These ratings are intended to highlight key overhead decisions. More careful evaluation should be performed after implementing these strategies in your application. Look ahead to Table 11-3 to see what this four-point rating means. We will build up this table in each of the following sections leading to the table.

A Frame Loop

Simply put, we propose that instead of having several data parallel loops in a frame, we have only two: one to move objects and a second to update positions for the next frame.

To compare threaded game architectures, consider data parallelism (Figure 11-24) and domain decomposition (Figure 11-25). The data parallelism structure indicates several parallel loops running in each frame. Operations on pieces of data are distributed in each parallel loop. After each parallel loop is executed, synchronization with the root thread occurs. It performs some serial computation and after several parallel loops, it synchronizes with the rendering thread to allow the next frame to begin. Each of these synchronizations, sometimes called *barriers*, is *terrible* (3 on the scale) because:

- The fastest thread must wait for the slowest thread every loop. There are more chances for load imbalance.
- Synchronization with the root thread is a much more contentious multiple-writer, single-reader (root thread) type.

  How many synchronizations are really needed? Note that for each frame there are at least two synchronizations: at the end of parallel interactions (S_I), and then at the end of the frame when all the object positions are updated for the next frame to start (S_F; F is for *frame*).

- S_I and S_F are sufficient to keep all threads synchronized on each frame.

With domain decomposition, the data is divided among the threads at the beginning into domains of objects. Also, fewer synchronizations are done in one large loop. This is a major improvement in scalability because it avoids all but one of the S_I synchronizations where physics threads have to wait for the slowest physics thread.

There is still an S_F frame synchronization between the rendering thread and the root thread.

In the example code, InteractTask (Example 11-54) and UpdateTask (Example 11-55) are the S_I and S_F phases. The call to spawn_root_and_wait(task) (Chapter 9) causes a barrier at the end of each phase.

Domain Decomposition Data Structure Needs

Data decomposition is a technique frequently used for very scalable computations. There are two points of definition: tasks that communicate most frequently are in the same domain; and the amount of work in a domain is fairly balanced. For scalability, the first point assumes that most communication occurs local to each domain; in other words, local to a single thread and requiring no synchronization. A smaller amount between domains should impact speedup less. Communication cost should include the cache effects of moving a cache line from one core to another, as well as synchronization.

There is a natural tendency to associate the term *domain* with a spatial domain. That may not be the case. It is possible, and demonstrated in the example, that spatially close objects may execute in different threads because the memory is still shared. It is also possible that a domain—a group of objects—may move (by task stealing) to a different thread even though its spatial-domain neighbors stay.

In this example, one root task creates a task for each domain in a k-d tree (see Figure 11-27). It starts by creating the root:

```
*new(tbb::task::allocate_root())
    InteractTask(m_bh, 0, m_bh, m_universeRadius, m_DummyCount);
```

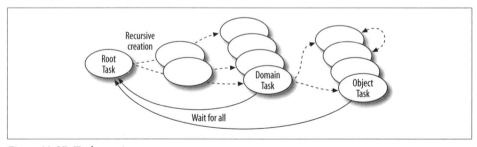

Figure 11-27. Task creation structure

A task tree of all the domain tasks is built recursively descending the k-d tree structure. See InteractTask (Example 11-54) or UpdateTask (Example 11-55). At each level, descendant tasks are built by creating a task_list with a for loop over the children:

```
for (i = 0; i < m_node->getChildCount(); ++i) {
list.push_back(*new(c.allocate_child())
                        UpdateTask(m_node->getChild(i)));
}
```

Because we need to enumerate the number of children that we want to wait for before proceeding, `c.set_ref_count((int)i)` is used for a continuation task:

```
tbb::task& c = *new(allocate_continuation()) tbb::empty_task( );
```

Then the children tasks are put into the ready queue:

```
c.spawn(list);
```

At the leaves of the tree, parallel execution of all the leaf objects (individual stars) in a domain task will be performed in this way. (It would be low overhead in Threading Building Blocks—in other words, only *not-good*—to create these tasks on the same thread on which they execute.) The root task waits for all `InteractTask` tasks to have completed, S_I, before the same task-building process is executed to update each object, S_F.

You can run the code and increase the number of objects to see how speedup increases with more objects. You can use the Intel Thread Profiler to see the threads and how they execute tasks. You can visually see where all the threads wait for the last task to complete. Run the code as normal with one thread per core. Also run it with multiple threads on a single core to see the threading overhead.

In the downloadable example code (not shown in this chapter), we wanted to illustrate how game data structures drive domain decomposition task creation. Above the individual object level, a k-d tree is built. This k-d tree is not very realistic in the example, in that it is only an eight-way decomposition, but it does accurately illustrate the interaction between tree traversal and task creation.

Creating a task graph can range from *bad* to *not-good*. If the root task must create the whole graph, there is greater overhead than if each task creates subtasks in parallel. Threading Building Blocks is designed to support the latter.

Think Tasks, Not Threads

You should think about game architecture in terms of tasks rather than threads. Each task should have several characteristics:

Parallel
> A task is a unit of work that is done repetitively and can be done independently.

Managed
> At the end of task execution, normally it will be recreated as a task in the next frame of work. A leaf- or object-level task should not create other tasks.

Autonomous
> The task should minimize synchronization with tasks on other threads. If a synchronization lock is needed between tasks, the locked region should be as small as possible. At runtime, if the same thread releases and claims a lock, it is *not-good* overhead compared to serial code. Or if one thread releases it and, after some delay (this is an uncontended lock), the next thread claims it, it is also *not-good*. It

is *bad* only if the lock is contended, such as when multiple threads are simultaneously interfering to get the lock. You can use the Intel Thread Profiler to measure this directly, which is how you can go about characterizing your own usage.

In the physics interaction set of tasks, we want to create tasks so that:

- There are several times more tasks than threads to allow task stealing for load balancing. (See the next section, "Load Balancing Versus Task Stealing.")
- Tasks that are close to each other in game space where they might communicate get scheduled on the same thread to maximize the opportunity for cache reuse and local synchronization.

The latter is achieved by using Threading Building Blocks task creation as the data structure is traversed.

In the example code that you can download, there is a frame loop that is not shown in the code in this book. The parallelism and management are as described in the previous subsection. Refer also to Figure 11-25. All objects are moved forward in time, together, by executing a parallel Threading Building Blocks task tree.

We are unable to reach the completely autonomous goal stated earlier because of the requirements of the physics. If the user at the user interface changes the number of objects, or if objects are absorbed by the black hole, the data structures must be changed for the next frame. The k-d tree is locked at each `SceneNode` node to allow simultaneous updates of the tree. `Lock( )` and `Unlock( )` bind to `EnterCriticalSection(&m_criticalSection)` and `LeaveCriticalSection(&m_criticalSection)`, where the `m_criticalSection` is local to the `SceneNode`. Then they drop down to the individual star level to lock and unlock `star private &m_criticalSections`. Now data structure changes are rare enough that this lock granularity does not impact performance.

Load Balancing Versus Task Stealing

Task stealing is *terrible* because it can result in a relatively large synchronization cost. But more importantly, it can move all the data in cache from one core to another. You should minimize the number of tasks stolen. Therefore, there are two levels of work distribution in the example:

- Balancing the amount of work within each domain task
- Task stealing of domain tasks

The work in each domain of data decomposition by a spatial data structure, such as a k-d tree, can be balanced by selecting an algorithm available in the data structure research. But because the work does not have to be perfectly balanced, and rarely is, it is good to create more domain tasks than physical threads. In the example, we demonstrate that Threading Building Blocks can be used to steal domain tasks from one thread to another when the first thread has less work to do in its normal domain.

The example shows that on average, m tasks are stolen. As long as m << n, the data decomposition is sufficiently efficient.

In addition, in the current k-d tree traversal, we assume that the k-d tree is roughly spatially balanced. But objects can move in space from one quadrant to another without moving in the k-d tree. Thus, the tree can become an incorrect k-d tree over time. Moving objects to their proper place in the k-d tree takes extra time and may not be necessary for threading efficiency. In some games, it may be necessary to keep the k-d tree correct for other purposes. So in the example code, if (!(balance_counter % 10)) means that every 10 frames we check when an object has moved to another domain. Then, it is removed from the tree and reinserted.

When you run the code, you can see in the data reported how many objects are currently in each domain. Note that as the serial version runs next to the parallel version, the number of objects in each domain is different.

Synchronization Between Physics Threads

There are several ways to make scalable communication. Applying the right technique depends on the game's rules. But with respect to scalability, there are two major cases. First, if there are a constant number of point-to-point interactions independent of the number of threads, the game would be scalable. Second, if there are effects that have a collective nature, such as gravity between objects—potentially n^2 point-to-point operations—the game is not likely to scale. (We consider this to be *worst*.) There are a variety of techniques to improve the scalability of such n^2 point-to-point operations. In selecting the right technique, you should also take into account that the serial computation of these effects can be more efficient (linear time) than the scalable point-to-point computation.

As an example, a real physics computation is rigid body physics. There are two cases. Each rigid body may lie within one or a few domains. In this case, it is scalable because the physics will be computed by each thread on bodies within its domain. If, however, the rigid body spans all domains substantially, an advanced technique must be used. In this case, you could consider the computations done in molecular dynamics (MD), which have similar characteristics. MD computations have been implemented in an extremely scalable manner in the NAMD application (*http://en. wikipedia.org/wiki/NAMD*), which won a Gordon Bell award for scalability. It is not likely that you will need that much scalability, so be selective in using these techniques.

In the example, in order to illustrate why object-to-object physics interaction alone can be hard, we used the gravity challenge, potentially n^2 communications. Our example code illustrates two implementation moves.

The first move is to split the physics into two phases, as described earlier in terms of S_I and S_F. In the first phase, compute all the interactions:

- Based on current state positions and velocities, these are stored in a `state[0]` structure.
- Compute the next state position and velocities. These are in `state[1]`.

In the second phase, transfer the next state into the current state so that the next frame can repeat.

In the second phase, we implemented a fast algorithm that does neither all-to-all synchronization nor only point-to-point. It uses something loosely based on the n-body *Barnes-Hutt* computation. It is inside the `pStar->Update` method for stars and is not shown in the code (though it is in the downloadable complete version of the code).

Integrating the Example into a Real Game

We do not claim that the example is fast for game engines, but rather that it has a better set of techniques to speed up a game engine. Although implementing these techniques in a real game will take time, it will also require applying these techniques and perhaps some others. We want to do two things to validate the example:

- Review the source structure of the game to determine which techniques we can apply and whether there are gaps in the techniques we need. The review must determine how much code restructuring is needed and the step-by-step sequence such that the game can be tested at each step.
- Update the example code to model the structure of the game at each step, plus the performance modeling needed to see whether the expected performance and scalability will be attained if the code is transformed.

Spatially decomposing a k-d data structure may be appropriate for physics and scene management, but how can you provide good scalability for other game components? The answer is not clear. Let's do a thought exercise. Suppose, for example, that online players only interact with players in the current neighborhood. Although they may see other players moving at a distance in other spatial domains, the group of players nearby have much more game play to be executed. It will be necessary to spread these closer players' game-play structures across tasks to get speedup.

To achieve this, it would be necessary for:

- The player's space structure to be load-balanced across tasks. There can be granularity problems.
- Tasks to execute the player's work space in a timely manner, interacting players to enter and leave the player space structure, and the work to remain balanced (by domain decomposition or task stealing).
- Tasks executing the player structure to synchronize with the spatial data structures. This is the most complex problem because even if the synchronization is not contended, there may be a cache-thrashing problem.

The granularity of tasks must allow threads that execute few player tasks to have more other tasks to execute in idle periods.

Synchronization between the data structures may mean that there is a direct trade-off between processing speedup and memory bandwidth utilized.

How to Measure Performance

Measuring performance in a scalable game is very easy from an end user's point of view. The gaming experience keeps getting better as more cores are added. But it is more important here to look at the developer's point of view, which is much more complex and will allow us to understand scalability in the full game.

Two types of overhead must be considered. The first overhead is observed in the threading primitives used. Here, there are also two types: when it recurs on every frame, synchronizations are an example, and when it depends on game play, task stealing is an example.

The second overhead concerns the additional computation needed in the threaded version. For example, if a game did not have a k-d tree and it was added just to provide a spatial decomposition, all computations with this tree would be overhead. In the ideal case, this type of overhead would vary no more than linearly with the number of threads. If this is the case, the overhead for one thread would be zero or almost zero.

Table 11-3 summarizes the aforementioned techniques in terms of the four-tiered overhead scale: *not-good* (the best of the four), *bad*, *terrible*, and *worst*.

Table 11-3. Summary of the techniques examined

Cost scale	Description
Not-good	Creating a task and executing it on the same thread
Not-good	Getting an uncontended lock
Bad	Getting a contended lock
Bad	Creating a task graph
Terrible	Task stealing; if it occurs, it will disrupt cached data
Terrible	Data parallel loop synchronization
Terrible	Computing frames that are not rendered
Worst	Nonscalable interactions between tasks

Physics Interaction and Update Code

The source code for the physics interaction (Examples 11-54 and 11-55) and update (Example 11-56) are presented here for you to study. You can download the complete source code from *http://www.threadingbuildingblocks.org/book*. Look for errata and notes at this web site as well.

For more in-depth reading on this topic, Intel engineers wrote several articles covering the topic of threading games, which you can download at the web site as well.

Example 11-54. Physics interaction code: InteractTask

```
class InteractTask : public tbb::task
{
  SceneNode* m_node;
  size_t m_i;
  D3DBlackHole* m_bh;
    float m_universeRadius;
size_t m_DummyCount;

public:     // Interact all stars in task
InteractTask(SceneNode* node,
             size_t i,
             D3DBlackHole* bh,
             float universeRadius,
             size_t DummyCount)
   : m_node(node), m_i(i),
     m_bh(bh), m_universeRadius(universeRadius),
     m_DummyCount(DummyCount)
  {}
   tbb::task* execute()
  {
    if (m_node->getChildCount()) {
// High in scene graph, Create parallel domain tasks for the children
      size_t i;
      tbb::task_list list;
      tbb::task& c = *new(allocate_continuation()) tbb::empty_task();
      for (i = 0; i < m_node->getChildCount(); ++i) {
        list.push_back(*new(c.allocate_child())
          InteractTask(m_node->getChild(i),
                       i, m_bh, m_universeRadius, m_DummyCount));
      }
      c.set_ref_count((int)i);
      c.spawn(list);
    }
    if (m_node->getUserID() > 0) {
      // Low-level object tasks, interact each star serially
      D3DStar* pStar = (D3DStar*)m_node;
      float elapsedTime = g_elapsedTime - pStar->getTimeStamp();
      // TODO: check accuracy of interaction and decide:
      // 1. Skip interaction for this short period of time
      // 2. Split this long period of time to parts and
      //    interact for each
      pStar->setTimeStamp(g_elapsedTime);
      pStar->setElapsedTime(elapsedTime);
      if (!pStar->isAlive() && !pStar->isDying()) {
        pStar->Reset(m_bh, m_universeRadius);
        pStar->NextState();
      } else {
```

Example 11-54. Physics interaction code: InteractTask (continued)

```
        // apply attraction to black hole
        pStar->Interact(elapsedTime, m_bh,
                        m_universeRadius, m_DummyCount);
        // apply attraction to every other star
        SceneNode* node = m_node->getParent( );
        for (size_t j = (m_i + 1); j < node->getChildCount( ); ++j) {
          pStar->Interact(elapsedTime,
                          (D3DStar*)node->getChild(j),
                          m_DummyCount);
        }
      }
    }
    return NULL;
    }
};
```

Example 11-55. Physics interaction code: UpdateTask

```
class UpdateTask : public tbb::task
{
  SceneNode* m_node;

public:  // Update all star positions based on
         // interactions in this frame
  UpdateTask(SceneNode* node)
    : m_node(node)
  {}
    tbb::task* execute( )
  {
    if (m_node->getChildCount( )) {
      // High in scene graph, Create parallel
      // domain tasks for the children
      size_t i;
      tbb::task_list list;
      tbb::task& c = *new(allocate_continuation()) tbb::empty_task( );
      for (i = 0; i < m_node->getChildCount( ); ++i) {
        list.push_back(*new(c.allocate_child( ))
          UpdateTask(m_node->getChild(i)));
      }
      c.set_ref_count((int)i);
      c.spawn(list);
    }
    if (m_node->getUserID( ) > 0) {
// Low-level object tasks, update each star serially
      D3DStar* pStar = (D3DStar*)m_node;
      // Matrix transformation
      pStar->Update(pStar->getElapsedTime( ));
    }
    return NULL;
    }
};
```

Example 11-56. Update code

```
void World::Update(void)
{
  static __itt_event ev = __itt_event_create("update", 6);
// Lock out changing k-d tree until interactions
// and updates are done.
Lock();
  __itt_event_start(ev);
  tbb::tick_count t0 = tbb::tick_count::now();
  if (isParallel() && !isChanged()) {
    InteractTask& task = *new(tbb::task::allocate_root())
                           InteractTask(m_bh, 0, m_bh,
                                        m_universeRadius,
                                        m_DummyCount);
    tbb::task::spawn_root_and_wait(task);
  } else {
// Sequential equivalent to threaded version in InteractTask
    for (size_t i = 0; i < m_bh->getChildCount(); ++i) {
      GroupNode* grp = (GroupNode*)m_bh->getChild(i);
      for (size_t j = 0; j < grp->getChildCount(); ++j) {
        D3DStar* pStar = (D3DStar*)grp->getChild(j);
        float elapsedTime = g_elapsedTime - pStar->getTimeStamp();
        pStar->setTimeStamp(g_elapsedTime);
        pStar->setElapsedTime(elapsedTime);
        if (!pStar->isAlive() && !pStar->isDying()) {
          pStar->Reset(m_bh, m_universeRadius);
          pStar->NextState();
          continue;
        }
        // apply attraction to black hole
        pStar->Interact(elapsedTime, m_bh,
                        m_universeRadius, m_DummyCount);
        // apply attraction to every other star in group
        for (size_t k = (j + 1); k < grp->getChildCount(); ++k) {
          pStar->Interact(elapsedTime,
                          (D3DStar*)grp->getChild(k),
                          m_DummyCount);
        }
      }
    }
  }
  tbb::tick_count t1 = tbb::tick_count::now();
  m_UpdateTime = (t1-t0).seconds();
  __itt_event_end(ev);

  t0 = tbb::tick_count::now();
  if (isParallel() && !isChanged()) {
    UpdateTask& task = *new(tbb::task::allocate_root())
                         UpdateTask(m_bh);
    tbb::task::spawn_root_and_wait(task);
  } else {
// Sequential equivalent to threaded version in UpdateTask
    for (size_t i = 0; i < m_bh->getChildCount(); ++i) {
```

Example 11-56. Update code (continued)

```
    GroupNode* grp = (GroupNode*)m_bh->getChild(i);
    for (size_t j = 0; j < grp->getChildCount( ); ++j) {
      D3DStar* pStar = (D3DStar*)grp->getChild(j);
      // Matrix transformation
      pStar->Update(pStar->getElapsedTime( ));
    }
  }
}
float elapsedTime = g_elapsedTime - m_bh->getTimeStamp( );
m_bh->setTimeStamp(g_elapsedTime);
m_bh->setElapsedTime(elapsedTime);
// update Black Hole
m_bh->Update(elapsedTime);
t1 = tbb::tick_count::now( );
m_TransformTime = (t1-t0).seconds( );

// Balance groups here (every 10 frame)
static int balance_counter = 0;
if (!(balance_counter % 10)) {
  for (size_t i = 0; i < m_bh->getChildCount( ); ++i) {
    GroupNode* grp = (GroupNode*)m_bh->getChild(i);
    for (size_t j = 0; j < grp->getChildCount( ); ++j) {
      D3DStar* pStar = (D3DStar*)grp->getChild(j);
      if (pStar->isAlive( ) &&
          !grp->isInGroup(pStar->getLocation(0),
                          pStar->getLocation(1),
                          pStar->getLocation(2))) {
        for (size_t k = 0; k < m_bh->getChildCount( ); ++k) {
          GroupNode* ngrp = (GroupNode*)m_bh->getChild(k);
          if (ngrp != grp &&
              ngrp->isInGroup(pStar->getLocation(0),
                              pStar->getLocation(1),
                              pStar->getLocation(2))) {
            grp->removeChild(pStar);
            ngrp->addChild(pStar);
          }
        }
      }
    }
  }
}
Unlock( ); // Ok, now permit changing the k-d tree.
}
```

Open Dynamics Engine

As a final example, let's take a look at how to thread the Open Dynamics Engine, an open-source physics engine that is available for download and experimentation from *http://www.ode.org*. The Open Dynamics Engine (ODE) is a physics engine with two main components: a rigid body dynamics simulation engine and a collision detection engine.

We will walk through an example, which is typical of how we approach the task of helping thread programs with Threading Building Blocks when we are asked to assist with code we have not seen before.

Having never used the code before, we downloaded it to take a look at what we could do. We ended up finding two alternative implementations: `parallel_for`, which is quick and easy to implement, and a more advanced use of the task scheduler to deal with dynamics. It is interesting that the tasks into which we break up our program are relatively the same, so the discovery of the `parallel_for` solution has the program ready for better task handling when we understand the application a little better.

Look for Hotspots

The first step was to use a performance analysis tool—the VTune Performance Analyzer in this case—to identify the hotspot in this library. Sampling found a hotspot in the dynamics simulation engine (a *hotspot* is a place where the program is spending a lot of time). The function containing the hotspot was `dInternalStepFast`.

`dInternalStepFast` is a solver function that works with two connected objects. Basically, it applies forces to the objects. There are several loops doing compute-intensive work. If you look more closely at the code, you will see that all these loops have data dependencies and the work is too fine-grained. So, you do *not* want to apply `parallel_for` there because it is unlikely that you will get good scalability. What we should do when we are discouraged in this way is look higher in the call tree—in this case, we wanted to see which function was calling `dInternalStepFast`.

Returning to VTune, we used information from a call graph view to identify the higher-level function that calls `dInternalStepFast`. That function is `dInternalIslandStepFast`. The call graph timing information showed that `dInternalIslandStepFast` itself did not take much time to execute: it goes through the list of objects and computes inertia tensor and rotational force for each one. Then, it calls `dInternalStepFast` for the object pairs.

Notice what we are doing: we are walking up the call graph to find as much parallelism as we can. The fact that we started our walk at a hotspot means this would be nice to run in parallel. Walking up the call graph looking for the best place to break into parallelism is typical. The higher we go, we hope, the more coarse-grained parallelism we may find.

At this point, we realized that `dInternalIslandStepFast` works with the groups of objects, not with the complete list. Returning to the call graph, we looked higher still. We noticed `processIslandsFast` (Example 11-57), which takes the list of all objects in the scene and searches for the *islands*. An island is a subrange of objects that have common joints so that objects from the different islands do not intersect

---

and islands can be processed independently (there are no data dependencies between them), which makes them *very good* choices for data parallel decomposition.

We decided to apply parallel_for (Example 11-58), which would take the std::vector of islands and call dInternalIslandStepFast for each island in parallel. We added a new class, process_island, and overrode its operator() to make it model the parallel_for Body Concept (Chapter 3). Operator() calls dInternalIslandStepFast for each island of the given subrange. Then our prototype was done. The modified processIslandsFast function was called processIslandsFastPfor (Example 11-59) in the modeling app.

Example 11-57. ODE: processIslandsFast

```
// Finds islands of connected objects and calls solver
void processIslandsFast (int counter, world_t& world)
{
    int obj_num = counter;
    for (size_t i = 0; i < world.size(); i++) {
        busy (search_time);
        if (i % counter == 0) {
            // Call solver for the found island
            dInternalStepIslandFast (obj_num, world);
        }
    }
}
```

Example 11-58. ODE: process_islands for parallel_for

```
// Body functor for parallel_for version
class process_islands
{
    islands_vector &p;
    int obj_num;
public:
    process_islands (islands_vector& params, int num):
                    p (params), obj_num (num) {}
    void operator() (tbb::blocked_range<int> &r) const
    {
        // Call solver for each island from the sub-range
        for (int i = r.begin(); i != r.end(); i++)
            dInternalStepIslandFast (obj_num, *p[i]);
    }
};
```

Example 11-59. ODE: processIslandsFastPfor

```
// Modified processIslandsFast: calls tbb::parallel_for
// for the array of islands
void processIslandsFastPfor (int counter, world_t& world)
{
    int obj_num     = counter;
    int num_islands = 0;
```

Example 11-59. ODE: processIslandsFastPfor (continued)

```
    for (size_t i = 0; i < world.size(); i++) {
        busy (search_time);
        if (i % counter == 0) {
            // Just register a new island
            num_islands++;
        }
    }
    islands_vector islands(num_islands);
    // Call parallel_for for all found islands
    tbb::parallel_for (tbb::blocked_range<int>(0, num_islands,
                                               grain_size),
                       process_islands (islands, obj_num));
}
```

Improving on the First Solution

Naturally, we wondered what we could do to improve our newly parallel program.

What's wrong with using parallel_for in this example, you ask? The problem is that the applications that would use ODE are dynamic: the number of objects in the scene changes, the number of islands also changes over time, and so on. It's hard to come up with a good grainsize parameter for parallel_for. Also, the more objects you have, the more time you spend searching for islands. What if we could make the island processing overlap with other operations? Our prototype does not allow this to happen, and it becomes a major problem.

The task scheduler interface is a natural place to go when you have a dynamic ability to find more tasks. Islands make good tasks, but in the parallel_for structure they are not balanced well because they pop up as surprises.

We created yet another class, process_one_island (Example 11-60), that has a class task as a parent. We overrode the pure virtual execute method where we just called dInternalIslandStepFast for the given island. So, we just described our own logical task.

 Aha! Slipping in a task when you can identify work is easy and can be very powerful.

We wanted processIslandsFast to spawn tasks. To do this we needed to create a root task. We wrote a new class for this root task, process_world, which would just call a modified processIslandsFast (processIslandsFastTask, shown in Example 11-61). The modified processIslandsFast needed to be changed to accept a new parameter—a reference to the root task, which is used to create, spawn, and wait for process_one_island tasks. The new children tasks were created and spawned as soon as the new island was found (so that we did not have to wait until all islands were found to start processing, like we did in the parallel_for case).

Example 11-60. ODE: process_one_island (task)

```
// Task: calls solver for the given island
class process_one_island: public tbb::task
{
    island_t &p;
    int obj_num;
public:
    process_one_island (island_t& params, int num):
                          p (params), obj_num (num) {}
    task* execute ()
    {
        dInternalStepIslandFast (obj_num, p);
        return NULL;
    }
};
```

Example 11-61. ODE: processIslandsFastTask

```
void processIslandsFastTask (tbb::task& tbb_root,
                             int counter, world_t& world);
// Root task: calls processIslandsFastTask to search for islands
// spawns process_one_island tasks for the found islands
class process_world: public tbb::task
{
    int counter;
    world_t& world;
public:
    process_world (int num, world_t& w) :
                   world (w), counter(num) {}
    task* execute ()
    {
        processIslandsFastTask (*this, counter, world);
        return NULL;
    }
};

// Modified processIslandsFast: spawns process_one_island task
// for the island new parameter "tbb_root" is added
void processIslandsFastTask (tbb::task& tbb_root,
                             int counter, world_t& world)
{
    int obj_num = counter;

    for (size_t i = 0; i < world.size(); i++) {
        busy (search_time);
        if (i % counter == 0) {
            // Spawn the solver task immediately,
            // not wait until all islands are found
            tbb::task& t =
              *new (tbb_root.allocate_additional_child_of (tbb_root))
                process_one_island (island_t(), obj_num);
            tbb_root.spawn (t);
```

Example 11-61. ODE: processIslandsFastTask (continued)

```
        }
    }
    // Join all the children tasks
    tbb_root.wait_for_all ();
}
```

We are seeing more parallel work now, and better resource utilization. The new version can adapt to the dynamically changing environment better than the `parallel_for` version.

The first attempt gave a 1.1X speedup, whereas the second effort gave us a 1.29X speedup when run with 400 simple objects on a quad-core system, all in the span of less than a day of effort.

The Code

To meet space constraints, we've published a complete standalone version of the program that actually uses delay loops to simulate being in the ODE package itself. This means that all the code listed strictly concerns the code that was written to introduce threading (two different ways) via Threading Building Blocks (see Examples 11-62 and 11-63). This *model program* contains none of the ODE but behaves like the ODE at a high level. The timing delays in the listing simulate the effects of the real calls in the ODE such that the speedup results seem consistent with the trials we ran. The web site for this book has instructions on how to download a modified ODE as well, which actually incorporates these changes into the whole ODE.

Example 11-62. ODE: includes and delay placeholders

```
#include <stdio.h>
#include <vector>
#include <windows.h>
#include "tbb\task_scheduler_init.h"
#include "tbb\task.h"
#include "tbb\parallel_for.h"
#include "tbb\blocked_range.h"
#include "tbb\tick_count.h"

typedef int object_t;
typedef std::vector<object_t*> world_t;
typedef std::vector<object_t*> island_t;
typedef std::vector<island_t*> islands_vector;

const unsigned int N = 20000; // Weight of the computation complexity

const int grain_size = 5; // Grainsize for parallel_for: hard to
                          // find a good number if the
                          // environment changes dynamically
```

Example 11-62. ODE: includes and delay placeholders (continued)

```
const int step_time   = 1; // Time to spend processing one object
                           // in dInternalStepIslandFast (solver)

const int search_time = 1; // Time to spend processing one object
                           // in processIslandsFast (islands finder)

void busy (int weight)
{
    for (int i = 0; i < weight; i++) {
        static volatile int x;
        for (int j = 0; j < N; j++)
            ++x;
    }
}

// Simulates solver
void dInternalStepIslandFast (int obj_num, island_t& island)
{
    for (int i = 0; i < obj_num; i++)
        busy (step_time);
}

// put Example 11-57 through Example 11-61 here //
```

Example 11-63. ODE: set-up

```
// after Example 11-62, and Example 11-57 through Example 11-61

void main (int argc, char **argv)
{
    unsigned int world_size  = 400;
    int tbb_num_threads = tbb::task_scheduler_init::automatic;

    // Process program input arguments
    unsigned int num = 0;
    for (int i=1; i<argc; i++)
    {
        if (_stricmp(argv[i],"-numThreads")==0) {
            if ((i < argc-1) && ((num = atoi(argv[i+1])) > 0))
                tbb_num_threads = num;
        }
        else if (_stricmp(argv[i],"-numObjects")==0) {
            if ((i < argc-1) && ((num = atoi(argv[i+1])) > 1))
                world_size = num;
        }
    }

    // Initialize the world with objects
    world_t world(world_size);

    if (tbb_num_threads != tbb::task_scheduler_init::automatic)
        printf ("Number of threads: %d\n", tbb_num_threads);
```

Example 11-63. ODE: set-up (continued)

```
    else
        printf ("Running default number of threads\n");

    printf ("Number of objects in the scene: %d\n", world_size);

    //**** Serial version:
    tbb::tick_count t1_serial = tbb::tick_count::now( );

    // Frame loop: simulates dynamically changing environment:
    // total number of objects is constant, number of islands varies
    for (unsigned int i = 1; i <= world_size/2; ++i)
        processIslandsFast (i, world);

    tbb::tick_count t2_serial = tbb::tick_count::now( );
    printf ("Serial time: %g seconds\n",
            (t2_serial-t1_serial).seconds ());

    //**** tbb::parallel_for version
    tbb::task_scheduler_init tbb_init(tbb_num_threads);
    tbb::tick_count t1_pfor = tbb::tick_count::now( );

    // Frame loop:
    for (unsigned int i = 1; i <= world_size/2; ++i)
        processIslandsFastPfor (i, world);

    tbb::tick_count t2_pfor = tbb::tick_count::now( );
    printf ("parallel_for version time: %g seconds\n",
                (t2_pfor-t1_pfor).seconds ());

    //**** tbb::task version:
    tbb::tick_count t1_task = tbb::tick_count::now( );

    // Frame loop:
    for (unsigned int i = 1; i <= world_size/2; ++i)
    {
        tbb::task& root =
            *new (tbb::task::allocate_root())
                process_world (i, world);
        root.set_ref_count (1);
        tbb::task::spawn_root_and_wait (root);
    }

    tbb::tick_count t2_task = tbb::tick_count::now( );
    printf ("Task version time: %g seconds\n",
                (t2_task-t1_task).seconds ());

}
```

CHAPTER 12

History and Related Projects

Nothing in this chapter is required reading to learn how to use Intel Threading Building Blocks. Instead, this chapter looks at some of the inspirations that shaped our thoughts at Intel and led to the design and implementation of Threading Building Blocks. A list of papers, articles, and books at the end of the chapter forms a bibliography to give some suggested further reading. The chapter also contains a brief explanation of lambda functions, whose inclusion in C++ is advocated by Arch Robison, lead developer for Threading Building Blocks, in his foreword to this book.

The information in this bibliography is likely to appeal most to those who want to contribute to Threading Building Blocks. There is much to be pondered in the design of Threading Building Blocks, and this chapter aims to clarify where to start.

Intel Threading Building Blocks draws from a great many sources. Figure 12-1 highlights the key influences of the past decade or so. The influences were in the form of inspiration and, other than McRT, they have no actual source code connection. Influences prior to 1988 are left as an exercise for other historians.

Threading Building Blocks is unique because it rests on a few key decisions:

- Support general C++ programs with existing compilers.
- Relaxed sequential execution (see Chapter 10).
- Use recursive parallelism and generic algorithms.
- Use task stealing.

This chapter gives insights into each one of these. The Quicksort example in Chapter 11 can give good insights into task stealing and recursive parallelism.

Libraries

1988, Chare Kernel, University of Illinois at Urbana-Champaign
> In 1988, it was simply a C library. The key notion was to break a program into small bits of work, called *chares*, and the scheduler would take care of packing

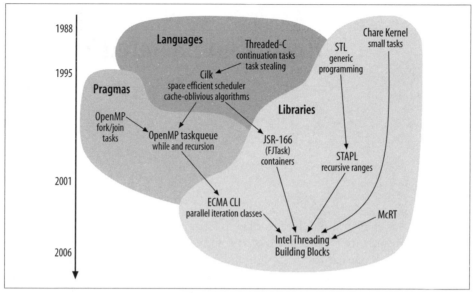

Figure 12-1. Key influences on design of Intel Threading Building Blocks

these efficiently (in both space and time) onto processors. Mapping tasks onto threads instead of programming threads directly is an important concept. The Chare Kernel was later extended with some features for marshalling to address distributed memory machines, becoming Charm++ (*http://charm.cs.uiuc.edu/research/charm/index.shtml*).

1993, Standard Template Library (STL) for C++, Hewlett-Packard

STL was presented in November 1993 to the ANSI/ISO C++ committee and HP made it freely available in 1994. It was adopted into the C++ standard. Arch Robison related: "I once heard Stepanov give a great talk on generic programming, where he went through how to write a really generic greatest-common-factor algorithm. [The paper at *http://www.stepanovpapers.com/gcd.pdf* is similar to that talk, but with more mathematical emphasis.] In its full glory, generic programming is not just parametric types, but programming with concepts." There is a very good explanation of generic programming in the box on page 2 of *http://www.osl.iu.edu/publications/prints/2003/comparing_generic_programming03.pdf*. More works by Stepanov on STL and generic programming are listed later in this chapter.

1999, Java Specification Request #166 (JSR-166), Doug Lea

It was actually not standardized until later, but 1999 was the year Lea first introduced it. FJTask was an attempt to put Cilk-style parallelism into the stock Java library. It was proposed for JSR-166, but it did not make it into that standard. An overview is available at *http://java.sun.com/developer/technicalArticles/J2SE/concurrency*.

2001, Standard Template Adaptive Parallel Library (STAPL), Texas A&M

STAPL introduced the notion of recursive parallel ranges ("pRanges") and the concept of using these ranges instead of iterators to bind parallel generic algorithms to parallel containers. STL lacks a recursive range. STAPL is more complex than Threading Building Blocks because it encompasses distributed memory architectures typical of High Performance Computing (HPC). Furthermore, STAPL supports the specification of arbitrary execution order for parallel task graphs. This allows the use of multiple scheduling policies to optimize execution time (*http://parasol.tamu.edu/stapl*).

2004, ECMA CLI parallel profile, Intel

This ECMA spec for the .NET virtual machine has classes for parallel iteration, designed by Arch Robison. See *http://www.ecma-international.org/publications/files/ECMA-ST/Ecma-335.pdf*, pp. 554–555.

2006, McRT-Malloc, Intel Research

A scalable transactional memory allocator, McRT forms the basis of the Scalable Memory Allocator supplied with Intel Threading Building Blocks. Sections 3 and 3.1 of a 2006 paper by Hudson, Saha, Adl-Tabatabai, and Hertzberg (*http://doi.acm.org/10.1145/1133956.1133967*) describe roughly what is in the Scalable Memory Allocator in Threading Building Blocks.

Languages

1994, Threaded-C, Massachusetts Institute of Technology

The Parallel Continuation Machine (PCM) was the runtime support for Threaded-C. It was a C-based package that provided continuation-passing-style threads on Thinking Machines Corporation's Connection Machine Model CM-5 Supercomputer and used work stealing as a general scheduling policy to improve the load balance and locality of the computation. This language is not to be confused with the *Threaded-C* for *EARTH* from McGill University and the University of Delaware. PCM is briefly mentioned in the history of Cilk on page 2 of *http://supertech.csail.mit.edu/cilk/manual-5.3.2.pdf*.

1995, Cilk, Massachusetts Institute of Technology

The first implementation of Cilk (*http://supertech.csail.mit.edu/cilk*) was a direct descendent of PCM/Threaded-C. Cilk fixed the difficulty of programming continuation tasks and came up with methods to tailor task allocation to caches without knowing the size of the caches with *cache-oblivious* algorithms. Cilk is an extension of C that supports very efficient fork/join parallelism. Its space efficiency is discussed in *http://supertech.csail.mit.edu/papers/cilkjpdc96.pdf*. FFTW (*http://www.fftw.org*) is an example of a cache-oblivious algorithm.

Pragmas

1997, OpenMP, by a consortium of major computer hardware and software vendors
> OpenMP supports multiplatform, shared-memory parallel programming in C and Fortran, offering a standard set of compiler directives, library routines, and environment variables. Prior to OpenMP, many vendors had proprietary compiler directives with similar intent, but they lacked portability. OpenMP embodies a fork/join philosophy. See *http://www.openmp.org*.

1998, OpenMP Taskqueue, Kuck & Associates (KAI)
> Proposed extensions for OpenMP to move beyond loops. The original paper (*http://www.it.lth.se/ewomp99/papers/grant.pdf*) is more programmer-friendly than the later compiler-oriented paper at *http://www.caspur.it/ewomp02/ PAPERI/EWOMP02-03.pdf*.

Generic Programming

Bjarne Stroustrup, creator of C++, once considered there to be three fundamental styles supported by C++—*procedural programming*, *data abstraction*, and *object-oriented programming*—but later said that *generic programming* has become a fourth style.

We can give credit to the Standard Template Library (STL), created by Alexander Stepanov, for popularizing this style. It fits very well with the principles of C++, which favors abstraction and efficiency together.

In STL and Threading Building Blocks, algorithms are separated from containers. This means that an algorithm takes a recursive range and uses it to access elements within the container. The specific type of the container itself is unknown to the algorithm. This clear separation of containers and algorithms is the basic idea of generic programming. Separation of algorithms from containers means that template instantiations result in relatively little added code and generally only that which is actually going to be used.

Threading Building Blocks does embrace the same principles as STL, but does it through the use of *recursive ranges*, not *iterators*. Iterators in STL (except for random access iterators) are fundamentally sequential, and thus inappropriate for expressing parallelism. Random access iterators can, of course, express parallelism, and blocked_range is carefully defined so that blocked_range works for ranges defined by [begin,end) iterator pairs. In fact, an early design of Threading Building Blocks used random-access iterators to express parallel ranges, but there was not a clean way to extend that to multidimensional ranges and more general ranges such as the one used for Quicksort.

Threading Building Blocks algorithms are written to use recursive ranges without any concerns regarding which container supplies the recursive range. The recursive ranges themselves are completely independent. They are related only in being required to supply the same required operations and obey the same semantics.

The design of Threading Building Blocks embraces these same principles to provide the separation of container and algorithms through the use of recursive ranges. Additionally, Threading Building Blocks has a focus on parallelism and specifying tasks instead of threads.

Concepts in Generic Programming

Generic programming is supported in C++ through the notion of templates. The templates provide abstraction while retaining the opportunity for optimal performance.

A *Concept* is a set of requirements on a type and is represented in this book in Pascal-Case (a style of combining words into keywords by capitalizing the first letters in each word). The requirements may be syntactic or semantic. For example, the Concept of *Sortable* could be defined as a set of requirements that enable an array to be sorted. A type T would be Sortable if:

- x < y returns a Boolean value, and represents a total order on items of type T.
- swap(x,y) swaps items x and y.

You can write a sorting template function in C++ and be assured that it can sort an array of any type that is Sortable.

We describe the requirements you should observe on types for Threading Building Blocks types in this book as *Concepts*. When these constraints are followed, Threading Building Blocks will work well. When they are violated, you may get a cryptic compiler error message or occasionally inefficient or incorrect code. There is a great deal of interest in designing a type system for C++ that can check template arguments for errors. In the future, we may have extensions to C++ that allow more type constraints in the template definitions. This will lead to more safety and better error messages from the compiler.

Pseudosignatures in Generic Programming

Two approaches for defining Concepts are *valid expressions* and *pseudosignatures*. The C++ standard follows the *valid expressions* approach that shows what the usage pattern looks like for a Concept. It has the drawback of relegating important details to notational conventions. This document uses *pseudosignatures* because they are concise and can be cut-and-pasted for an initial implementation.

You can find information on where to learn more about *pseudosignatures* versus *valid expressions* in the paper by Siek et al. in the "Further Reading" section of this chapter. Table 12-1 shows pseudosignatures for a *Sortable* type T.

Table 12-1. Pseudosignatures for example Sortable Concept

Pseudosignature	Semantics
`bool operator<(const T& x, const T& y)`	Compare x and y.
`void swap(T& x, T& y)`	Swap x and y.

A real signature may differ from the *pseudosignature* by relying on implicit conversions allowed by C++ to deal with the difference. For an example, type U, the real signature that implements `operator<` in Table 12-1, can be expressed as `int operator<( U x, U y )` because C++ permits implicit conversion from `int` to `bool` and implicit conversion from U to `(const U&)`. Similarly, the real signature `bool operator<( U& x, U& y )` is acceptable because C++ permits implicit addition of a `const` qualifier to a reference type.

Models in Generic Programming

A type *models* a Concept if it meets the requirements of the Concept. For example, type `int` models the Sortable Concept in Table 12-1 if there exists a function `swap(x,y)` that swaps two `int` values x and y. The other requirement for Sortable, specifically x<y, is already met by the built-in `operator<` on type `int`.

The library sometimes requires that a type model the `CopyConstructible` Concept, which is defined by the ISO C++ standard and provides fundamental operations for creating and referring to the type. Table 12-2 shows the requirements for `CopyConstructible` in pseudosignature form. For a type to model the `CopyConstrutible` Concept, it needs to implement each operation specified in Table 12-2. This way, containers and algorithms that expect `CopyConstructible` types will be able to use your types, too.

Table 12-2. CopyConstructible requirements

Pseudosignature	Semantics
`T( const T& )`	Construct copy of T.
`~T( )`	Destructor.
`T* operator&( )`	Take address of T.
`const T* operator&( ) const`	Take address of T.

Caches

The speed of processors has grown to be much faster than main memory. Making all of memory nearly as fast as a processor would simply prove too expensive for most computers. Instead, designers make small amounts of memory, known as *caches*, operate nearly as fast as the processor. The main memory can then be slower and more affordable. The hardware knows how to move information in and out of caches as needed, thereby adding to the number of places where data is shuffled on its journey between memory and the processor cores. Caches are critical in helping overcome the mismatch between memory speed and processor speed.

Virtually all computers use caches only for a temporary copy of data that should eventually reside in memory. Therefore, the function of a memory subsystem is to move data needed as input by each processing core to caches near that processor core, and to move data produced by the processing cores out to main memory. As data is read from memory into the caches, some data needs to be evicted from the cache. Cache designers work to make the data evicted be approximately the data least likely to be used again.

Once a processor accesses data, it is best to exhaust the program's use of it while it is still in the cache. Continued usage will hold it in the cache, whereas prolonged inactivity will likely lead to its eviction and future usage will need to do a more expensive (slow) access to get the data. Furthermore, every time an additional thread runs on a processor core, data is likely to be discarded from the cache.

Threading Building Blocks is designed with caches in mind and works to limit the unnecessary movement of tasks and data. When a task has to be passed to a different processor core for execution, Threading Building Blocks moves the task with the least likelihood of having data in the cache for the processor core from which the task is stolen.

It is interesting to note that parallel Quicksort (Chapter 11) is an example in which *caches* beat *maximum parallelism*. Parallel Mergesort has more parallelism than parallel Quicksort. But parallel Mergesort is not an in-place sort, and thus has twice the cache footprint that parallel Quicksort does. Hence, Quicksort usually runs faster in practice.

Keep data locality in mind when considering how to structure your program. Avoid using data regions sporadically when you can design the application to use a single set of data in focused chunks of time. This happens most naturally if you use data decomposition, especially at the higher levels in a program.

Costs of Time Slicing

Time slicing enables there to be more logical threads than physical threads. Each logical thread is serviced for a time slice—a short period of time defined by the operating system during which a thread can run before being preempted—by a physical thread. If a thread runs longer than a time slice, as most do, it relinquishes the physical thread until it gets another turn. This chapter details the costs incurred by time slicing.

The most obvious cost is the time for *context switching* between logical threads. Each context switch requires that the processor save all its registers for the previous logical thread that it was executing, and load its registers with information for the next logical thread it runs.

A subtler cost is *cache cooling*. Processors keep recently accessed data in cache memory, which is very fast, but also relatively small compared to main memory. When the processor runs out of cache memory, it has to evict items from cache and put them back into main memory. Typically, it chooses the least recently-used items in the cache. (The reality of set-associative caches is a bit more complicated, but this is not a cache primer.)

When a logical thread gets its time slice, as it references a piece of data for the first time, this data is pulled into cache, taking hundreds of cycles. If it is referenced frequently enough not to be evicted, each subsequent reference will find it in cache, and take only a few cycles. Such data is called *hot in cache*.

Time slicing undoes this because if Thread A finishes its time slice, and subsequently Thread B runs on the same physical thread, B will tend to evict data that was hot in cache for A, unless both threads need the data. When Thread A gets its next time slice, it will need to reload evicted data, at the cost of hundreds of cycles for each cache miss. Or worse yet, the next time slice for Thread A may be on a different physical thread that has a different cache altogether.

Another cost is *lock preemption*. This happens if a thread acquires a lock on a resource and its time slice runs out before it releases the lock. No matter how short a time the thread intended to hold the lock, it is now going to hold it for at least as long as it takes for its next turn at a time slice to come up. Any other threads waiting on the lock either busy-wait pointlessly or lose the rest of their time slice. The effect is called *convoying* because the threads end up "bumper to bumper" waiting for the preempted thread in front to resume driving.

Quick Introduction to Lambda Functions

Adding lambda functions to C++ would let a programmer write a loop body *in-place* instead of having to write a separate STL-style function object. Similar capability is found in the *anonymous method* in C#, in the *inner* class in Java, and in the primordial *lambda expression* of LISP.

For example, currently a programmer who wants to convert a sequential for loop into a parallel_for has to write something like this:

```
// Without lambda expression
class ApplyFoo {
public:
    int my_x;
    ApplyFoo( int x ) : my_x(x) {}
    void operator()(const blocked_range<size_t>& r) const {
        for(size_t i=r.begin(); i!=r.end(); ++i)
            Foo(i,my_x);
    }
};
void ParallelApplyFoo(size_t n, int x) {
    parallel_for(blocked_range<size_t>(0,n,10),
                ApplyFoo(x));
}
```

In particular, the programmer has to deal with *capturing* the value of parameter x in ParallelApplyFoo so that it can be referenced from ApplyFoo. The addition of lambda expressions, as recently proposed to the C++ Standards Committee, would enable the preceding example to be written more concisely as:

```
// With lambda expression
void ParallelApplyFoo(size_t n, int x) {
    parallel_for(
        blocked_range<size_t>(0,n,10),
        <>(const blocked_range<size_t>& r) {
            for(size_t i=r.begin(); i<r.end(); ++i)
                Foo(i,x);
        });
}
```

The <> directs the compiler to convert the expression after it into a function object that does everything the handcoded ApplyFoo would do. In general, lambda expressions let programmers pass blocks of code as parameters without having to write the function-object boilerplate.

Further Reading

Acar, U., G. Blelloch, and R. Blumofe (2000). "The Data Locality of Work Stealing." Proceedings of the Twelfth Annual ACM Symposium on Parallel Algorithms and Architectures, 1–12.

Amdahl, G. M. (1967, April). "Validity of the single-processor approach to achieving large scale computing capabilities." AFIP Conference Proceedings, 30. Reston, VA: AFIPS Press, 483–485.

An, P., A. Jula, et al. (2003). "STAPL: An Adaptive, Generic Parallel C++ Library." Workshop on Language and Compilers for Parallel Computing, 2001. Lecture Notes in Computer Science 2624, 193–208. .

Austern, M. H., R. A. Towle, and A. A. Stepanov (1996). "Range partition adaptors: a mechanism for parallelizing STL." *ACM SIGAPP Applied Computing Review*. 4, 1, 5–6.

Blumofe, R. D., and D. Papadopoulos (1998). "Hood: A User-Level Threads Library for Multiprogrammed Multiprocessors." From *http://citeseer.ist.psu.edu/blumofe98hood.html*.

Blumofe, R. D., C. F. Joerg, et al. (1996). "Cilk: An Efficient Multithreaded Runtime System." Proceedings of the 5th ACM SIGPLAN Symposium on Principles and Practice of Parallel Programming, 207–216. *http://supertech.csail.mit.edu/papers/cilkjpdc96.pdf*.

Boehm, H. (2006, June). "An Atomic Operations Library for C++." C++ standards committee document N2047.

Butenhof, D. R. (1997). *Programming with POSIX Threads*. Reading, MA: Addison Wesley.

Flynn, M. J. (1972, September). "Some Computer Organizations and Their Effectiveness." IEEE Transactions on Computers, C-21, 9, 948–960.

Garcia, R., J. Järvi, et al. (2003, October). "A Comparative Study of Language Support for Generic Programming." Proceedings of the 2003 ACM SIGPLAN conference on object-oriented programming, systems, languages, and applications. *http://www.osl.iu.edu/publications/prints/2003/comparing_generic_programming03.pdf*.

Gustafson, J. L. (1988). "Reevaluating Amdahl's Law." Communications of the ACM, 31(5), 532–533.

Halbherr, M., Y. Zhou, and C. F. Joerg (1994, March). MIMD-Style Parallel Programming Based on Continuation-Passing Threads, Computation Structures Group Memo 355. *http://csg.csail.mit.edu/pubs/memos/Memo-355/memo-355.pdf*.

Halbherr, M., Y. Zhou, and C. F. Joerg (1994, September). "MIMD-style parallel programming with continuation-passing threads." Proceedings of the 2nd International Workshop on Massive Parallelism: Hardware, Software, and Applications, Capri, Italy.

Hansen, B. (1973). "Concurrent Programming Concepts." ACM Computing Surveys, 5, 4.

Hoare, C. A. R. (1974). "Monitors: An Operating System Structuring Concept." Communications of the ACM, 17, 10, 549–557.

Hudson, R. L., B. Saha, et al. (2006, June). "McRT-Malloc: a scalable transactional memory allocator." Proceedings of the 2006 International Symposium on Memory Management. New York: ACM Press, 74–83. *http://doi.acm.org/10.1145/1133956.1133967.*

Intel Threading Building Blocks 1.0 for Windows, Linux, and Mac OS—Intel Software Network (1996). From the Intel product web site, *http://www.intel.com/cd/software/products/asmo-na/eng/294797.htm.*

"A Formal Specification of Intel Itanium Processor Family Memory Ordering" (2002, October). From Intel web site: *http://www.intel.com/design/itanium/downloads/25142901.pdf.*

ISO/IEC 14882:1998(E) International Standard (1998). Programming languages—C++. ISO/IEC, 1998.

ISO/IEC 9899:1999 International Standard (1999). Programming languages—C, ISO/IEC, 1999.

Järvi, J., and B. Stroustrup (2004, September). Decltype and auto (revision 4). C++ standards committee document N1705=04-0145.

Kapur, D., D. R. Musser, and A.A. Stepanov (1981). "Operators and Algebraic Structures." Proceedings of the 1981 Conference on Functional Programming Languages and Computer Architecture, 59–63.

MacDonald, S., D. Szafron, and J. Schaeffer (2004). "Rethinking the Pipeline as Object-Oriented States with Transformations." Ninth International Workshop on High-Level Parallel Programming Models and Supportive Environments.

Mahmoud, Q. H. (2005, March). "Concurrent Programming with J2SE 5.0." Sun Developer Network. From *http://java.sun.com/developer/technicalArticles/J2SE/concurrency.*

Massingill, B. L., T. G. Mattson, and B. A. Sanders (2005). "Reengineering for Parallelism: An Entry Point for PLPP (Pattern Language for Parallel Programming) for Legacy Applications." Proceedings of the Twelfth Pattern Languages of Programs Workshop. *http://www.cise.ufl.edu/research/ParallelPatterns/plop2005.pdf.*

Mattson, T. G., B. A. Sanders, and B. L. Massingill (2004). *Patterns for Parallel Programming*. Reading, MA: Addison Wesley.

McDowell, C. E., and D. P. Helmbold (1989). "Debugging Concurrent Programs." Communications of the ACM, 21, 2.

Meyers, S. (1998). *Effective C++*, Second Edition. Reading, MA: Addison Wesley, 1998.

Musser, D. R., and A.A. Stepanov (1994). "Algorithm-Oriented Generic Libraries." Software—Practice and Experience, 24(7), 623–642.

Musser, D. R., G. J. Derge, and A. Saini, with foreword by Alexander Stepanov (2001). *STL Tutorial and Reference Guide, Second Edition: C++ Programming with the Standard Template Library*, Boston, MA: Addison Wesley, 2001. *PDF*.

Narlikar, G., and G. Blelloch (1999). "Space-Efficient Scheduling of Nested Parallelism." ACM Transactions on Programming Languages and Systems, 21, 1, 138–173.

"OpenMP C and C++ Application Program Interface, Version 2.5 (May 2005)." From the OpenMP web site: *http://www.openmp.org*.

Ottosen, T. (2006, September). Range Library Core. C++ standards committee document N2068.

Plauger, P. J., M. Lee, et al. (2000). *C++ Standard Template Library*, Prentice Hall.

Rauchwerger, L., F. Arzu, and K. Ouchi (1998, May). "Standard Templates Adaptive Parallel Library," Proceedings of the 4th International Workshop on Languages, Compilers, and Run-Time Systems for Scalable Computers (LCR), Pittsburgh, PA. Also Lecture Notes in Computer Science, 1511, Springer-Verlag, 1998, 402–410.

Robison, A. D. (2006). "A Proposal to Add Parallel Iteration to the Standard Library." From the Open Standards project: *http://www.open-std.org/jtc1/sc22/wg21/docs/papers/2006/n2104.pdf*.

Robison, A. (2003, April). "Memory Consistency & .NET." *Dr. Dobb's Journal. http://www.ddj.com/dept/windows/184405316*.

Samko, V. (2006, February). "A proposal to add lambda functions to the C++ standard." C++ standards committee document N1958=06-028.

Schmidt, D. C., and I. Pyarali (1998). *Strategies for Implementing POSIX Condition Variables on Win32*. Department of Computer Science, Washington University, St. Louis, MO.

Schmidt, D. C., M. Stal, et al. (2000). Patterns for Concurrent and Networked Objects. Pattern-Oriented Architecture, 2.

Shah, S., G. Haab, et al. (1999). "Flexible Control Structures for Parallelism in OpenMP." Proceedings of the First European Workshop on OpenMP. *http://www.it. lth.se/ewomp99/papers/grant.pdf*.

Siek, J., D. Gregor, et al. (2005). "Concepts for C++0x." From *http://www.osl.iu.edu/ publications/prints/2005/siek05:_concepts_cpp0x.pdf* (see section 3.3.2 regarding pseudosignatures versus valid expressions).

Stepanov, A. A., and M. Lee (1995). "The Standard Template Library." HP Laboratories Technical Report 95-11(R.1).

Stepanov, A. A. (1999). "Greatest Common Measure: The Last 2500 Years." *http:// www.stepanovpapers.com/gcd.pdf*.

Stroustrup, B. (1994). *The Design and Evolution of C++*, also known as D&E. Reading, MA: Addison Wesley.

Stroustrup, B. (2000). *The C++ Programming Language*. Special Edition. Reading, MA: Addison Wesley.

Stroustrup, B., and G. Dos Reis (2005, April). "A Concept Design (rev.1)." Technical Report N1782=05-0042, ISO/IEC SC22/JTC1/WG21, available from *http://www. open-std.org/jtc1/sc22/wg21/docs/papers/2005*.

Stroustrup, B., and G. Dos Reis (2005, October). "Specifying C++ concepts." Technical Report N1886=05-0146, ISO/IEC SC22/JTC1/WG21, available from *http:// www.open-std.org/jtc1/sc22/wg21/docs/papers/2005*.

Su, E., X. Tian, et al. (2002, September). "Compiler Support of the Workqueuing Execution Model for Intel SMP Architectures." Fourth European Workshop on OpenMP, Rome. *http://www.caspur.it/ewomp02/PAPERI/EWOMP02-03.pdf*.

Sutter, H. (2005, January). "The Concurrency Revolution." *Dr. Dobb's Journal*. From *http://www.ddj.com/dept/cpp/184401916*.

Sutter, H. (2005, March). "The Free Lunch is Over: A Fundamental Turn Towards Concurrency in Software." *Dr. Dobb's Journal*.

Voss, M. (2006, December). "Enable Safe, Scalable Parallelism with Intel Threading Building Blocks' Concurrent Containers." From DevX web site: *http://www.devx. com/cplus/Article/33334*.

Voss, M. (2006, October). "Demystify Scalable Parallelism with Intel Threading Building Blocks' Generic Parallel Algorithms." From DevX web site: *http://www. devx.com/cplus/Article/32935*.

Willcock, J., J. Järvi, et al. (2006). "Lambda Expressions and Closures for C++." N1968-06-0038.

Index

A

A-B-A problem, 125
abstraction, 8, 25–27
accessor, 96
  class, 97
acquire method for locks, 113
Aha! factor in examples, 177
algorithm structures, 26
algorithm templates, 29–64, 65–79, 169
aligned_space template class, 109
allocator arguments, 81
Allocator Concept, 106
Amdahl, Gene, 14, 292
Amdahl's Law, 14–18
  Gustafson's observations and, 16–18
Application Layer Gateway (ALG), 242
assembly languages of parallelism, 4, 136
atomic and constructors, 125
atomic operations, 22, 112, 122–129
  convoying, minimizing, 118
  interleaving, 123
  mutual exclusion, versus, 123
  priority inversion, minimizing, 118
  thread-safe reference counting, 123
atomic template class, 127
auto_partitioner class, 38, 45, 52, 59
automata, 192
automatic grain size, 38

B

bibliography, 292–295
blocked_range, 35
  template class, 54
blocked_range2d, 49
  template class, 56–58
blocking, 133
blocking style, 141
  children, with, 145
body object, 33
Boost Threads, 4
breadth-first execution, 142
breadth-first theft and depth-first work, 144

C

C++, 1, 5
cache, 8, 289
  aligned allocator, 103
  cooling, 290
  lines, 102
calloc, replacing, 104
Chare Kernel, xvi, 283
Charm++, xvi, 284
Cilk, 285
coarse-grained parallelism, 11, 20
compare_and_swap, 124
comparison sort (see parallel_sort)
compatibility, 3

We'd like to hear your suggestions for improving our indexes. Send email to *index@oreilly.com*.

About the Author

James Reinders, Chief Evangelist for Intel Software Development Products, is a senior engineer who joined Intel Corporation in 1989. He has contributed to a number of projects, including the world's first TeraFLOP supercomputer (ASCI Red), and compilers and architecture work for the iWarp, Pentium Pro, Pentium II, Itanium, and Pentium 4 processors. He has years of experience in processor architecture, optimizing compilers, parallel computer architecture, and making products for software developers.

Reinders is also the editorial columnist for the monthly "The Gauntlet" at *www.go-parallel.com*, and is the author of *VTune Performance Analyzer Essentials* (Intel Press) and a contributor to *Multi-Core Programming* (Intel Press).

Colophon

The animal on the cover of *Intel Threading Building Blocks* is a wild canary (*Serinus canaria*), a small songbird in the finch family. It is also known as an island canary or Atlantic canary because it is native to islands off western Europe, particularly Madeira, Azores, and the Canary Islands, for which the bird was named. The name comes from the Latin *canaria* ("of the dogs"), first used by Pliny the Elder in his *Naturalis Historia* because of the large dogs roaming the Islands. Canaries live in orchards, farmlands, and copses, and make their nests in bushes and trees.

Although the wild canary is darker and slightly larger than the domestic canary, it is otherwise similar in appearance. Its breast is yellow-green and its back is streaked with brown. Like many species, the male is more vibrantly colored than the female. The male also has a sweeter song. When the Spanish conquered the Islands in the 15th century, they domesticated the birds and began to breed them. By the 16th century, canaries were prized as pets throughout Europe. (Samuel Pepys writes about his "canary birds" in a 1661 diary entry.) Five hundred years of selective breeding have produced many canary varieties, including the bright yellow type common today. The small birds are popular pets because they can live up to 10 years, require little special attention, and are considered to have the most melodious song of all birds.

As late as the 1980s, coal miners used canaries as a warning system, with two birds in each coal pit. According to the U.S. Bureau of Mines, canaries were preferred to mice because they are more sensitive to fumes and more visibly show distress in the presence of gas. A canary in a mine would chirp all day, but if the carbon monoxide level rose, it would stop singing and sway on its perch before falling dead—warning the miners to get out fast.

The cover image is from J. G. Wood's *Animate Creation*. The cover font is Adobe ITC Garamond. The text font is Linotype Birka; the heading font is Adobe Myriad Condensed; and the code font is LucasFont's TheSans Mono Condensed.

Related Titles from O'Reilly

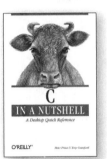

C and C++ Programming

C in a Nutshell

C Pocket Reference

C++ Cookbook

C++ in a Nutshell

C++ Pocket Reference

C++: The Core Language

Mastering Algorithms with C

Objective-C Pocket Reference

Practical C Programming, *3rd Edition*

Practical C++ Programming, *2nd Edition*

Practical Perforce

Programming Embedded Systems, *2nd Edition*

Secure Programming Cookbook for C and C++

STL Pocket Reference